With the Understanding Also

With the Understanding Also

Occam's Razor Meets King James

Burton E. Turner

Unless otherwise noted, all scripture reference is of the King James Version (KJV)

WestBow Press books may be ordered through booksellers or by contacting:

WestBow Press
A Division of Thomas Nelson & Zondervan
1663 Liberty Drive
Bloomington, IN 47403
www.westbowpress.com
1 (866) 928-1240

ISBN: 978-1-4908-8261-1 (sc)
ISBN: 978-1-4908-8263-5 (hc)
ISBN: 978-1-4908-8262-8 (e)

Library of Congress Control Number: 2015908670

Print information available on the last page.

WestBow Press rev. date: 3/25/2016

Contents

Preface

Truth Is Captive

We've often heard that necessity is the mother of invention. The first thing printed on Gutenberg's press was the Holy Bible. Gutenberg felt that the truth was being withheld from the people of the world by the elite of the church. He wanted the people to be able to hold the truth of the Word in their own hands. In the fifteenth century, Gutenberg wrote, "God suffers because of the great multitudes whom His sacred Word cannot reach. Religious truth is captive in a small number of manuscript books which guard the treasures."

This work responds anew to this ages-old problem.

Knowledge, Understanding, and Wisdom*

Knowledge without understanding is like a gondola without a balloon.

This is the driving force behind this work. There is no doubt that wisdom requires knowledge. The point of the gondola comment above is the relationship of wisdom to knowledge. Knowledge, while not always doing so, must go hand in hand with understanding. We often see that a person can have a great education and actually have little knowledge. Knowledge gives one the ability to answer the question "why?"

---

* See the Appendix for Proverbs 7:1–9:12 in which Wisdom speaks to us in the first, second, and third person.

Knowledge is the understanding of the education acquired in life. *Wisdom* is knowledge rightly applied to life. Ergo, wisdom never changes—wherever knowledge may take us.

Herein, we will study and know what the Bible says. The Holy Scriptures *can* be understood. We have to understand what the Bible says in order to hitch a balloon to our gondola. With our knowledge—and our understanding of that knowledge—we can rightly apply the wisdom of the Word to both our faith and lives.

In this book, I have sought to answer the question "why?" in ways that many readers may not have seen, about things that they may not have thought about before. Understanding is key to a deep-rooted faith. "Blind faith" is no faith at all.

The Foundation of Study

Let's say that you decide to "root out" the deeper meaning of some ticklish or difficult passages to find the truth in them. Those sections of Scripture may seem difficult for various reasons:

- They are genuinely difficult to understand.
- They rebuke the reader's behavior.
- They seem to disagree with the reader's beliefs.

In every Bible study, the choices are:

- Adjust my beliefs as I increase in understanding.
- Adjust or "jigsaw" Scripture to better fit my existing belief (which, by the way, takes a lot more time and effort).
- Ignore the passages and study around them (Occam's Broom).
- Start a new religion that discounts the difficult passages. (This is more common than you'd think.)

This study gets to the root of every subject covered in this work, meeting them head on and in depth. This work is not a compilation of Sunday school lessons. However, each subject will be more than fruitful for the "unashamed workman."

On a Personal Note

The purpose of this work is to make some things known that have been given to me through prayerful study of the Holy Scriptures. However, I cannot—nor will I ever—presume to have sole possession of specific God-given facts, meanings, or interpretations. Nor can I presume that the thoughts and/or interpretations herein are original to me simply because I hadn't heard them before.

I continually thank God for the knowledge that I did not produce this work on my own. I will never claim to have known anything herein except that God gave it to me to share (Matthew 5:15). I pray that you will see the light of the candle and none of the candlestick.

A Brief Introduction

There Is Absolute Truth

The purpose of our study is to make sure that you feel you have a faith you can call your own. If you consider this work to be confrontational, your feelings are your own. You should dig a little deeper. Most certainly, however, this work will touch on some things that will at least cause raised eyebrows in many readers.

Herein you will find only statements of fact, using the Bible as the only source of proof. You will find no conjecture, hyperbole, or exaggeration, only reason and logic. We will use the history found in the Bible as proof of our modern applications. The Bible is the Word of God, and we will neither add to it nor subtract from it. *Ad hoc* hypotheses find no home here.

This study is not intended to be argumentative. Whatever your beliefs, if they truly be beliefs, you should fearlessly read on. If, in your private honesty, you are seeking truth, insight, or both, stay tuned to that spot in your heart. This work will speak to it.

The purpose of this work is to help and cause the reader to "go ye and learn what that meaneth" (Matthew 9:13). Further, while you might think that practicing Christianity is hard, a life of following Jesus is easy. He said so Himself.

Again, this study is for examination and, hopefully, the increase of one's personal faith. There are those whose faith will be shaken. Some will have their faith changed by this work. Still others will find their faith strengthened.

The reality is that the nature of truth is proactive rather than reactive, without making a move. This is simply because the truth exists. The truth, guarded and guided by the Holy Spirit, changes lives.

This work may bring to light error of one sort or another. Where error exists, I pray that this work will help it to be seen. I have here put pen to paper because I, along with many others, believe that the truth is again being held captive by intention, tradition, or error. There are also religious beliefs—some even labeled as Christian—in the world today, as in times past, that deify idols. Still others do not fear to mock the one true God.

"And we have the word of the prophets made more certain, and you will do well to pay attention to it, as to a light shining in a dark place, until the day dawns and the morning star rises in your hearts" (2 Peter 1:19 NIV).

Something for Everyone

This study also will show you, in no uncertain terms, how first to attain a right faith in God's truth and how to both procure and assure for yourself the gift of salvation. This, of course, is what we're all here for. This is God's will; it's as simple as that. People spend their lives "seeking God's will," and we're told in 2 Peter 3:9 exactly what that is.

I assure you that this work goes far beyond God's plan of salvation. For instance, one of the things we'll look at is the difference between God's *will* and God's *plans*. We'll also be looking at things that many people, myself included, consider to be totally irrelevant to salvation. These thoughts were given to me to give to whomever has ears to hear. I can also tell you that this work is not a waste of time, mine or yours. All parts of this work are either historically relevant or theologically pertinent. Most times, they are both.

You may be one of the many who say, "I don't believe in organized religion" or even "I don't believe in God." If so, read this work. You may find better reason to believe what you previously believed. Or you might change your mind.

As the author and primary researcher of this work, I will tell you that during my research I even changed my own beliefs on a couple of things. They were *aha* moments when the lightbulb came on. It's thrilling to realize the truth about something—even more if it changes your previously held ideas and beliefs.

Some Will (First) Be Offended

In Luke 12:51–53, Jesus said, "Suppose ye that I am come to give peace on earth? I tell you, Nay; but rather division: For from henceforth there shall be five in one house divided, three against two, and two against three. The father shall be divided against the son, and the son against the father; the mother against the daughter, and the daughter against the mother; the mother in law against her daughter in law, and the daughter in law against her mother in law."

I've heard this put many ways: "The truth will offend until there are no more to be offended." I offer no disclaimers about speaking the whole truth of Scripture. I do not deride those who believe otherwise. However, the truth will stand when all else is shaken down around it.

Christian Maturity

In the process of maturing spiritually, all people face four primary growth processes. They are:

- growth in our understanding of God;
- growth in our understanding of Jesus, the Christ;
- growth in our understanding of the Holy Spirit; and
- growth in our understanding of the Scripture that will lead us to the three above.

Growth in any of these areas seems often to produce an unfavorable human reaction. At each "eureka," we tend to stop to congratulate ourselves, so to speak, and then to be content with what we have learned. It seems that we get to a point where we feel that we know enough or even that we have found all that is important to know. Paradoxically, it is when we begin to feel the most satisfied that we should begin to feel the most uncomfortable.

It is satisfying to believe that we understand everything that we need to understand and that we have a correct understanding. It is easier to defend what we know than to recognize that we need to increase our understanding further.

To stop the learning process and build defenses for what we believe–rather than to seek further knowledge and grow greater in our understanding—is a basic human characteristic. The key phrase here is "to stop."

Pausing to mark a tree on the trail or to record a map of the trail to that point is not the same as pitching camp and building a fort. The latter indicates that you do not intend to travel further for quite some time, if ever.

The largest single argument against defensive behavior is the simple fact that truth needs no defense, nor does it need a defender. Yes, there are those who would detract from the truth, and those who would listen to those detractors. This does not change the truth. We will see, as Lancelot said, "But at the length truth will out."

The seeker who realizes that the more he learns, the more he finds to learn, is gaining wisdom from the process.

When we think we've got things all figured out, both our understanding and maturity are stunted. We may even continue to study earnestly, but the purpose of our study changes from spiritual growth to a need to defend what we have come to believe. When our purpose for study changes from seeking to defending, our wisdom actually begins to decrease.

Our faith gains no ground if we stop to dig spiritual and philosophical trenches.

Some Things Never Change

God never changes. God's moral laws have never changed. Jesus said that not one "jot or tittle" would change or go away. There are certain things (if correct) that should not change in one's Christian beliefs. God's plan of salvation tops the list for obvious reasons.

One Thing to Remember

As you proceed through this study, pray that God will allow you to see His truth. It's not that this study claims to be some "holy grail" of knowledge, but there will be times when you may need to adjust some thoughts because of your beliefs or even about your beliefs.

In other words, whether or not for the reason of this study, you must decide within yourself if you will adjust your beliefs to fit any new knowledge and understanding of the Scripture, or if you will alter your interpretation or translation to prove your current beliefs to be correct. That is, you must decide if you will choose truth or rationalization.

I, with your help, ask a blessing on these words and on both your reception and perception—in Jesus' name.

PART I

Salvation

This section is listed first because there's nothing more important than salvation—to God or humanity.

Some theology has gone astray, even with something as simple as God's plan of salvation. Therefore, we must address the theological truth of salvation before we go further.

This section manifests the difference between the milk of the Word and the meat of the Word, which Paul wrote about to the Corinthians in 1 Corinthians 3:2. The same example is used in Hebrews in a situation that may better fit this section. The author said that those to whom the book was addressed (Hebrews 5:12) should have been knowledgeable enough to be teachers, but they were still only drinking the milk of the Word rather than having progressed to eating the meat of the Word.

This section is the milk of the Word. This is the "What must I do to be saved?" section. For those who do not know this, salvation is the basic requirement. To those who are "young" in Christ it gives both security and the real ability to explain it to others.

A study of salvation will be the whole purpose of this first section.

1

There Are Minimum Requirements?

When seeking the truth of salvation, people ask many questions, the most popular being the question in the title of this chapter. In a word, the answer is yes.

Minimum Means Minimum

In Luke 17:7–10, Jesus related a "what if" story. "What if" we had a servant who had worked all day. Would we reward that servant for doing his job by telling him to sit and have dinner with us? Or would we expect the servant to continue doing his job by preparing our meal and then eating after we had been served?

Jesus was asking if we would reward someone for simply doing what was required by his job description. The answer is no, we would not reward the servant, nor would he expect us to.

Jesus' point was that the servant who performs only to the level expected will receive only the pay agreed upon when he was hired. This servant will simply "break even." He has done his job in a way that we would mark as "satisfactory" on an employee evaluation. The servant has done all that was required in a satisfactory fashion, and nothing more. The boss got a day's work for a day's pay.

The King James Version calls this employee "the unprofitable servant." This is a very accurate wording. In our modern times, the word *unprofitable* generally indicates that something or someone is losing money. However, the actual definition of the word simply means that whatever it was did not make a profit. The satisfactory servant did not perform above par, but he did perform *at* par. The servant deserved a day's pay, but nothing more.

"It's My Money," Says Jesus

Jesus "goes you one further" with the parable of the vineyard workers in Matthew 20:1–15. With this parable, Jesus established who decided what a day's pay was.

Jesus told of the landowner who went out early in the morning, looking for workers for his vineyard. He found some at the "day labor" corner and agreed to pay them a denarius for their work for the day. The landowner obviously felt that he needed more workers, because he went out "in the third hour" to shop in the marketplace and found a few more workers. He told them to go to work and said he'd pay them what was right.

The landowner went out again at the sixth and the ninth hours and repeated his offer to the workers he found at those times. He also went out in the eleventh hour for some reason, and he seemed surprised to find a couple of men still standing around. The landowner asked these men if they'd not worked all day. The men replied that they had not, and when he asked them why, they said, "Because no man hired us." This is where we get our modern analogy of the "eleventh hour."

The landowner, being generous and not wanting to see any man go home empty-handed, made the same deal with them that he had made with the men from the earlier times of the day. "I'll pay you what is right," he said. These men went to work, because they too did not want to go home empty-handed.

The story ends with the last men getting paid first. We very often repeat what Jesus said: "The first shall be last, and the last shall be first." However, we rarely speak of what that means.

Many people believe this statement means that on the day of judgment the older-in-Christ Christians will be allowed to see the fruits of their labors. I like that idea, myself. However, we now see that it actually means that the first will be *indistinguishable* from the last.

Jesus told us that even the very last men to come to work were paid the same wage agreed upon by the first workmen. The last men had only worked for an hour but were each paid a denarius, just like the men who had worked all day.

The men hired in the morning grumbled and asked why they had not been paid more or more accurately, why the latecomers hadn't been paid less. The first men did not desire more than the agreed-upon wage, but they certainly wanted to be paid more than those who had only worked one hour. The situation seems terribly and typically human.

In Matthew 20:13–15, Jesus said, "But he [the landowner] answered one of them, 'Friend, I am not being unfair to you. Didn't you agree to work for a denarius? Take your pay and go. I want to give the man who was hired last the same as I gave you. Don't I have the right to do what I want with my own money? Or are you envious because I am generous?'"

With this parable, Jesus made the point that there is a reward for all who "work in the vineyard." More than that, He made it abundantly clear that there is a minimum reward.

The parable of the prodigal son has a place here, but I won't belabor this point.* As we continue through these Bible studies, we'll see a tremendous overlap of teachings. You may see things that others haven't. The point is this: "If you seek Him, He will find you." You'll see the "fingerprints of God" all over the Bible before you're through.

Minimum Here, Minimum There: What's Your Point?

We've heard from the lips of Jesus that there is a minimum performance requirement for a minimum reward. What should be equally evident is the fact that if a person does not perform the minimum requirements, that person will not attain even the minimum reward. In terms of the parable, Jesus was saying that the workers had to have worked in the vineyard—no matter how long—in order to be paid.

We see that God (the landowner), with His loving generosity, sees no difference—in terms of reward—between Christians who come to salvation early in their lives and those who come at or near the end of their lives.

---

* See chapter 31, "The Prodigal Son."

A Couple of Questions

What reward are you talking about? In any study of Christianity, the reward most spoken of is that of salvation and living eternally with God in heaven. You'll find no difference here. Other rewards are spoken of in the Scripture, but if they are found in this work, they will be properly identified.

Why are you calling it a reward if it's a minimum thing that everybody gets? To a person who believes that the human animal is a selfish and therefore sinful creature, we live in a putrid world. To a person who believes that God desires for everyone to "come to everlasting life" (2 Peter 3:9), forgiveness and the love that produces it are the greatest things ever to be seen on this earth.

The fact that the forgiveness that leads to salvation is even offered to humanity is a wonder in itself. Our God, who *is* love, gives us a chance to take His forgiveness and thereby gain everlasting life.

2

What Must I Do to Be Saved?

What's the Big Deal?

We've talked about salvation. To be sure we're on the same page, let's address its definition. Salvation means living eternally in heaven with God.

Well, that's the short version. There are other studies that answer questions like "Where is heaven?" and "What will we do when we get there?" It appears to most people that the true believer is only mildly curious about these things–or more probably, gives such questions little thought at all.

My point here is that the important thing is to "get in the gate." Nothing else matters! If you feel that there is something more important than getting into heaven, you are wrong. The train is leaving the station! Get on board! If it sounds as if I think this is important, you are absolutely correct.

Do You Practice Religion or Follow Jesus?

You may say, or you may have heard others say, "I don't agree with organized religion." Perhaps a small analogy will help you see the difference between religion and the example given to us by Jesus, along with the doctrine established by the apostles as inspired by the Holy Spirit.

A former Buddhist explained it by saying that he likened his spiritual life to drowning in a lake. The story goes something like this. "Buddha came to the side of the lake, stopped, and called to me. He told me to start swinging my arms and kicking my legs, but I had to make it to shore by myself. Jesus not only came to the lake, but he jumped into the lake, swam to me, and pulled me to shore. Jesus then taught me to swim so I could go out and rescue others who were drowning!"

The point is this: religion, no matter whose, is a liturgy—a checklist of things—that must be done to supposedly bring one closer to whatever god is being worshipped. Religion, then, by definition, is man reaching for God. Christianity, as shown to us by Jesus, stands alone as God reaching for man.

Take It to the Bank

Let's say that you've heard of some place where a man is giving away a fortune. When you ask around, you realize that not as many folks as you'd have thought have heard of this fellow. At the least, they don't want to talk about it if they have.

However, a good number of the folks you talk to say they've heard of this fellow, but they simply don't believe it. They say that nobody would do such a thing. Besides, they believe they're doing all right without any such fortune.

An interesting number of people say that they know of people who have gone to see this man but that it sure doesn't look like their lives have changed in any way. If the guy really was giving away a "fortune," that fortune must be bogus.

Let's say that you think it might be worth a look anyway. You visit with some people who genuinely received this "fortune" (their piece of it, anyway) and now simply sing the praises of the guy who wrote their check. You can see how people might easily "jump on the bandwagon" when they first hear the story.

However, you want to see if this thing is genuine. After all, there's got to be some kind of initiation or requirement to join this club and get whatever it is you get. Maybe you have to put down some kind of deposit or something. But these people keep saying that it's simply a gift. You think it might be worth investigating.

Well, after a couple more visits with these folks, your life seems to change, even though you haven't even asked for a check yet. These folks have welcomed you as a friend. They've invited you to dinners, functions, and so on. You realize that you're not as interested in your old friends. It seems that you are actually beginning to believe that this "fortune" thing is for real. A couple of these guys that you've become a little more friendly with have asked you if you've asked for a check yet, because you're beginning to look like you're part of the group.

A few days later, you ask one of these guys, "What must I do to get a check?" He says, "It's so simple that I don't understand why everyone doesn't get a check." He begins to count on his fingers, saying:

1. "You have to hear about the check-writer and the checks. Of course, you've done that."
2. "You have to believe that both the check and the check-writer are real and good. If you do, you receive your check, absolutely free. We've got an endless supply, preprinted and signed." He pulls one out of his pocket and gives it to you.
3. "You have to go to the bank."
4. "You have to endorse the back of the check."
5. "You have to present the check to the bank so they can cash it."
6. "Then you simply take your fortune and use it to show that you have it."

That seems too easy, you think. But it's great! It *is* free!

"But ...," he says.

Aha, you think. *Now the other shoe is about to drop.*

He continues: "There are people out there who think you do not have to take the check to the bank. They just continue living their lives the way they always have. It seems odd that they wouldn't go ahead and cash it, but they will tell you that they've already received their fortunes just by being given the check. There are also people out there who don't endorse the check. They even go to the bank from time to time, but without endorsing the check, they cannot get it cashed. Some of these people actually believe they have received their fortunes just by believing the check is good and by acting like they've cashed it when they come to the meetinghouse. And as amazing as it seems, there are some people—actually, a lot of people—who believe that they don't have to present their check to the teller. How odd that these people believe they can receive their fortune without some form of proof that they've got it coming!"

"The big deal," he adds, "is that you need to go about your life in a new way. You need to show people that your life has changed and help them to see how to get a check of their own. A great many people actually cash their check and then put the fortune to no good use at all—like they've buried it in the backyard or something. They are as broke as they were before they cashed their check. I believe you've met a few of them already. The reason I said all that was to warn you that those people I mentioned will actually do their best to convince you that they are right. They may even doubt their own correctness, but if they can convince you, then it makes them more comfortable with being incorrect. It's the old 'misery loves company' thing. Do not let anyone convince you that there is any other way of getting your fortune, or you will never have it—even if you try to believe that you do."

It's Not Just a Scenario. It's the Truth!

It's just that easy—either to be right or to be wrong.

Think on this. If you receive a check from someone on your birthday, is it a gift? If someone gives you and your spouse a check and says, "I'll pay for dinner," is that a gift? If you get a check as a Christmas bonus, is that a gift? The truth is that in these and other instances where you are given a check without doing anything to earn it, you can't call them anything but a gift.

For this study, salvation is the gift. In the analogy of taking a check to the bank, salvation is the check.

At this point, some people may ask, "If salvation is the check, what does the rest of that list mean? I thought you said we didn't have to do anything to earn it?"

In return, I must ask, "Do you genuinely believe that taking a check to the bank to cash it is working for or earning that money?" Of course, you don't. It is still a gift. The fact that you present yourself to the bank, endorse the check (with matching identification), and present the item to the teller is merely proof to the bank that you are the person the check is made out to.

Having made the analogy, the question becomes, "What must I do to be saved?"

The reply is much the same as the one in the analogy. The man said, "It's so simple that I don't understand why everyone doesn't get saved (a check)." He begins to count on his fingers, saying:

1. You must hear the gospel—that Jesus is the Christ, the Son of the living God (Romans 10:17). (You hear about the fortune.)
2. You must believe that Jesus came to be our example and to die as the perfect sacrifice as propitiation for our sins (1 John 4:10). (You believe that the giver and the check are real.)
3. You must repent of your sins (Acts 2:38). (You go to the bank.)
4. You must confess that you believe (Matthew 10:32). (You endorse the check.)
5. You must be baptized in the name of the Father, Son, and Holy Ghost for the remission of your sins (Matthew 28:19). (You present the check to the teller and gain your fortune.)
6. You must live as a new creature, spreading the gospel in your daily life by your example as a follower of Jesus, the Christ (Revelation 20:12). (You live as an example of your good fortune.)

But I Was Told Otherwise

As in the story of taking a check to the bank, a person must follow all the required steps in order to receive the gift of salvation. The warning is not so much to ensure that you understand the answer to the question of how to get a check; it is more to warn you that someone might tell you that you can do less and still receive your fortune.

You may have heard myriad reasons why there is some other way to attain salvation. We'll not go into them here; that's for the next chapter of this section. But we will certainly show why and how the simple steps shown here that lead to salvation, sure and certain.

Examining the Steps to Salvation

A question often arises when we begin this area of study. The question usually goes something like this: "Why do you say that a 'laundry list' of things to do is wrong, yet here we are with a list of things to do?"

This is a good question, if asked honestly. The answer is simply that the plan of salvation is a once-and-for-all list of what we must do to be saved.

The laundry lists of the various religions of the world are used for the *practice* of those religions. They list the things you must do each time you perform "worship" as well as each day of your life outside of worship. Various aspects of a this-or-that practice may include "kneel and say," "stand and say," "sit and repeat," and so on. Daily life includes things likes "don't eat that," "pray at set times," "pray these exact words," and so forth.

The "plan of salvation" examined in this work is given as an enumerated list to show the plan in a logical sequence. The steps often run into each other as the person becomes a believer. This is to say that, internally, the personal process for going from unbeliever to saved believer is usually smooth and often uninterrupted. It is only for the purposes of this work that we individualize each component of the plan.

Step 1: You Must Hear the Gospel

We'll examine the second step in far greater detail because the second step is the "linchpin" of the entire issue of salvation. However, logic dictates that in order for a person to believe something, he must first hear of it.

The reason we list it here is that it is duly noted in the Scripture. Paul wrote of the progression toward faith in Romans 10:12–17. The last verse reads, "So then, faith comes by hearing and hearing by the Word of God."

In that passage of Romans, Paul also noted that not all who hear will believe or apply what they hear. God will not force anyone into His gracious offer, but it's there for one and all.

Step 2: You Must Believe

Faith is defined by Webster as "complete trust or confidence in someone or something." It's a simple thing, isn't it? It's a yes or no answer, one might say. The simple question with the simple answer is: do you have faith in God? However, if you stop and think of it, that's quite a different question from "do you believe in God?"

It seems that we should actually say that the second step toward salvation is faith rather than belief. Let's look at that. Those two things—belief and faith—while quite similar, are a bit different in meaning. Let's look at how belief comes first and leads to faith.

Note that you cannot have faith that God will do anything without first believing in God—and further, without believing that He can do that thing, whatever it is. Hebrews 11:6 states this explicitly. "But without faith it is impossible to please him: for he that cometh to God must believe that he is, and that he is a rewarder of them that diligently seek him." Notice, however, that one can certainly believe both of these things and yet not have faith that God will perform in any given fashion.

One of the best examples of belief and unbelief, biblically speaking, is in Mark 9:17–26. The story goes like this. A man brought his son to Jesus. The boy was possessed of a demon that made him fitful. Jesus was not there at the time, and the disciples who were there tried and failed to call out the demon. When Jesus arrived, the disciples were saying, "I don't know what's wrong. We've been doing this for a while now, and it has always worked before." The man who had brought his son, and others of the crowd, were probably calling them frauds or worse.

Jesus arrived and said, among other things, "Bring the boy to me." In verses 21–24, the story goes like this. Jesus asked the boy's father, "How long has he been like this?" "From childhood," the man answered. "The demon has often thrown him into fire or water to kill him. But if you can do anything, take pity on us and help us."

I can just picture Jesus turning to look straight at the man and repeating the question with an almost insulted expression: "If you *can*?" Jesus then looked back at the boy and said, "Everything is possible for him who believes." You can almost see the boy's father dropping to his knees as he immediately exclaimed, "I do believe; help me overcome my unbelief!"

Here we see that Jesus accepted, without argument, belief and unbelief that coexisted side by side in the same person. Jesus commanded the demon to come out of the boy and not to return. The demon shrieked and did not hesitate to leave. The boy lay lifeless until Jesus helped him up. Though no one spoke of a celebration, I'm sure there was one. Jesus melted into the crowd without another word.

So, we see that it is obviously more important *what* you believe than *how much* you believe. Though we don't have specific evidence that the man didn't believe anything more than that Jesus was capable of healing his son, the fact that he brought his son to Jesus says that much. The man admitted that he needed deeper teaching, and Jesus made sure that the man would return to get it by showing His benevolent mercy in the form of healing.

We also finally see that we can believe and not have faith. James 2:19 bears this out. James noted that demons also believe in God and tremble, but their belief in God does not earn them any form of salvation.

Webster says that hope is "a wish or desire accompanied by confident expectation of its fulfillment." One can believe in anything without any hope of anything. Faith goes hand in hand with hope, leading to deeper faith.

So, we've seen how the spark of belief will lead to strong belief. In verses 28–29 of the above story, Jesus explained that there are levels of faith as well. The story goes on to say that after Jesus and the disciples had gone indoors, they asked Jesus why they couldn't get the demon to leave. Jesus had made it look so easy. "And he [Jesus] said unto them, 'This kind can come forth by nothing, but by prayer and fasting'" (Mark 9:29).

The point is that prayer, to Jesus, meant something much more than it does to most of us. He proved it when, in the King James Version, He coupled it with fasting. Jesus was not speaking of the prayer that you say before dinner. He's not even speaking of the prayers that are offered in church. Jesus was telling the disciples that they simply did not have the faith in the power of His holy Father that He did, a powerful faith that was continually strengthened by ceaseless, prayerful communion with God.

In Mark 9:29, Jesus was speaking of the continued prayer of communication with God that feeds the strength of faith, which feeds the strength of prayer, which feeds the strength of faith, which feeds the strength of prayer, *ad infinitum*, until we are called to see the glory of God face-to-face.*

---

* An in-depth study of prayer is in chapter 12, "Prayer: Is This Thing On?"

Jesus was saying that a young-in-Christ Christian will simply never have the peace, understanding, knowledge leading to wisdom, and unshakeable, unbeatable faith of a person who has spent year upon year studying, loving, believing, trusting, and obeying God with an ongoing communication through Jesus on a level that is coveted by many of the faith.

In a total sidebar here, let me add this. This story is absolute proof of demons among us, in that Jesus spoke directly to the demon rather than to the boy possessed. Jesus never spoke to the eyes of the blind man or the legs of the lame. The illnesses were inanimate; they were healed. The demons heard and obeyed.

The real "take-away" from this is that you don't have to have some kind of mountain-moving faith in order to believe that Jesus is the Son of the living God and that He died as the only perfect sacrifice for the remission of our sins. However, you must believe both that you are a sinner and that you need the saving forgiveness that comes by repentance and proof of your belief.

Step 3: You Must Repent

A man told me years ago that the man who doesn't make mistakes isn't doing anything. In Romans 3:23, Paul said, "All have sinned and fallen short of the glory of God."

I suppose there are a few people out there who truly do not have a conscience, but be assured that they are merely a handful of the billions that have lived throughout history. If you have a conscience, you know right from wrong. Even those seeming not to have a conscience know how they would like to be treated. In our present day, a principal problem concerning salvation is the relativism of the so-called postmodern thought about truth.

Secularists, humanists, and postmodernists (a rose is a rose is a rose) say that truth is invented. They say that truth comes from man and will always be defined by the perceptions and perspectives of the observer. Of course, this means that in a worldly worldview, truth is relative. Therefore, since those who hold to this worldview believe truth to be relative, they also believe that absolute truth does not and cannot exist.

The point is that there are those who will tell you that you have nothing to live up to and, therefore, nothing to repent for. Please realize that it is merely our technological advances in communication that make these views seem prevalent. The truth of God is as real as gravity; defy either one, and you will witness consequences—whether you believe them to exist or not.

The word *repent* is not defined as simply saying "I'm sorry" but as a life-changing remorse that makes one wish to never do it again (whatever "it" is). The word *repent*, originally written in Greek (seventy-seven times in the King James Version of the New Testament) as *metanoeō*, transcribes directly to "feeling a moral compunction to think differently."

God doesn't require that you bring a list of your failures and wrongs and then ask His forgiveness for them. God only requires that you have a contrite heart in order to forgive you for your failures and wrongs, which may range from stealing a pack of gum to murdering someone. This does not give anyone permission to wrong others, but God's forgiveness does not exclude any wrong that a repentant heart brings to Him.

Let's say that you haven't killed anyone, robbed anyone, stolen any cars, or the like. If you think of it, there are a great many ways to hurt yourself and others without physical injury to person or property.

The Bible told us about this long ago. In Proverbs 23:7, the writer was speaking of "a man with an evil eye," but the application can be for us all. We're also told, "As a man thinks in his heart, so is he." This verse basically points out that we truly are what we are when no one is looking. It shows that a good man is good to his core and that wrongs are wrongs, even if they are only in our heart. That realization is tough to take and easy to dismiss if we've got a hateful heart. Jesus reaffirmed that *thoughts equal action* in the fifth chapter of Matthew.

The point is that recognizing that the house needs painting does not get the house painted. Recognizing that I am a sinner does not make me sorry for it. There comes a point at which most people do wish to do something about their sins. At that point, repentance comes immediately.

Step 4: You Need to Make a Confession

Watch almost any cop show, and you'll see the investigators striving to get a statement of confession from the alleged perpetrator. A confession may not be the only way to get a conviction, but it is the surest way.

God seeks a confession as well. However, the difference between the rules of God's plan of salvation and the US court system is this: the only thing that even allows us a hearing before the throne of God is a confession. Other evidence, either good or bad, will not be heard. Think about that for a moment.

An important note here is that the confession we speak of—the confession that saves one's soul—is twofold. The first part is the confession of sin that goes hand in hand with repentance. In fact, they are often considered to happen simultaneously. The other part of the salvation confession is the believer's confession *before others* that Jesus is the Christ, the Son of the living God. Jesus said in Matthew 10:32, "Whosoever therefore shall confess me before men, him will I confess also before my Father which is in heaven."

This is why the repentant believer seeking salvation is asked, "Do you believe that Jesus is the Christ, the Son of the living God?" Answering yes to this question is only the first of many times he will make this confession, but it is certainly the most important time he will do it—for the salvation of his immortal soul.

Step 5: You Must Be Baptized

I have likened some people's reaction to this step to a child hearing that he has to eat his peas.

It is absolutely unbelievable how many people will tell you that you do not need to be baptized to be saved. Baptism, in the take it to the bank story, is presenting the check to the teller. You present yourself to God and literally walk in the footsteps of Jesus through the processes of:

- His death: You "die to sin," in that you repent and confess, and the "sinful person" in you is crucified.
- His burial: You are "buried" in the water of baptism.
- His resurrection: You are "raised" to walk in newness of life.

Can you cash a check without presenting it to the bank to "transform" it to currency? Then how can you expect God to transform you without presenting yourself to Him?

Jesus was baptized—not that He needed it. He came to earth to exemplify how to live (Matthew 3:13). Jesus said that we are to be baptized (Mark 16:16). Every account of conversion in the New Testament includes baptism.

Baptism is the final act—not the only act—of the plan of salvation.

Step 6: You Must Share the Gospel

In 2 Peter 3:9, Peter told us of God's will: "The Lord is not slack concerning his promise, as some men count slackness; but is longsuffering to us-ward, not willing that any should perish, but that all should come to repentance."

The point is that we are here on earth to glorify God. God obviously wants everyone to be saved. You and I must do our part. If this is the first time you've heard the story of Jesus, you've now heard it; someone has told it to you, even if it's just in this book. You must be sure that those you love and those you have contact with hear the story too.

You don't have to become a preacher or anything like it. Francis of Assisi is sometimes credited with saying this: "Preach the gospel at all times, and sometimes use words." In 1 Peter 3:15 (KJV), Peter said, "And be ready always to give an answer to every man that asks you a reason of the hope that is in you." You must live like you've received your fortune, and then others will simply want to know how you got it. You have "preached" the Word by the way you live your life.

And the Point Is?

If you are satisfied that you now know the true, biblical, God-given plan of salvation but have not yet given your life to be transformed by the blood of Jesus, stop reading and find someone who believes as you now do, someone to baptize you, by immersion, for the remission of your sins, in the name of the Father, the Son, and the Holy Ghost.

Basically, the rest of this work can wait. Heed this: if you are not saved at this point, you need to do nothing else until you are! There are some people out there who will tell you that baptism is a matter of convenience. The most polite thing I can say about that is, "They are wrong!" Go now and get your check cashed. Gain the fortune that is your soul's salvation.

We will speak to the detractors of God's plan of salvation in the next chapter of this section. If you need to stop here, we'll wait for you, okay?

3

THAT'S NOT THE WAY I HEARD IT

What's in It for Me?

That seems to be a very popular question nowadays. If you wish to look at it that way, then the answer is still the same: eternal salvation.

We spoke of the importance of being a saved creature. This is truly the most important thing in your life. Again, we can prove this with God's Word. In the Sermon on the Mount in Matthew 6:25–34, Jesus talked of trusting God for everything, even for your daily needs. He gave examples from the world around us. After listing the reasons, He said in verse 33, "But seek ye first the kingdom of God, and his righteousness; and all these things shall be added unto you."

Jesus' point, and the point here, is that He told us to seek God first. However, if you continue with worldly pursuits, you must, at the very least, seek salvation. If you truly have sought and received salvation, God will become more and more important to you. You'll start saying a blessing at dinnertime, begin to enjoy the fellowship of the church, and so on.

Now, think about this as well. God sees your heart. God knows if you are confessing to Him only for show. I'm here to tell you that if your "come to Jesus" moment is less than sincere—if you are using God and His church for some other gainful purpose—you will rue the day. It's not that the sky will open and you will be struck dead (though it has happened before), but you will know in your heart that you have wronged God Himself, and you will begin to see failures of your own making, bad decisions, and so forth. You will come to know the opposite of blessing until you make a right confession. By the way, the opposite of blessing is no blessing. You will not be cursed until the day of judgment, but you will certainly not be blessed.

The thing to consider about not having God's protection is that you are literally defenseless against Satan and his whims. Satan will continue to make sure that you see sinful activity as the more attractive and easier way to live. Cheating on your taxes, indulging in an occasional fling on a business trip, taking two bags of fertilizer when you only paid for one: these things begin not to even register on your conscience meter—if you're not already to that point.

What do others (your kids, your friends, your business associates) see in your example of how to live? The way you live is literally equal to the person you are. If I seem to belabor the point, it's because it is so important.

But *They* Said ...

Previous chapters have told of the unadulterated truth—and simplicity—of the plan of salvation. Here, I'll show you how the world, through the years, has attempted to improve on God's plan. Doesn't it sound funny to say that we could ever presume to improve upon anything designed by God?

Step 1: You Must Hear the Word

You must understand the story of God, the Son, who came to earth and lived a perfect life. He was crucified and buried by man, was resurrected by God on the third day, lived on earth again for a little while to be seen by men, ascended to heaven on a cloud, and now reigns in heaven.

There are a great many adulterations of this story. Most actually come from distortions by men who simply couldn't wrap their minds around the Trinity and the idea that God the Father, God the Son, and God the Holy Spirit, all being God, are a singular entity. Men like Joseph Smith Jr. and Charles Russell simply said that they didn't have to believe that part—or anything else they thought they needed to change.

Of course, there are those who are not even saying that God is a god. Allah is not God; Allah is a big rock (meteor?) in Mecca. Mohammed actually consulted Christians to try to make his new religion, Islam, more believable. In fact, Jerusalem was the original place for Muslims to pray to. Buddha is not God, but he did say that there is no god. In fact, Buddha was a disgruntled Hindu, probably because Hinduism has too many gods to keep up with. And so it goes.

We are not going into a study of religion, but I can tell you what Jesus said about it. Jesus said in Matthew 7:21–27 that there will be people who act like they are doing God's work, but because they have not obeyed God and have taken their own path, they will, at their judgment, be unknown to God.

So much more can be said about this, but suffice it to say that, yes, you must hear the Word. However, hearing the wrong story or a partially right story does you no good. Indeed, it can cost you your eternal soul.

Step 2: You Must Believe the Word

Again, I must emphasize that believing the wrong story is as bad as ignoring your salvation completely. Being close may count in the game of horseshoes, but it does not count with God. Being partly saved is to be totally lost. Being partly lost is like being partly pregnant. Can it be any clearer?

Later in this work, we will be looking at the problems that many theologians have brought to Christianity through the centuries since Jesus walked the earth. In this chapter, we will look at the specific reasons that so many people have come to believe adulterations of the truth about how we gain salvation—since salvation is obviously the first step for getting into heaven.

Step 3: You Must Repent of Your Sins

This seems rather obvious, but there are those who believe, as we noted previously, that truth is relative. In a world with a "moving target" morality, we can't really feel right about repenting of something that we can sanitize with rationalization. Our society today makes it easy to believe lies that say, "That isn't really wrong." Many people simply feel that they have nothing to repent of. Even worse off are those who say that their feelings are proof that they don't even need a deity.

How you repent is also important. Once you have followed Jesus' example through baptism (steps of salvation), repentance will, more often than not, be a private, prayerful act between you and God through Jesus, our Savior. If you have *not* received your salvation, you may repent or confess to God whenever you want, but you will be asked again, at the point of your baptism, if you repent.

The point is that repentance is not the "be all and end all" of salvation. At the peril of your soul, *do not* believe that you may simply say a prayer and be saved. (We'll talk more about prayer in chapter 12.) Once you have believed that you need to be saved, repentance is a natural progression, not a destination.

Step 4: You Must Confess

Repentance and confession, as mentioned previously, go hand in hand. Therefore, you must certainly realize that the confession you make will be affirmed at the time of your baptism. This must be done with the person who will baptize you and is obviously a witness.

Remember that we spoke of this salvation confession as being twofold. First, you must confess your sin and your need for salvation. Second, you affirm that Jesus is the Christ. In Matthew 10:32, Jesus said, "Whosoever therefore shall confess me before men, him will I confess also before my Father which is in heaven." It is so like God to make the largest thing in your life the simplest of acts. But you must prove by your word that you have a right to the free gift of salvation.

Step 5: You Must Be Baptized

I cannot put it any more plainly than this: if you have not been baptized, you are not saved.

However, this statement is neither inclusive nor exclusive. There are those who have been baptized to become a member of a congregation or for other reasons; they are *not* saved. There are those who have been sprinkled rather than immersed; they are *not* saved.

There are those who have undergone baptism, believing that they were already saved and really didn't need to be baptized to be saved. Their baptism was only a ceremony that took place at the first or last of the month, or whenever it was convenient for the church and the pastor. Sometimes their purpose in being baptized was to obtain church membership and to be allowed to partake of the Lord's Supper at that location. They are *not* saved.

There are those who believe that baptism by itself—a simple, physical act—saves a person. These are baptized thinking that they are purchasing "fire insurance." They are *not* saved.

And then there are those who start this plan of salvation process for *any* reason in any church, right or wrong, and end up knowing in their hearts that they have been baptized correctly (immersion) for the remission of their sins by following Jesus to the grave. That is to say that they have recognized baptism as the final step to becoming saved. They *are* saved.

Let's look at how the apostle Paul viewed baptism.

One of the strongest churches of the first century was the church at Ephesus. Early in his ministry, Paul came to that group of disciples and saw that they had been baptized only by John's baptism.

John's baptism was, indeed, a baptism of repentance. John baptized the people with the admonition that they should look for the coming of the Christ and His baptism of the heart, a baptism of the Holy Spirit. In Acts 19:4, we read: "Then said Paul, John verily baptized with the baptism of repentance, saying unto the people, that they should believe on him which should come after him, that is, on Christ Jesus."

The believers saw that they had not been complete in their salvation. In the very next verse, we see their reaction: "When they heard this, they were baptized in the name of the Lord Jesus."

Matthew Henry spoke well on this passage in his commentary.

> Though we do not now expect miraculous powers, yet all who profess to be disciples of Christ, should be called on to examine whether they have received the seal of the Holy Ghost, in his sanctifying influences, to the sincerity of their faith. Many seem not to have heard that there is a Holy Ghost, and many deem all that is spoken concerning his graces and comforts,

> to be delusion. Of such it may properly be inquired, "Unto what, then, were ye baptized?" for they evidently know not the meaning of that outward sign on which they place great dependence.

Perhaps a person is truly repentant at the point of receiving John's baptism. Just because other people believe that this person was baptized for the right reason does not mean that the person baptized believes it—or should, for that matter.

We have pointed to Scripture that verifies that such a person did not receive John's baptism for a wrong reason. However, we also see that this same person, in terms of the gospel, was not baptized for the right reason either, that reason being to show proof to God that he will follow Jesus to the cross and die to sin. The right kind of baptism also shows that a person understands the commands of Jesus and realizes that his sins are not forgiven until he rises from the watery grave. John's baptism is not that of the Holy Spirit.

If doubt exists on any level concerning one's previous baptism, it is advised that a person be baptized once more to affirm a true belief in the true gospel. It's hardly an embarrassment. Folks will be proud of your desire to more completely please God, and you may actually cause others to be saved by your own action.

Baptism is the physical proof to God that you will follow Jesus, beginning with following Him to the cross, crucifying your old self by repentance, being buried with Him, and rising from that burial as a "new creature." This is the same as presenting your check to the bank. If you keep the endorsed check in your pocket, you will never receive your fortune.

Why are there such differing thoughts about baptism?

More specifically, where does the belief come from that says a person doesn't need to be baptized? The most often used verse of the Bible is Jesus' Great Commission in Mark 16:16: "He that believeth and is baptized shall be saved; but he that believeth not shall be damned."

The person who is splitting hairs agrees that Jesus said "believes and is baptized." However, that person continues, "*But* Jesus also said, 'He that believeth not shall be damned.'" The hair-splitter then says, "I believe, therefore I will not be damned. I do not need to be baptized to believe."

It seems to me that it takes far more faith to twist the truth like that (and then believe the distortion) than to simply read the Word and believe the simple truth. Notice that Jesus didn't mention repentance or confession either, but the believer knows that those steps are there as well.

There are those who point to Cornelius (Acts 10) and say that the Holy Spirit came to him and his family and friends *before* they were baptized. They say that one need not be baptized with water to receive the baptism of the Holy Spirit. Note that the argument always contains the phrase "before they were baptized."

To those hair-splitters, we answer the question of when *does* one receive the gift of the Holy Spirit with a resounding: who cares?

Remember that God sees the heart. If God sees that you truly believe that Jesus the Christ is the Son of God and that you are about to be baptized into Him for the remission of your sins, do you think He cares whether you receive the Holy Spirit before or after baptism? Neither do we. The point is that baptism—for the right reason—is a requirement of the plan of salvation.

There are other verses that have been distorted by those I call hair-splitters. People who hold to this distortion do not readily preach the belief of this "near truth," but they stand very ready to defend their "I need no baptism" position.

Here, I will ask those of the "I need no baptism" belief if they would recognize and act like Paul when he said in 1 Corinthians 8:13, "Wherefore, if meat make my brother to offend, I will eat no flesh while the world standeth, lest I make my brother to offend."

The point of that passage is that the true follower of Christ simply will not do what might offend another believer—except on occasions when it would be unscriptural not to do so—for the simple reason that it may shake a weaker brother's faith, which this "I need no baptism" belief certainly does.

Baptism is such a simple act, yet it is so divisive. Why not just go ahead and agree with baptism as the act of salvation that it is, and be baptized. Unite the church in a way that has not been seen since the first century! Thousands and tens of thousands of churches, which call themselves by many names, are divided on this single point alone.

I repeat: if you are not baptized for the right reason, you are not saved.

What about "sprinkling?" Why is sprinkling not considered baptism?

First and foremost, look at the definitions of both sprinkling and baptism. To put them together and say "a sprinkling baptism" is to speak of an impossible action.

In terms of a burial, sprinkling is like tossing a handful of dirt on the body, but baptism is like filling the grave.

Examining the Greek words *bapto* (primary verb) and *baptizo*, we realize that neither have anything to do with sprinkling. These are the two words from which *baptism* comes.

Bapto means to dip or immerse, and *baptizo*, used only in the New Testament concerning the church's baptism, means to overwhelm. *Whelm* literally means to submerge or bury. The word *baptism* obviously means "to totally immerse." Even today, the word *overwhelmed* is taken to mean something like "underwater" or "totally covered up."

The most obvious reason for immersion is for what it represents. You follow Jesus through His death on the cross by repenting and confessing your sins and thereby dying to the sinful world. You follow Jesus to the grave and are "buried with Him" in the "watery grave." You again follow Jesus in His resurrection by rising from that watery grave. This exemplifies to both God and man that you have crucified the old man of sin in your life and are now beginning to live "in newness of life" (Romans 6:3–6).

What about infant baptism?

An appeal to logic poses another question. Why would Jesus say, "He that believes and is baptized shall be saved," if the believing conscience were not involved? Infant baptism is useless because the only thing the baby believes is that the water is cold and annoying!

This may be a hard pill to swallow for many people, but given the foregoing truth about baptism, we realize that anyone who relies on infant baptism for salvation will be eternally disappointed, to say the least.

Where you are baptized is not important.

Notice that we've been viewing the "how" of baptism, with no mention of the "where." The "when" is, of course, as soon as you truly understand and repent. Do not delay. If someone says "tomorrow," "the end of this month," or anything other than "meet me where there's water," keep looking until you find a Christian who understands, as you do, the urgency of being saved.

Where you are baptized is irrelevant. A proper baptism for the proper reason can be performed in a swimming pool, at a riverside, in a horse trough, or even in a church baptistery. For instance, the eunuch listened as Philip "preached unto him Jesus." The eunuch understood and recognized that he should not wait.

The story continues in Acts 8:36–38: "And as they went on their way, they came unto a certain water: and the eunuch said, See, here is water; what doth hinder me to be baptized? And Philip said, If thou believest with all thine heart, thou mayest. And he answered and said, I believe that Jesus Christ is the Son of God. And he commanded the chariot to stand still: and they went down both into the water, both Philip and the eunuch; and he baptized him."

Step 6: Live a Right Life

This is actually a two-part thought that represents one's lifetime commitment to God and retention of a saved state. A person cannot simply claim to have been changed and not act accordingly.

A good many people have a mistaken view of salvation. These believe that salvation, once claimed, can never be lost. If we were speaking of any manmade social club, we would expect an initiate to live within the bylaws of that organization. A large number of organizations even require membership renewals. Why would we hold God to a lower standard? In other words, one must continue to live a life that shows an espousal to God's will. The doctrine of *once saved–always saved* is error. The point of living a right life is to physically and visibly manifest the love of God in service to our fellow man.

The second part of living a right life that *keeps* us saved is continual prayerful communication with God and continual prayerful repentance.

The Truth Is the Truth

It has been asked in many different ways: if no truth exists, why are so many people searching for it?

Truth is not relative. Truth is absolute. Truth exists, and if anything is not the truth, what is it? If it is not the truth, *it is a lie*. In John 8:43–45 (NIV), Jesus said to the Pharisees, "Why is my language not clear to you? Because you are unable to hear what I say. You belong to your father, the devil, and you want to carry out your father's desire. He was a murderer from the beginning, not holding to the truth, for there is no truth in him. When he lies, he speaks his native language, for he is a liar and the father of lies. Yet because I tell the truth, you do not believe me!"

We have already seen how Jesus feels about the person who looks good but does not practice "the whole truth." Here's what He said on another occasion in Luke 6:46–49 (NIV):

> Why do you call me, "Lord, Lord," and do not do what I say? I will show you what he is like who comes to me and hears my words and puts them into practice. He is like a man building a house, who dug down deep and laid the foundation on rock. When a flood came, the torrent struck that house but could not shake it, because it was well built. But the one who hears my words and does not put them into practice is like a man who built a house on the ground without a foundation. The moment the torrent struck that house, it collapsed and its destruction was complete.

On another occasion, in John 14:15 (NIV), Jesus said, "If you love me, you will obey what I command." He also said in John 14:21, "Whoever has my commands and obeys them, he is the one who loves me. He who loves me will be loved by my Father, and I too will love him and show myself to him."

Now, I'll repeat what Jesus said in Mark 16:16: "He that believeth and is baptized shall be saved; but he that believeth not shall be damned."

PART II

God's Logic

This section looks directly at why it was necessary to have a plan of salvation in the first place. It also considers the way words, once again, have come to mean things other than the definitions they began with.

This section will also address a major mistaken thought of how we came to the different interpretations of the Scriptures. This begins our study of things that will not, in and of themselves, keep a person out of heaven for believing one way or another. However, clarity brings understanding, and understanding brings a stronger faith.

After this study, you may find that you actually believe otherwise on this or that point. That's fine. The idea is that you now have a belief that is beginning to take root in your own study of the Word. Again, you must have a faith of your own or you do not have a genuine faith at all. Part II could easily have been entitled "Christianity: Past, Present, and Future."

4

Seeking Balance? So Is God.

Firm but Fair

I've seen, in both the profit and nonprofit corporate worlds, that one of the highest attributes of any management personnel is that of being "firm but fair." This phrase says that the rules apply to everyone and that everyone means *you* too. If we really think about it—and even though we often think otherwise—the word *firm* is actually a very good word to have in your résumé.

Those who have raised kids—or have only been around them for any time at all—come to realize that fairness is the greatest single attribute of grown-ups sought by children. Think about it. Kids may gripe about doing something, but as long as everyone has to do it, they will do what is required of them. By the way, all children consider a coin toss to be the fairest decision-making tool because it is fair and equal.

Logically, God Almighty, being God over all, had to stipulate to the first human the same rules, regulations, blessings, curses, promises, and rewards that He has for us today. God has changed His mind on a few occasions, but He has never relented on any punishment or lessened any reward that He has established as a statute.* We will see proof of this in Scripture as well.

God (Jesus) is "the same yesterday and today and forever" we're told in Hebrews 13.

---

* See chapter 22, "Testing, Testing," for the example of Miriam in Numbers 12.

What Is Balance?

We humans have a perspective on sin and forgiveness that is much different from God's. In human terms, we think that the things of this world are relative. If we walked at seventy miles per hour, that speed would not be considered fast at all. We have a court system laden with relativity in the form of relative levels of crime: murder, manslaughter, justifiable homicide, and so on.

The perfect physical (human) example of balance that we can truly understand is our pH scale. Water, the universal neutral, registers a pH (potential of hydrogen) of seven. Anything above seven is alkaline (base), and below seven is acid. For those who wonder, each whole number increases the amount by an exponent of ten.

The plain truth of the pH scale is that anything that's not neutral is alkaline or acid—period. If one wishes to return to neutral from either side of the scale, a person must add enough of the opposite pH to neutralize the original.

Let's use this pH scale as an example. God is neutral (no sin). No matter which direction we go, we are going away from God. We'll go deeper into this subject in the study to follow, but right now, suffice it to say that we humans have more than missed the mark in most cases. Man has his own ideas about what it means to return to God, and he has applied them, over and over, in a way similar to a child adding salt because the food seems too "peppery."

God's plan is the only way to "return to neutral." That certainly makes sense when you pause and think that it's God we want to be with.

God uses the simplest of scales: the balance scale. You see it all the time in various depictions of justice and equal measure. In fact, in Daniel 5:27, Daniel interpreted God's writing on the wall to King Belshazzar: "Thou art weighed in the balances, and art found wanting."

What Is Wrath?

The dictionary says that the word *wrath* in its biblical use means "seeking divine retribution." This doesn't quite sound like anger, does it? Well, just to be sure, let's dig one word deeper. *Retribution* means "something justly deserved; a recompense."

Wrath, by definition, looks like simply "making things even" or "getting even." I remember the FBI man in the movie *National Treasure* saying, "Somebody's gotta go to jail." The simple truth is this: if you sin, you gotta pay. The payment for sin is your blood (your life). In Romans 6:23, Paul said, "The wages of sin is death."

The simple "wrath of God" is like putting a man on one side of a scale, and putting all that he has done–or *not* done—on the other side. You may ask, "What do you mean: *not* done?" One must always remember that the minimum requirement earns minimum reward. (See chapter 1-1).

No matter how you slice it, definition is in the mind of the interpreter. This is another good reason to learn for yourself rather than simply taking the preacher's word for it. If anyone tells you that *wrath* is anger, you will know that they are not totally correct. In speaking of God, they will be almost totally incorrect.

We see wrath as anger or punishment because the price of sin is our eternal soul. This actually seems fair to the believer, because the believer also sees that one's eternal reward is received by giving one's life to God through Jesus. To the unforgiven, though, the amount due seems harsh and therefore seems to be associated with anger.

More often than not, man seems to have decided whether or not God is angry. Man continually asks questions like: "would God do that (whatever *that* is) if He weren't angry?"

God is never cold, but He is absolutely *firm* in every aspect of His being. How many times a day do children all over the world wail and cry when a rule is enforced? Children often get angry and, therefore, come to believe that parents are angry as well. By believing that parents are angry, children shift blame to the parent rather than believe that they themselves have done anything wrong. In the worst-case scenario, fear and blame come to overrule the relationship.

In that light, it's very easy to see how the word *wrath* has come to mean "anger" rather than its original, true meaning of "settling the account."

What Does All That Mean?

We see that God is the ultimate example of fairness in that His rules have been applied to everyone equally—and firmly—without deviation since the beginning of humankind. We'll see more on this later as we continue our study.

God sees compliance or noncompliance with His stipulations as if they are placed on a balance scale. We can do more than God asks, exactly what God asks, or less than God asks. It's as simple as that.

We see that God's wrath is simply the act of God putting things or people on the scale and, if it is out of balance, applying whatever is necessary to bring it to the point of balance. If we have done less than God requires, He will take our life (our blood, as we'll see more clearly in the next chapter) to settle the difference. Later in this study, we'll also see that if we exceed the minimum, God will reward us handsomely.

5

Judaism: The Blood

In the Beginning

For us, it all started with God. But also remember that God has no beginning.

Adam and Eve ate from the Tree of Knowledge of Good and Evil. This was humanity's first sin and Satan's first victory. Satan had brought death to the world. We'll not go into theology here, only history. God confronted Adam (Genesis 3:9–11), and Adam said, "I was naked." God cursed the Serpent, made both Eve and Adam promises about being human, and cast them out of the garden. In verse 21, we're told that God made them "coats of skin."

Blood had to be shed—meaning that an animal or animals had to be killed—in order for God to make the "coats of skin" for Adam and Eve. This shedding of blood to cover the evidence of the sins of Adam and Eve was the first blood sacrifice for the sin of humanity. From the very beginning, the shedding of blood was associated *by God* with the covering of sin.

Notice that I said "covering of sin." There is no mention of forgiveness.

Noah built an altar after the flood and offered to God one of every clean animal that came from the ark as a burnt offering, and God "smelled a sweet savor." This was the first sacrifice after the flood. Blood was shed once more. We have little doubt that Noah knew what and how to sacrifice, in that it was the first thing he did when he got off the Ark. Noah knew how to praise God. Long before the flood, Noah, no doubt, had been taught proper sacrifice and had also taught his sons. Specifically, they remembered the "firstfruits" and "unblemished" offerings.

To see proof, let's back up to chapter 4 of Genesis. Cain and Abel offered sacrifices of the very best they had, their "firstfruits." Abel was a shepherd, and Cain was a farmer. Cain actually came first with his firstfruits of the field. Abel came afterward and offered a blood sacrifice.

God looked upon their sacrifices, and Abel's, being a blood sacrifice, was accepted. Cain's sacrifice was made up of plants, and probably frankincense and other items that were considered very nice gifts, but it was "not respected" (rejected) by God because it was not a blood offering.

People say that Cain's sacrifice was not accepted because his attitude was not right. Notice, though, that there was no record of Cain's attitude until God did not accept his sacrifice. Cain thought he was doing well until he saw otherwise.

When his sacrifice was "not respected," Cain got mad. God asked him why. God even offered him a substitute (Genesis 4:7), just as He did later for Abraham. God didn't accept Cain's offering, but God saw that his intentions were good and offered to help. God told Cain that "sin lieth at the door." The Hebrew word for "sin" or "sin offering" was the same and the meanings were used interchangeably. Also, the word for *lieth* (as in "lies down") is a Hebrew word indicating a four-legged (nonhuman) thing lying down. God told Cain that if he would simply go and get the lamb in front of his house, he would have a pleasing sacrifice.

Notice a correlation between then and now. God furnished a substitute for the sacrifice of Cain. God offered a substitute for the sacrifice of Abraham. God offers us a substitute for our sacrifice as well: the Lamb of God.

The rest is history, or so they say. Cain killed Abel. This was the first murder, and it was a red-letter day for Satan. After all, death is Satan's atom bomb. Not only did this incident involve death, but it was death of the worst kind: a violent death.

Cain refused to do things God's way, thinking he would do best to simply do away with the competition. It was a human reaction repeated by the temple leaders concerning Jesus. God showed Cain otherwise, and to this day, God still will only accept a blood sacrifice.

We see that the Hebrews used the same word for *sin* and *sin offering* with interchangeable meanings. They also saw that the consequences of sin went hand in hand with the sin itself—as should we. A good example is occasion when Aaron spoke to Moses in Numbers 12:11: "Alas, my lord, I beseech thee, lay not the sin [punishment] upon us, wherein we have done foolishly, and wherein we have sinned." Aaron was actually asking Moses not to lay the punishment for their sin on them.

Through the Years

Life went on, up through the Tower of Babel and the sons and grandsons of Terah (beginning in Genesis 11:27). One son of Terah was Abram. Along with his nephew Lot, Abram and Sarai went to Canaan. Famine took them to Egypt. They left Egypt, not leaving on good terms, and returned to Canaan. Lot left Abram and went his own way to Sodom.

Abram built an altar in Hebron—once again for blood sacrifice. This indicates that he settled there. And so went history through Abraham and Isaac, Jacob and Esau, and on through Joseph in Egypt.

Exodus began the story of Moses. Then came the law of Moses. In Leviticus and Deuteronomy—and to some degree in Numbers—we find the "guidelines and guardrails" for living the life that God saw best for humankind.

The law of Moses was initiated for the chosen people, the Hebrews, to follow. The Hebrews went through quite a bit of history being led by patriarchs, judges, kings, and prophets, and they continued under various leadership with the law they had been given at Mount Sinai.

The Hebrews' problem—as it is with all of us—was that they were human. Not only did they continually fail to keep the law, but they continued to attempt to improve upon it with various and sundry amendments.

The Old Testament Ends

The Old Testament record ended circa 430 BC with the book of Malachi. Malachi is our view of God's last recorded admonition to His people under the Old Covenant, all the way through to the "day of the Lord."

The point I make here is that the first thing God brought up in the book of Malachi was the fact that the sacrifices—while meeting the stipulation of the law—were not as they should be. Blood sacrifice of animals has been essential to all human communication to and worship of God since the beginning of time—until God brought His new covenant.

Jesus Was a Jew

Which sect Jesus belonged to is irrelevant, but most people say that He was Essene. The point is that Jesus came to earth because people kept messing up every plan of righteous living that God put on the table.

God could have decided that it wasn't worth His effort, which He had done before. God could have waved His hand and sent us all to our real reward, but He didn't. Instead, He came as Jesus. He lived and then died as a blood sacrifice, which was exactly what He required to satisfy His own rules of atonement. However, this new covenant sacrifice permitted real forgiveness because it involved real atonement.

Here's a little vocabulary help.

- *Atonement* is "payback." Atonement is the act and responsibility of the sinner.
- *Forgiveness* is "to remember no more." Forgiveness is the act of God through and by His gracious nature.

So, How Does This Work?

Wrath means to seek atonement. *Atonement* of blood is required before forgiveness can be given. Atonement is a "balanced scale." *Forgiveness* is only God's to give. Forgiveness cannot be given if the "scale of judgment" is unbalanced to the sinful side.

Jesus came and lived and died as the perfect sacrifice—offered once and for all humanity.

Remember the pH scale? The only thing that will bring a human to "neutral" is the blood of a human. Animal blood would suffice, but it sufficed only in that it "covered" sin; it did not truly atone unto forgiveness. We'll see later that true faith is required for forgiveness to enter the picture.

Since Jesus came, *born-again** *followers of Jesus need only pray for God's forgiveness in the name of Jesus, and it shall be given to them.*

Next, we'll look at how Mosaic law—or Judaism, as it is now called—and the teachings and practices of Jesus all meshed together very smoothly. That is, until humanity messed things up once again.

---

* Chapter 2 addresses how to be born again

6

Judaism: The Practice

The Law: Don't Do That, and You Have Done It Right

The law was all that humankind had to live by, from the time Adam and Eve sinned until Jesus arrived. In a great many areas of our lives, we still use the law of Moses as a guideline.

Paul likened the law to a schoolmaster or tutor in Galatians 3:24. Think of our own human upbringing. Behaviorally, the first thing a baby is taught is "no." The baby is told, "Don't touch that," "Don't do that," "Don't eat that," "Don't pull that"—and the list goes on.

I often liken the law to guardrails. Have you noticed that there are no guardrails in areas of a roadway where you really should be able to stay on the road? The "don't" aspect of the law is evident when you examine it in this way. Look at Galatians 5:22–23: "But the fruit of the Spirit is love, joy, peace, longsuffering, gentleness, goodness, faith, meekness, temperance: *against such there is no law*" (emphasis added). It seems that highway engineers determine where there are hazards that might hurt us, and they put guardrails there to keep us from running off the road into a ravine.

The law of Moses is like that. Actually, all laws are like that. In fact, if statutes don't point out things that are wrong, those statutes are called *instructions*, not laws. Nonetheless, the law of Moses was followed by God's chosen people and a few Gentiles until the coming of the new covenant. That same law of Moses, with human alterations and amendments, is followed by people of the Jewish religion (and others of Middle Eastern origin) to this present day.

The inherent problem with the law is best summarized in this adage: "We cannot legislate morality." The law attempts to show us what is right by pointing out when or where we are going wrong. I think of the time when the "warning track" was placed in the rules of baseball. After the warning track was added, the outfielders could see and feel when they were getting close to the outfield wall. This lowered the number of injuries of fielders who suddenly "met the wall" without warning.

The biggest problem with morality versus law is that the law cannot show us where the middle of the road is. The law can only point out when we are going off the road. The law cannot, in all practicality, carry a "warning track" for each statute. A person is either on one side of the law or the other. Crossing from one side to the other can be (and usually is) painful, since there is no "warning track" for the law.

This has been an on-going problem with the law since the beginning of the need for laws. Laws point out what is wrong. In fact, Paul told us in Romans 8 that before he knew the law, he was sinless—at least in his own mind. He said that until he knew that some things were wrong, he certainly didn't think they were wrong. How could he? Therefore, the law essentially made him a sinner.

Note that there is a monstrous difference between saying, as Paul did, that "the law made me a sinner" and saying that "the law made me sin." Some people have even gone so far as to say that this means that God makes us sin. Of course, Paul simply meant that the law pointed out what was sinful, and there were plenty of laws about plenty of the things he had done to violate those laws. However, even as it was in Paul's case, ignorance of the law is no excuse.

Sacrifice According to the Law

We've already seen that sacrifice has existed almost from the beginning of time—from the time sin entered the world, to be exact. We've seen that the covering of Adam and Eve with skins was the first blood sacrifice for sin—and that there is no mention of their sin being forgiven. The reason is that the blood of animals simply covers sin; it does not truly atone for it to the point where God forgives that sin. We'll come to understand that a person's faith has to be added in order to "balance the scales" under the first covenant.

The next recorded sacrifices were those of Cain and Abel. We know how that went. Noah made an altar with offerings after the flood. The story of Abraham and Isaac is the next recorded sacrifice (Genesis 22). Another offering recorded in Genesis was that of Jacob in his dispute with Lathan (Genesis 31).

Genesis ends with Joseph's death. The law, especially pertaining to sacrifice, was handed down from father to son throughout this period of history. We call this period, appropriately, the Patriarchal Age.

More Than Just the "What"

While the Hebrew people were living in Egypt, they were also growing as a nation and a nationality all their own. The family leaders (patriarchs) continued to deliver the law to their families, and those families thrived. Life was good until, in Exodus 1:8, "there arose up a new king over Egypt, which knew not Joseph."

Times got tough for the Hebrews. Moses was born, left Egypt, met and worked for Jethro, returned to Egypt, and—according to God's plan—led the Hebrews out of Egypt.

The "passing over" of the angel of death was a milestone in the history of the Hebrew nation. God marked it as such by declaring it to be the beginning of the new calendar year for the Hebrews. He further instituted the ordinances of the Passover remembrances. Obviously, this was the beginning of a new era of the Hebrew nation. Moses led them into the wilderness, and at Mount Sinai, God gave the Hebrews the Ten Commandments and the complete law of Moses.

It is believed that the law in the book of Leviticus was recorded (or at least dictated) by Moses, as were Genesis, Exodus, Numbers, and Deuteronomy, thereby forming the Pentateuch. These, of course, are the first five books of the Old Testament.

The Leader Was the Law

It's obvious how important sacrifice was to the Hebrews. The first two books of history that Moses wrote were Genesis, which ended with the death of Joseph in Egypt, and Exodus, which begins with the Jews' freedom from Egypt and ends with the laws (beginning with the Ten Commandments in chapter 20) given by God to Moses. Sacrifices and offerings punctuate the progression of these two books.

Exodus contains the rules for building the Tabernacle: construction materials, location, and so on. Those instructions were followed by requirements for properly dressing the priests, who came from the tribe of Levi. The law instructed that things be done "exactly so" in an effort to quash any "rabbit trails" or alternatives humankind might consider cute—which they eventually did within Christianity. We also find rules concerning the Ark of the Covenant, curtains, candlesticks, consecration of priests, and so on. Exodus ends with the history of the peoples' weakness and the preparation of the Tabernacle for worship.

Leviticus (meaning "of the Levites") starts with no frivolity. In the first seven chapters, Moses listed the various sacrifices (offerings) and described why and how each was to be performed. The book ends with Leviticus 27:34: "These [previous chapters] are the commandments, which the LORD commanded Moses for the children of Israel in mount Sinai."

Numbers has census information, along with more history and much more instruction on the various feasts and the offerings thereof. This is followed, through chapter 36, with more rules of law.

Moses lived for 275 years. Deuteronomy is Moses' effort to review and reinforce the law of Leviticus and the follow-up in the book of numbers. Deuteronomy seems repetitious, and it is so by design. Deuteronomy reinforces the law so there can be no question of accuracy or application.

From the time of the written law, the Hebrews were led by its statutes and institutions more than by men. The Hebrews' worship was an integral part of daily life. It has continued until this day within Judaism among the children of Isaac, and within Islam among the children of Ishmael. The specific lifestyle dictated by Old Testament law and tradition is replete with ritual. Ritual is the best way to never forget any part of a study, practice, or worship.

The people—who were guilty of more than the occasional transgression—ritually practiced the law. Over time, the rituals and legality grew further and further away from God's "spirit of the law." Legalism came more and more into play, until when Jesus came along, He would have nothing to do with the temple leaders.

Meanwhile, Back at the Altar

This was not intended to be a history of legalism, but the history is important. We see that no matter what else may have changed over the millennia of Hebrew history, sacrifice—more specifically, blood sacrifice—remained a central tenet of a faith in God.

As we've seen, Leviticus abounds with instructions of sacrifice. We've also seen that the priests were to dress and act specifically. The High Priest would regularly offer sin sacrifice for himself and the people. The patriarchs of the tribes would also offer sacrifices for the benefit of the families. Sacrifice was common in Hebrew life.

In the "seventh month on the tenth day," on one day only, the High Priest was allowed to go into the Holy of Holies in the Tabernacle (in the Temple after it was built) to offer sacrifice for himself first and then for the sins of the people. The "scapegoat" carried the sins into the wilderness. These sacrifices were the only way that God could abide being near the Hebrews. God and sin are what we, in modern terms, would compare to matter and antimatter. Sin had to be covered by the blood of sacrifice and carried away, annually, into the desert.

By the way, the idea of going to "face God" was so serious to the Hebrews that a rope was secured to the high priest's ankle before he went into the Holy of Holies so that his body could be pulled out if God was displeased with the amount of sins carried to Him.

In Hebrews 10:3–4, the writer said that the problem of animal sacrifice was twofold. He wrote: "But in those sacrifices there is a remembrance again made of sins every year. For it is not possible that the blood of bulls and of goats should take away sins."

7

Judaism: New and Improved

If Only I Could

A snowstorm was passing through a farmer's land, and it was blowing as much as snowing. Earlier in the day, the farmer saw it coming, and when the storm actually got there, he was prepared for it—at least as much as he could be. Electricity either hadn't been invented or, at the least, had not been run to his place. He was alone with the animals.

He'd secured a few kerosene lamps around the stalls and had stuffed hay into the biggest openings between the slats of the barn walls in an effort to make the barn as hospitable as possible for two carriage horses, his milk cow, and a few chickens.

As the snow blew, the farmer peeked out of the house—to see nuthin,' he reckoned. He did see something, though. He saw a small flock of sparrows flitting around the side of the barn. The birds were apparently attracted to the light and the possibility of shelter. One would fly at a beam of light coming between a couple of slats. Then another would try, and then another. The farmer worried that if they continued like that, they might hurt themselves or, worse, wear themselves out and die trying. The man wasted no time getting bundled up and going outside to see what he could do to get the birds into the safety of the barn.

The farmer first tried to shoo the birds toward the front of the barn. The flock split and then gathered, over and over, sometimes closer to the front and sometimes farther away from the only way in. The farmer didn't want to scare them like that, so he went around, opened one door, got a lantern, and went back to the birds.

The man tried to simply lead them to the front of the barn by waving the lantern, rather like luring a fish. The birds appeared interested, but it was one step forward and two steps back. He noticed that the open door cast a little light out on the snow, so he ran around to open the other door.

After opening the doors as wide as possible, the farmer simply stepped away to see if they'd come around on their own. The birds continued their fruitless effort of flying into the wall. He gave them a wide berth and got behind them. He shooed them again, and the flock split again and again.

The farmer saw what was happening. He was not communicating with the birds. The birds wanted the shelter, but they feared the man as he tried to get them to come to the safety of the barn. He heard himself say, "If only I could be one of them. They would follow another bird, because they would not fear it. If I were a bird, I could communicate with them."

It's A Story, But It's The Story Of God!

The farmer saw in the birds the same thing that God saw in humankind, and specifically the Hebrews. The Hebrews wanted to follow God, but they could not see the life that they needed to live, because they had no example to follow.

Humanity came to wrongly believe that God and His salvation had to be attained by acting "just so." This continued until the time of Jesus. By then, the Pharisees had even written additional "laws" to "clarify" the law of Moses contained in the Levitical and Deuteronomic recordings. They were "banging their heads against the wall" like the sparrows.

God knew that He was going to have to live among the humans in order to show them the kind of life he desired them to live. God also knew that a new and different system of sacrifice was going to have to be initiated, because humanity was becoming less God-oriented and more ritual-oriented. Forgiveness was not an issue to the people, because the chosen people (the Jews) were perfectly willing to "roll forward" their sins year to year. The Jews had come to believe that rituals were what pleased God.

Take note of the major point of this discussion: Blood sacrifice, no matter what, was required for all but the "meal offering," for which blood was never required. The burnt offering, peace offering, guilt offering, and sin offering were—and are—blood sacrifices to this day.

"Okay, so change it," you say. Remember that God never changes. Blood is and always will be required for these offerings of humankind—through the end of time. Once more, note the equity and fairness of God. God knew that the blood sacrifice of an animal would not atone for the sins of a person, but He proved that it would "cover" the sin temporarily until a person's death. In death comes the final atonement, the judgment. The author of Hebrews reminds us that the blood of bulls and goats will never atone to the point of forgiveness (Hebrews 10:4).

God, like the farmer of the story, wanted simply to show that if a person did not transgress the law, this would be a good life to be pursued. God wanted to show humans how easy it was to get into heaven.

Well, humanity proved to be stiff-necked, hard-hearted, and just plain stupid when it came to thinking of the law in godly ways. Just as it is today, the people of that time felt that if they performed to the letter of the law, they had done all that was required of them. The Hebrews and, later, Jews had proven throughout their history that they would do little more than live with the ritual of the law.

As time progressed, God saw that humanity's spiritual life was regressing rather than improving. The book of Malachi shows that God was far less than pleased by the chosen people's efforts to live within the law.

Jesus Changed Everything While Changing Little

In order to actually atone for human sins and thereby forgive them, God had to see a human sacrifice. Remembering again that God never changes, we know that He will only accept a blood sacrifice "without spot or blemish." This stipulation had to include a human sacrifice. The only way this was going to happen was if God came to earth, lived as a man—but without sin–and died as a willing sacrifice for all the sins of humankind.

The writer of Hebrews goes to great lengths to explain these things. I'll not include the extensive writings here, but you should go specifically to chapters 9 and 10 of the book of Hebrews for even deeper explanation. The point is that the burdensome rituals of sacrifice were removed by the perfect sacrifice of Jesus.

"And almost all things are by the law purged with blood; and without shedding of blood is no remission" (Hebrews 9:22). The writer is saying that, under the law, nearly everything required a "blood of animals" sacrifice of some kind. Hebrews 10:18 says, "Now where remission of these is, there is no more offering [bulls and goats] for sin." Here, he was saying that the sacrifice of Jesus removed the need for animal sacrifice. He was not saying that there is no need for sacrifice, only that there is no need for the imperfect *animal* sacrifice.

Jesus, the angels said, was named Emmanuel, which means "God with us." Jesus, God the Son, came to show us the way "to the barn door." Jesus came to show us how to travel intentionally in the middle of the road rather than bouncing off the guardrails of the law like a pinball.

Jesus told us over and over—and showed us—how to live in a way pleasing to our Father in heaven. He moaned again and again when we just didn't get it. He pointed out that we needed to spend more time in prayer, as He did when the disciples couldn't get the demon to leave the boy. He kept trying, over and over, to get the temple leaders to understand that God didn't want the legalism to continue. Jesus said—on more than one occasion—that God "desires mercy, not sacrifice."

The Change of the Chosen

Jesus never spoke against the law, only against the temple leaders. Jesus lived by the precepts and tenets of the original covenant. For a person of faith, the first covenant was "A-Okay"—if that person followed the spirit of the law rather than the ritual of the law.

Jesus did, however, speak to the "glad tidings" of God's kingdom—a fulfillment of the law that had never been seen before—at two points in the Scripture. "The law and the prophets were until John: since that time the kingdom of God is preached, and every man presseth into it" (Luke 16:16). "Think not that I am come to destroy the law, or the prophets: I am not come to destroy, but to fulfil" (Matthew 5:17).

During all the time of Jesus' ministry, He passed no judgment on the people at the expense of the temple leaders—until the week of His death. By God's plan, Jesus will judge "the quick and the dead." Jesus finally relented during that last week and passed judgment on the temple leaders and their followers. This is what I call the "change of the chosen."

For over two thousand years, the Hebrews and, later, Jews were the chosen people. Jesus tried and tried to get the temple leaders—the scribes, Pharisees, Sadducees, and others of importance—to see His explanation of what God wanted our lives to be like. Jesus pointed out to everyone that the Law and the Prophets hung on only two commandments, which he identified in Mark 12:29–31. He continually manifested this, in word and deed, multiple times elsewhere in other gospels. Jesus was the living essence of the phrase "practice what you preach."

The "change of the chosen" is shown to us explicitly in Matthew 21. Jesus tried, one last time, to get the temple leaders to understand that He was the Messiah. In verses 45–46, we're told that they actually did "get it." However, their worries about job security and their pride of position kept them from admitting that Jesus was the Messiah.

The temple leaders' fear of the followers of Jesus also kept them from simply arresting Jesus to shut Him up. After all else failed, Jesus told them in Matthew 21:43,

"Therefore say I unto you, The kingdom of God shall be taken from you, and given to a nation bringing forth the fruits thereof."

With this one sentence, Jesus pronounced the greatest change in human history. From that point onward, the Jews were no longer the chosen people.

Why We Can Say That Little Changed

Yes, Jesus came and offered a new covenant. However, being true to His nature, God did not change anything concerning the rules of worship. If it slipped by you previously, note here that God still requires blood sacrifice to this day for all the occasions—the burnt offering, peace offering, guilt offering, and sin offering—required under the Old Testament law. Paul's more proper translation calls the period of the Old Testament the period of the first covenant."

The major point of salvation under the second covenant is this: Jesus, after judging the temple leaders in Matthew 21:43, sealed His own fate in

God's plan. Jesus would have to give His life's blood as sacrifice to atone for all the unforgiven sins of the world. This is why Jesus is referred to as the Lamb of God. Jesus would be sacrificed just like the many lambs that had been sacrificed before that time.

I don't take any real issue with those who see Jesus as a personal scapegoat. While the scapegoat was not directly sacrificed, it did bear the sins of the people, and ultimately it surely did die. If we think of it that way, then Jesus took the multiple parts of the Day of Atonement and combined them all into His own personal sacrifice.

Note here that while it was the blood sacrifice of the unblemished and sinless Jesus—no doubt the greatest gift humanity has ever received—the sacrifice was a sin offering above all else. The only difference was that the burden of sin that God placed on Jesus consisted of the sins left unforgiven or unatoned since the beginning of time! His sacrifice, being perfect, was also for the sins of anyone who would claim and receive forgiveness in the future.

Given that a perfect human sacrifice has been made, the blood sacrifices of animals are no longer required. The perfect sacrifice was "once for all," as the author put it in Hebrews 10:10.

Note also that the structure of sacrifice has not changed, either. In the time that preceded Jesus, the priests made sacrifice for the people they were responsible for, and the High Priest went into the Holy of Holies annually to make sure that any sin that may have been "missed" was put to the altar as well.

The only change to the structure of worship was not with the sacrifice but with those of us who ask for forgiveness.

- We who have received the gift of salvation are made saints.
- As we become saints, we are also made members of God's royal priesthood.
- We are responsible for ourselves and our own sins alone. We present our sacrifices to God as priests.
- We make our personal sacrifices to God in and with our personal temple, our body.
- We still have a High Priest. His name is Jesus. As our high priest, Jesus intercedes for us to God, just as it was done well over two thousand years ago. Jesus intercedes for us, yes, but now we get

to go into the Holy of Holies to meet with God personally—along with our High Priest, Jesus, of course. No one can enter the Holy of Holies without the High Priest.

Judaism Does Not Equal Christianity

Well, that's one of those "yes and no" type of statements.

Judaism and Christianity are different, because the temple leaders felt the need for job security at the time of the ministry of Jesus. The temple leaders and the Sanhedrin enjoyed their position in Jewish society. These leaders chose to be rid of Jesus rather than to espouse the new covenant that He brought to them. The temple leaders were blinded by their own brilliance. Gamaliel was so very right in Acts 5:33–42. To be truthful, we have to say that *modern* Judaism does not equal Christianity. Technically speaking, Judaism was the first "splinter" religion.

Jeremiah told of God promising "a new covenant." The Jews should have been more than ready to be more than receptive. However, we all know how things turned out.

So, who's right: Judaism or Christianity? It's a shame that this question even exists. If the Jews of today were still faithfully practicing Judaism as it was two thousand years ago, they could still be acceptable to God, even without Jesus. However, we're reminded by Paul on numerous occasions that if one practices any of the law rather than following the new covenant, the law must be followed "to the letter."

Jesus despised the leaders of the temple because they had distorted the law. That distortion continues. Modern Jews no longer give blood sacrifices, and they have altered other practices as well. An example that comes to mind is the adding of an orange to the Passover seder.

The judgment is of the truth, not of this work. It is not for us to say any more than what we have been told. Jesus said in Mark 16:15–16, "Go ye into all the world, and preach the gospel to every creature. He that believeth and is baptized shall be saved; but he that believeth not shall be damned."

The ultimate question is to ask if the unsaved person has rightly heard the gospel of Jesus. You have just read of the judgment of those who accept it and those who refuse. Those who have never heard the gospel of Jesus will be judged by a different yardstick of God's own making. We get a glimpse of that different yardstick in Hebrews 11.

Paul also discussed being with or without the law in Romans 2.

The point of this chapter concerning God's logic is to show that Christianity is what I have come to call "new and improved Judaism." We Christians need to realize that we are worshiping God in the same way as those who worshipped Him thousands of years ago.

New and Improved Judaism

There are slight–though *very* significant—differences between the practices of the Judaism that Jesus came to improve and the Christianity we now practice. Just as with anything else, if our God moves, the move is significant. The differences are:

- Jesus, through His self-sacrifice, made a blood offering that would be acceptable to God for absolute atonement for the sins of anyone who would claim the benefit of His sacrifice. Of course, as shown earlier in this work, the simple steps to becoming saved must be followed to gain this favor of God.

  Make no mistake; salvation is an offered favor of God. We humans can do absolutely nothing to make ourselves acceptable to God, except by the plan that our gracious God provided. Jesus Himself thereby eliminated for us the necessity of an individual, physical blood sacrifice for each and every transgression. There is little doubt that, with the Pharisees making things so difficult, most Jews at the time of Jesus found the sacrifices to be more hardship than worship.

- Jesus did what God had previously tried to do with the law. Jesus gave us a perfect example of how to live a life pleasing to God. He showed us where the "middle of the road" is. That is to say that Jesus showed us how to stay on the road and never hit a "guardrail" of the law. Jesus showed us that if we follow His example, we need never worry about breaking the law.

- In Matthew 5:17, Jesus said, "Do not think that I have come to abolish the Law or the Prophets; I have not come to abolish them but to fulfill them." Perhaps it might be better to translate the action rather than the words, in that Jesus came to genuinely "fill full" the law.

  Jesus actually "fleshed out" the law. Think of what the law gave us. In the law, we could never see God. Some of us got closer than others did, but the most any of us could get was a rough outline of what God actually desired of us. In the law, we got only a fuzzy image of God's true form. We were given a reverse image of God in that all we saw was "not God." We were told, over and over, what *not* to do. The law showed us what God was not.

  Jesus gave us more. The law had given us only a skeleton or framework on which to hang our imagination of the life that God desired. There were those who were "spot on" mentioned in the eleventh chapter of Hebrews. However, even these "faithful" didn't see the true picture of God's desires. If you had asked these people in Hebrews 11 what they did to gain God's favor, I'm sure that they could give you little more than a humble "I don't know. I just help where I can."

  Jesus came and showed us the way—to live, worship, think, pray, and love. Suffice it to say that He showed us what we'd been looking for in the thousands of years previous. Jesus showed us God and how to properly live for and worship Him. Jesus Himself said in John 14:9b, "He that hath seen me hath seen the Father; and how sayest thou then, Shew us the Father?"

  Visualize the law as a skeleton, and then try to see God. It can't be done. At best, you might see some sort of shape—an arm or a leg or a body. But now visualize Jesus standing in front of that skeleton, or better yet, actually wrapping His body over and around that skeleton of the law to give it substance. Now you can no longer see the law; you can only see Jesus. God was successful.

The birds now can clearly see the way into the barn.

- Jesus also eliminated our need for the help of any other earthly being (except for a teacher or witness, as with Philip and the eunuch) in order to gain salvation. We note that earlier in history, Jesus was given by God the priesthood (the order of Melchizedek) that existed from the beginning of human worship.*

Because Jesus became human and totally understands what it is to be human, He is now our High Priest, and we who are saved are the royal priesthood. Jesus is our intercessor. There is *no one* who stands between us and God, as long as we approach while holding the hand of (praying in the name of) our firstborn brother, Jesus.

- In His own words, Jesus said that He hadn't come to destroy the law or to belittle anything the prophets of old had told us. He did, however, do away with all the nit-picky aspects of the law.

  I say "nit-picky" seriously as well as figuratively. "Nits" are the eggs of lice. To pick these out of someone's hair is quite tedious. The Pharisees had gone so far down the list of what was clean and unclean that they had ruled that a gnat was unclean. They had even amended the law to say that you had to filter your drink through a cloth to ensure that you didn't ingest a gnat.

  Jesus pointed out the hypocrisy of the Pharisees as He was pronouncing the woes upon them in Matthew 23:24: "Ye blind guides, which strain at a gnat, and swallow a camel."

- Jesus knew that changing the way men looked at the law was His goal. He called the law a burden and compared it to "the way" in Matthew 11:28–30 (NIV): "Come to me, all you who are weary and burdened, and I will give you rest. Take *my* yoke upon you and learn from *me*, for I am gentle and humble in heart, and you will find rest for your souls. For *my* yoke is easy and *my* burden is light" (emphasis added).

  Throughout His ministry, Jesus pointed to how simple life can be. He cut the commandments of the old covenant down to only two. One could easily call it a single, two-part commandment. The Pharisees made obeying each and every article of the law so important that it was actually oppressive. A Pharisee lawyer

---

* See chapter 9, "The God We Call Jesus – Melchizedek." Also in section 3, take a deeper look at the Trinity in "Father, Son and Holy Ghost."

thought that Jesus might be tricked into picking one commandment as the most important. This would mean that the other commands were less important to Him, and then they could say that Jesus had said that all parts of the law were not equal.

Jesus answered the Pharisee's question in Matthew 22:37–40: "Jesus said unto him, 'Thou shalt love the Lord thy God with all thy heart, and with all thy soul, and with all thy mind. This is the first and great commandment. And the second is like unto it, Thou shalt love thy neighbour as thyself. On these two commandments hang *all* the law and the prophets'" (emphasis added).

Jesus crystallized Christianity down to two points: (1) Love God, first and foremost, and (2) love your neighbor as yourself. Christianity had been boiled down to doing the right thing.

- Like a relief pitcher in baseball, Jesus figuratively patted the law on the back and said, "Good job, Law. Now, give me the ball. You pitched a great game, but I'll take over. I'll finish this." Jesus, the Lamb of God, met death as the universal sacrifice, once and for all (Hebrews 10:10). Human blood was given for human sin. Atonement was obtained, and God could allow Himself to forgive and forget these two categories of sins:

    - All the unforgiven sin that God had placed on Jesus, which includes all the unforgiven or unatoned sins of the faithful from the beginning of time.
    - All the sin of anyone who claims the benefit of the perfect sacrifice of Jesus through His plan of salvation.

Because of His manifest love for us—and His sacrifice because of that love—Jesus, our High Priest, now sits in heaven on the great white throne. He proved that He would rather die than live without you

PART III

God

Where does one begin in talking about God?

We will begin by pointing out that this section is written to both the scholar and the student. By design, it is far deeper than what you'll learn in Sunday school. As in other sections of this study, I don't feel that the information is original to this work, in that all knowledge comes from God. I certainly cannot determine if others have been given the same information to spread elsewhere. I do believe, however, that a great many readers will find what they consider to be new information or, at the least, a different point of view.

This work is not designed to be another exhibition of the beaten path. It is intended to step off the beaten path and view that beaten path with new eyes. Understanding with even deeper knowledge and wisdom is what we all seek, and you will find some of that herein.

There are things within this section—as there are scattered through this study—that are moot points. This means that they are arguable but that the argument does nothing to change what is important. However, if you allow yourself to be receptive rather than argumentative, you may find yourself in agreement, having no argument at all. Jesus said in John 14:1, "Let not your heart be troubled: ye believe in God, believe also in me."

If this is true in your own heart, you believe the most important thing.

Part III first discusses the character and power of God (YHWH) and our relationship with Him. It also provides a detailed study of the God we call Jesus, the works and benefits of the Holy Spirit, and the Godhead of the Holy Trinity.

8

YHWH: The "I Am"

Our Awesome God

As the title of this chapter says, God is the great "I Am." He was, is, and always will be—all at the same time. When we say "all at the same time," it is purely because of our need to define—in our meager, human way—eternity. God does not require our definitions to function. It's almost "creepy," so to speak, that we can't seem to mention God without also mentioning time in some way or another.

God was limitless, timeless, and beyond restriction until the "time" that He decided to create people and place them in the universe created for their pleasure. Before that point in time, there had been no time. Even today, God lives in eternity. However, when He relates to us in our world, in our universe, He requires of Himself to work within humanity's time constraints and with things like covenants, agreements, and promises.

While God is still the God of all, YHWH Elohim, El Shaddai, becomes a constitutional monarch when He operates in our world of His creation.

What's that? A constitutional monarchy is a system of government in which the powers of a monarch (single ruler) are restricted to those granted under the constitution and laws of the nation. The point is that God loves us so much that He placed these constitutional restraints upon Himself in order to care for us.

Restraints on God?

This is an interesting and rarely considered aspect of our Father, God. God has made agreements with various men throughout history. Some of those agreements, or covenants, were applied to entire groups of people, such as the Israelites. Some were made with individuals, such as Abraham, Isaac, Jacob, and so on.

Anytime an agreement or covenant is made, the parties to it agree to be bound by one another's actions. A typical example would be the time when God agreed to make Israel a great nation—*if* Israel kept the commandments of God.

Allow me to interject a note that God, with a simple wave of His hand, can literally destroy our entire universe. He loves us, though, and will not—until the time of final judgment. The word *longsuffering* (patient) is used many times to describe God. How true that is concerning humankind! We see throughout the history of the Scriptures that God's patience will not abide all things and certainly will not abide forever in reference to issues such as covenant failure.

However, God wants everyone to acknowledge Him here on earth and thereby to come and live with Him forever. The problem with this is that in order to get into heaven, one must be sinless. Throughout history, we see our God working with humankind to help them at least get to a state of righteousness (Romans 4:3) and at best get to a sinless state.

One can never meet an obligation if it is not known. Further, obligations must not only be known but understood clearly, in no uncertain terms, by both the one owed the obligation and the one providing or performing the obligation. This is the purpose of the covenants that God has established with humankind through the years.

The point is that God, in order to keep His side of the bargain, must live within the constraints of caring for us in the ways He has guaranteed to His followers while our souls live here on earth.

Has God Given Us a Covenant?

In a word, yes. God's will is clearly shown in 2 Peter 3:9. Peter told us that "the Lord is … not willing that any should perish, but that all should come to repentance." This means that God wants all of us to live with Him for eternity.

However, we must remember that in order to get into heaven, a person must be sinless. This requirement is on our side of the covenant.

God, in his loving kindness, has not left us to our own devices. God has given us explicit instructions on how to live a right life. First, He gave us the law to point out the wrong things we are not to do, and second, He came to earth as Jesus to literally show us what were the right things to do.

You and I know that we can't live a sinless life, but the wisdom of God has provided us with a means of wiping the slate clean. If you have not read Part 1 on salvation, please do so now. Your soul is more important than any discourse you may find here.

God's Character

God is pure and true. That statement about sizes everything up—except for the question, "What does that mean?"

Pure is a word that we hardly ever think of, the reason being that literally nothing this side of eternity—on, in, or above this earth—is pure. Purity has all sorts of definitions, especially in science where you'd expect a more strict definition. Science says that you can have pure alcohol if you have a mixture of only ethanol, or methanol, or some other form of alcohol with no other additive. This concept in science is the reason that many people believe the error that there are different paths to heaven. They consider that any mixture of efforts, all of which involve "seeking" God, is pure.

However, let's leave our human definitions behind. When we say that God is pure, we refer to another level that is far removed from our comprehension. God is eternally unadulterated by any sin. God's purity is so pure that it has a brilliance of its own; we call it *glory*.*

God is incapable of sin. God cannot even look on sin. This is why the sky turned dark at the crucifixion of Jesus. Jesus was given the sins of the world, and at that point, God could no longer look at His Son. As God turned His face away, His glory left that place. The sky turned dark and

* See chapter 28 for a deeper discussion of God's glory.

remained so until Jesus died and God returned His gaze. God's purity is sinless to the nth degree of infinity.

God cannot sin. Therefore, God cannot lie. The point goes well beyond that. Realize that we cannot get poison from a pure spring. *Nothing evil comes from God.* For the person who blindly says, "God is in control," this idea is sometimes hard to grasp.

We have an actual discussion of sin in chapter 15. Here, we simply state that we must remember that God uses a balancing scale and allows the chips to fall where they may concerning the consequences of sin. The Bible is replete with stories of the consequences of sin. However, those stories are there to teach us the single important point that sin very often has immediate consequences that do not come from God.

Paul wrote to the church in Corinth:

> Now these things were our examples, to the intent we should not lust after evil things, as they also lusted. Neither be ye idolaters, as were some of them; as it is written, The people sat down to eat and drink, and rose up to play. Neither let us commit fornication, as some of them committed, and fell in one day three and twenty thousand. Neither let us tempt Christ, as some of them also tempted, and were destroyed of serpents. Neither murmur ye, as some of them also murmured, and were destroyed of the destroyer. Now all these things happened unto them for ensamples: and they are written for our admonition, upon whom the ends of the world are come. Wherefore let him that thinketh he standeth take heed lest he fall. (1 Corinthians 10:6–12)

God does not have to look for Satan; nor do we. We're told that Satan "as a roaring lion, walketh about, seeking whom he may devour" (1 Peter 5:8). Satan is more than happy to visit any due consequences on every sinner on the face of the earth. Notice, though, that Satan cannot overstep the bounds placed on him by God. If God's protection is on this or that person, Satan must seek God's permission before causing any consequence.[†] The story of Lot is a very clear example.

While you think on God, think powerfully on the fact that Satan cannot do to God's children what God will not allow him to do.

---

† See part I on how to receive the protection of God Almighty.

The "Omni" Words

God gave us time. Before God made humans, there was no time, only eternity. At the end of time, there will still be eternity.

Without going through the creation account and all the reasons for it and the miraculous nature and time frame of it, we'll simply explain the heading of the section:

- God is *omnipotent.*
- God is *omnipresent.*
- God is *omniscient.*

Human misunderstandings have made us think many things about those three words.

When we apply our English language to translation, we almost invariably try to oversimplify the meaning using the fewest words possible—and the smaller the better. It's the nature of our language. The only places where verbosity is acceptable seem to be in poetry and legalese. When we give thought to the Holy Scriptures, we often carry with us this "English" attitude, this desire to simplify and conquer. Our wish to simplify, coupled with our desire to understand, will (and quite often does) confound our already illogical paths of human reasoning.

We will look at these three words as descriptions applied to our God.

Omnipotent

Most people are a bit surprised to learn that *omnipotent* does not actually mean "strongest of all." It can be construed to that point, but let's look at the more literal translation from the original works.

The word *shaddai* in the King James Version of the Bible translates to "almighty" in all instances of the Hebrew (forty-seven times). The word given to us from the Greek (ten times) as "almighty" is *Pantokratōr*, which actually translates to "all-ruling" or "ruler over all." We have long considered *almighty* to mean the same.

A ruler, of course, has power over his kingdom. In the sense that God is ruler over all, He is also all-powerful. The point is that being all-powerful, in this case, has nothing to do with being able to perform physical acts of strength. I personally remember someone, years ago, wondering if God could "make a rock so heavy that He could not pick it up." To me, saying such things brings to mind Jesus saying to Satan in the desert, "It is written again, Thou shalt not tempt [test] the Lord thy God" (Matthew 4:7).

God reigns over the heavens and the earth. Therefore, He has absolute "power of the throne" and certainly can designate authority in any way He sees fit. God has given Jesus "all authority" until after the judgment, which is when Jesus will hand authority back to God (Luke 10:22).

The word *omnipotent* does not mean that God can do anything. We're told in Titus 1:2 that God "cannot lie." In 2 Timothy 2:13, we're told that God "cannot deny Himself." Certainly we can see that God cannot do anything that is against His nature or His essence.

The word *omnipotent* does mean that God is the ruler of heaven and earth and commander of life itself. No being in all eternity can rule or overpower God. Just ask Satan. (We'll talk more about that later.)

Omnipresent

How can this be? God has a body, and we can prove it over and over with Scriptures that mention the various body parts of God. In the Scriptures, we hear of the "strong arm of God," "His nostrils," "His feet," "His ears," "His hand," and so on. We were made in His image, and we have all these parts as well. How then can a "personage" be in all places at the same time?

David put it best in Psalm 139:7–10. He wrote, "Whither shall I go from thy spirit? or whither shall I flee from thy presence? If I ascend up into heaven, thou art there: if I make my bed in hell, behold, thou art there. If I take the wings of the morning, and dwell in the uttermost parts of the sea; Even there shall thy hand lead me, and thy right hand shall hold me."

Notice that David used the words "from thy spirit." David had no formal training on the Trinity, but he certainly recognized what he called God's Spirit. Have you noticed that, even today, Christians that are less than comfortable talking about the Holy Spirit use the term *God's Spirit*?

The Holy Spirit is everywhere. It's as simple as that. The Holy Spirit is everywhere we go—and everywhere we can't go—and in places we've never heard of or seen. We are blessed that we have the security of knowing that as long as we never leave God, God will never leave us, no matter where we go.

This is the "gift of the Holy Spirit" in Acts 2:38.

Omniscient

God knows everything. Actually, it's not quite that simple. Ask theologians and philosophers, and you'll get explanations that resemble what I call "pretzel logic." The definitions depend on the strict and careful use of the words in those explanations, and the explanations depend on themselves for justification.

We have Scriptures showing God's superior and infinite power of perception. The author of Hebrews (4:11) spoke to the fact that God even knows our intentions: "And [He] is a discerner of the thoughts and intents of the heart." In 1 John 3:20, John said, "For God is greater than our hearts, and he knows everything." David told us in Psalm 44:21 that God knows the "secrets of the heart." And in Psalm 139:12, David spoke of God perceiving everything when he said, "Even the darkness will not be dark to you; the night will shine like the day, for darkness is as light to you." David was saying that God is not only everywhere (verses 7–10), but that He sees in the darkness as if it was the light of day.

So, let's "put a bow on it," then. God is ruler over all and can perceive everything down to the intentions of our individual hearts. We've already seen that God's Spirit is everywhere. We see, in 1 Corinthians 2:10, that God's Spirit "searches all things." Therefore, according to Scripture, we must say that if something can be known—even if it's thought or intention—God immediately knows it.

Let's reinforce that point. If only one person in the entire world has a particular thought, God not only knows that thought, but He also knows the person's intent in that thought. Again, if a single person has a single thought, it can be known—and God knows it.

Given the Scripture's descriptions, God is omniscient as well as omnipresent and omnipotent.

Focusing on Omniscience

A great many people overreach when they think of the word *omniscient.*

We just discussed the fact that God perceives even the thoughts of people. God's perception is so far beyond keen that He even knows the *intentions* of the heart, whether they are malevolent or benign.

God has also said, from His own lips, that He has made plans and determines the future. "Remember the former things of old: for I am God, and there is none else; I am God, and there is none like me, Declaring the end from the beginning, and from ancient times the things that are not yet done, saying, My counsel shall stand, and I will do all my pleasure" (Isaiah 46:9–10).

Our own human dependence and/or frailties cause us to lean toward interpreting that Isaiah passage—and other passages—as meaning that God knows all, and that "all" includes the future. This is not a true interpretation. Some readers may just now have raised an eyebrow. Let's revisit and clarify the word *omniscience* with a bit of explanation and a number of Scriptures.

In various Bible reference materials, Bible dictionaries, and such, we find a tremendous amount of hot-potato rambling under the guise of definition. *Dictionary.com*, a more secular publication, defines *omniscient* this way:

1. having complete or unlimited knowledge, awareness, or understanding;
2. perceiving all things. [Perceive = become aware or conscious of (something).]

This definition states exactly what *omniscient* means. To be sure, many of us certainly feel better knowing that this is not a salvation issue.* However, there are those who believe that the future is predestined and that even salvation has been decided for us.†

---

* If something is "not a salvation issue," a belief of any sort on the issue is irrelevant to the salvation of one's soul.

† See also chapter 14, "Chosen, Elected, Called, Appointed, Predestined."

Various Schools of Thought on God's Omniscience

Large numbers of people view God as having seen the future for everyone. These people also see God as having "picked their mate before they were born," and so on. Basically, they say that God has an individual plan for them from the time of their birth. Others say that He has had a plan for them from the beginning of time.

There are variations on this thinking that run the gamut from "God sees the future" scenarios to how much of one's personal life is directly controlled by God's foreknowledge—or by His action as determined by His foreknowledge. The gist is that God knows your personal future and will guide your life accordingly—if you're one of the lucky ones. You have no free will, but it sometimes feels like you do.

Another school of thought believes that God sees the future but ignores it so we can have free will. There are also different ideas as to God's use of this information.

Yet another line of thought believes that God fixed the future at the beginning of time. This belief says that there is nothing that can be done to change anything. There is no possibility of free will.

Still another line of thinking believes that God *can* see the future but that He simply chooses not to so that we can have free will.

What Scripture Says about God's Omniscience

Some particular Scriptures conflict with the thoughts above when they are juxtaposed for comparison. We'll look at each one with context and expansion, as necessary. We'll discuss them here in the order they appear in the Bible.

Genesis 6:5. After He created Adam, God began to realize that man was not as dedicated to God as God was to man. In Genesis 6:5, we see that God was fed up. We're told that "GOD saw that the wickedness of man was great in the earth, and that every imagination of the thoughts of his [man's] heart was only evil continually."

All of humankind was thinking evil. Only Noah was righteous enough to save. This begins the Bible story of Noah and the ark. God had come to the realization that humanity wasn't worth saving, and Genesis 6:6 says that "it repented the LORD that he had made man on the earth, and it grieved him at his heart."

Genesis 22. In this chapter, we see the story in which Abraham was told to sacrifice his son Isaac. Abraham proceeded to do as he was told, and when the Lord saw the intention of his heart, the angel of the LORD called his name and told him to stop. Then, in verse 12, we read that the angel of the LORD said, "Do not lay a hand on the boy. Do not do anything to him. Now I know that you fear God, because you have not withheld from me your son, your only son."

The Lord provided another sacrifice, just as He had done for Cain. But unlike Cain, Abraham offered a proper sacrifice with the ram that the Lord had provided.

Exodus 32. In this chapter, we see that people had begun worshipping the golden calf that Aaron had made for them. God was angered and told Moses to get off the mountain and leave Him alone. He told Moses that He was going to destroy the people and make Moses the new Noah—meaning that God would try again with Moses as another new beginning of God's people.

Moses pled with God to remember His covenant with Abraham, Isaac, and Israel (Jacob), and verse 14 tells us, "And the LORD repented of the evil which he thought to do unto his people."

Numbers 13 forward. From Numbers 13 forward, God told Moses to send spies, one from each tribe, into the "land of milk and honey" to search the land. When the spies returned, only two—Joshua and Caleb—stood on the side of faith in God. The other ten spies said that the people looked tough and the cities had walls and that they'd better not go in there. The people called out to stone Joshua and Caleb, saying that they'd have been better off staying in Egypt.

God was enraged because of the people's continued lack of faith. In Numbers 14:12, God told Moses, "I will smite them with the pestilence, and disinherit them, and will make of thee a greater nation and mightier than they." Moses again begged for pardon, and it was granted. In Numbers 14:20, we read: "And the LORD said, I have pardoned according to thy word."

1 Samuel 15. In this chapter, Saul was commanded to utterly destroy Amalek. Saul decided to do differently and messed up once again by not following God's command. Samuel came and corrected the situation as best he could by killing King Agag. Verse 35 says, "And Samuel came no more to see Saul until the day of his death: nevertheless Samuel mourned for Saul: and the LORD repented that he had made Saul king over Israel."

1 Chronicles 21. David, often identified as "a man after God's own heart" (Acts 13:22), was quite a sinner. Perhaps his sins were no greater in strength or number than other people's, but his sins were certainly well documented.

In 1 Chronicles 21, David was tempted by Satan to take a census. The problem was not with the census but with the sin of pride. David took the census to show himself how powerful he was—not because of God but because of his own mighty armies. Another problem lay in the fact that God had established the proper rules for taking a census, which David was not following. Joab knew the problems involved in taking an improper census, but he did the king's bidding.

God gave David a choice of punishments, and David chose God's punishment: pestilence in the form of an angel's (Mi-ki-el's) sword. In 1 Chronicles 21:15, we are told, "And God sent an angel unto Jerusalem to destroy it: and as he was destroying, the LORD beheld, and He repented him of the evil, and said to the angel that destroyed, It is enough, stay now thine hand. And the angel of the LORD stood by the threshingfloor of Ornan the Jebusite."

As it is with any good parent, God can somewhat predict what His children will do. On the other side of the coin, however, even the best parent will *not* be able to predict every child's action in every situation. And neither will God. You'll note, further, that our God of mercy can be swayed by our prayers and intercessions.

Now, let's examine the six passages above.

Genesis 6:5. God saw—because He perceives all things—that humankind had not and would not come closer to Him but would only wander further and further away. God decided to start over with Noah, the only man who had remained truly faithful to Him. In Genesis 6:6, we see that God was sorry that He'd even created humans.

Would God be repentant over something He knew was going to happen?

Genesis 22. God told Abraham to sacrifice Isaac. God was testing Abraham's faith. God was about to embark on a great and glorious plan, and He needed to know if Abraham would stay faithful to the end. God saw Abraham's heart and knew that he intended to sacrifice his son. Most people see this as "just another Bible story."

It was so very much more than that. This momentous occasion was a turning point in the history of humanity. This was as important to history as the "change of the chosen" (chapter 7) and even the crucifixion itself. In fact, the very future of humankind as we know it was at stake.

God needed to know if humanity was worthy of the very real effort that the salvation of humanity would require. Abraham proved that he would give his son for the love of God. Consequently, God knew that He could rightly give His own Son for the love of humanity. Abraham proved to God that Jesus would not die in vain. Notice in the middle of Genesis 22:12 that God (the angel of God) said, "*Now I know that you fear God*, because you have not withheld from me your son, your only son" (emphasis added).

Would God have said "Now I know" if He had known already?

Exodus 32. God told Moses in no uncertain terms (Exodus 32:7–10) that He was about to destroy the Hebrew nation, if not the entire earth, as He had done to the earth of Noah's day. Moses remembered that Abraham had bargained with God over Sodom and Gomorrah, and Moses also knew that he'd done a little bargaining on his own when he got God to send Aaron along to Egypt. Moses began to bargain with God once more. And God changed His mind in Exodus 32:14: "The LORD repented of the evil which he thought to do unto his people."

Would God have been sorry for planning something that He knew He was not going to do? Would He even have told Moses about it to begin with?

Numbers 13 forward. God had led the people of Israel to the Jordan River, to the "land of milk and honey." Twelve spies had come back from a look around Canaan, carrying bountiful crops and telling everyone, "We came unto the land whither thou sentest us, and surely it floweth with milk and honey; and this is the fruit of it" (Numbers 13:27).

Imagine Moses' (not to mention God's) surprise when they began whining as they continued their report: "Nevertheless the people be strong that dwell in the land, and the cities are walled, and very great: and moreover we saw the children of Anak there. The Amalekites dwell in the land of the south: and the Hittites, and the Jebusites, and the Amorites, dwell in the mountains: and the Canaanites dwell by the sea, and by the coast of Jordan ... We be not able to go up against the people; for they are stronger than we" (Numbers 13:28–29, 31).

You can bet that God was angry! He had built the ladder to success and had placed the Hebrew people two-thirds of the way up it, for God had already given them the land. All they had to do was go and take it. The problem was that *they were telling God how big the problems were rather than showing the problems how big their God was.*

God was about to wipe out the whole lot of humanity again—for the second time during the life of Moses—when Moses stepped in again and begged pardon for the people. God relented and repented on His plans. This situation almost exactly repeats the one in Numbers 16:41–50. Three times God decided to destroy the Hebrew people—if not the entire world.

There is much more to be learned from this story, but in this segment, we will simply ask these questions: Would God have repented of His decision to send pestilence and to disinherit and destroy the people if He had known that He was not going to do it? Would God have even spoken of wiping out the people if He had known that it was not going to happen? Does God make empty threats?

1 Samuel 15. Saul proved, over and over and over, that he was not a king who would follow God's commands. Saul remained God's choice until the attack on the Amalekites. After Samuel did Saul's dirty work by killing Agag, the Lord withdrew His anointing, and Saul was left to his own wits, which served him poorly from beginning to end. We saw earlier in 1 Samuel 15:35: "And the LORD repented that he had made Saul king over Israel."

Would God have been sorry for installing Saul as king if He had already known that Saul was going to have so little regard for God's commands? Would God even have installed Saul at all?

1 Chronicles 21. When God gave David a choice of punishments, he chose God's punishment rather than humanity's because "very great are His mercies." God sent the pestilence, and seventy thousand men died. All the while, David and the elders were engaged in intercessory prayer, begging for God's mercy and forgiveness. God saw the devastation, and He restrained the destroying angel at the threshing floor of Ornan. The angel of the Lord told David to buy that piece of ground, build an altar to the Lord, and offer sacrifices. And the plague of the angel of the Lord was stayed.

Once more, God had decided to destroy the people, and this time they were Judeans. Why are we told that God decided that enough was enough—if He already knew how much of Jerusalem He was going to allow to be destroyed? Why would God start something He knew He would not finish? If God had already seen Himself stopping and deciding to show mercy, wouldn't He have told the angel to destroy only a quarter or a half of the population?

Major Points

There are two points in discussing the six passages above.

The first is to show that God does not know our moves before we make them. However, I emphatically believe that God knows our choices the very moment that we even hint at our intent, even before we have actually made the decision. God plans for all eventualities the moment a thought crosses our mind. As we discussed earlier, this shows that if something can be known—a thought or even an intention—God knows it! Simply put, we can keep no secrets from God.

The second, which is not unrelated to this discussion, is to show that our God, while vengeful, is always merciful. God will change His mind and His plans if we give Him good reason.

Sovereign God Almighty

Let's take a moment to think about the phrase "sovereign God Almighty." The biggest problem with any God-sees-the-future scenario is that if we say something like "God sees the future and acts accordingly," we are saying that God is *reacting* to future events. To say such is to say that something is controlling God and making Him do what He does. If so, God is not truly sovereign. There is no other way to interpret this idea. There is also no greater untruth.

In no way are we taking anything away from God. We have not put Him in a box. Rather, we have released Him from the box of our own creation with this understanding. We can now see God as even greater.

We are showing here that God does not know our future thoughts and decisions. However, to say that God cannot control or determine the future is to speak absolute error! We showed earlier that in Isaiah 46:9–10, God said, "Remember the former things of old: for I am God, and there is none else; I am God, and there is none like me, *Declaring the end from the beginning, and from ancient times the things that are not yet done*, saying, My counsel shall stand, and I will do all my pleasure" (emphasis added).

Now *that* sounds like a sovereign God!

Notice the wording of that passage in Isaiah. God doesn't say that He sees "the end from the beginning." He says that He "*declares* the end from the beginning." God goes further to say that after He declares His plan, He will most certainly cause it to happen. God states, "My counsel shall stand, and I will do all my pleasure."

One can readily see from the Scripture that God declares His plan and then enacts it with anyone who can do as He commands. Occasionally (how often, we'll never know), one man will fail (like Saul), and another (like David) will step up to complete whatever part of the plan the former person was (or was not) working on.

God in no way states that He knows what is going to happen. God does, however, state—in no uncertain terms in the next verse (11)—that He will go to any length to affect the successful end to His plan. He says that He might call a ravenous bird from the east[‡] or that He will find a man like

---

‡ To say something came from the east in biblical times was the same as saying "from out of nowhere."

Noah, Abraham, Moses, or the like and bring him in from a far country (exactly what God did with Abram) to make His plan complete. At the end of verse 11, God said, "I have spoken it, I will also bring it to pass; I have purposed it, I will also do it."

An example that comes to mind is in Jeremiah 29:11 (NIV). God was telling Jeremiah to tell the people, "For I know the plans I have for you," declares the LORD, "plans to prosper you and not to harm you, plans to give you hope and a future."

God was telling the people that He had plans for them, the chosen people. Plans for them to prosper and to give them a future. The King James Version puts it this way: "to give you an expected end." God did not tell them—or us—that He had seen what was going to happen but that He had planned and expected a good end, selected of His choosing, *if* the people came back to Him.

A grand master in chess can "see" about twenty-six moves ahead in any given game. How much more of a chess player might God be? God's plan is so complete that He anticipates every possible move: "If he zigs, I'll do this; if he zags, I'll do that; and if he stops, I've got a guy who can take his place."

God can plan so well that one can easily see how it might look like God has seen the future. In truth, God's plan is so complete that the future will happen—according to God's will—*whether you and I are a part of it or not.* (We will address this subject further in chapter 13: "God's Plan ≠ God's Will."

Now We Can Put a Bow on It

God's plans are perfect. It's the humans who are used to fulfill God's plans who are weak or downright bad. When instructed to "not look back," we do. When instructed to "enter by the straight gate," we don't. These are the eventualities that God plans for.

Our largest single example of the fact that God changes His plans based on our action is the new covenant. In Hebrews 8:6–13, the author precisely explained that the old covenant was "faulty" and that Jesus had come to institute and mediate a new covenant. *God's side of the covenant has not changed.* God has kept His side of the bargain through thousands of years of our history. God changed the new covenant requirements on our side in order to help us remember *Him* rather than rituals.

God does not want any of us to fail. God's will is stated clearly in 2 Peter 3:9: "The Lord is not slack concerning his promise, as some men count slackness; but is longsuffering to us-ward, *not willing that any should perish, but that all should come to repentance*" (emphasis added).

No, God does not want any of us to fail when we become a part of His plans, nor does He want a single soul left behind. However, He has contingency plans in place for any and every possibility. God's plans will succeed, with or without you and me. The point is that we must offer ourselves to God so we may be a part of His plans. His train is leaving the station, and it's up to us to get on board. Pause and wrap your mind around that.

Some people say that if they were to believe that God cannot see the future, they would feel that God is not as "in control" as they'd thought. Actually, the opposite is true for the believer. This concept proves that *God is in absolute control.* God is not *reacting* to the future; He is *planning* for the future. God is planning for *every* eventuality of the future. If we become—and remain—a part of God's plan, we will not, cannot, fail![§]

One very important point here is that if you are not a part of God's plan, you will receive little or no help in this life. There are those who will attain success—as the world sees success—without God.[§] Their success is earthly, and their reward is earthly as well.

The greater point is that we cannot get to heaven on our own terms. Heaven—and everything else—belongs to God, and He has established the very simple "entrance requirements."

Another thought to ponder is that we may be tested at one time or another, just as Abraham was tested, to see if our steel is tempered and our faith is strong. But you can now see that the greater the test, the greater a thing God wants to use you for.[¶]

---

§ See also chapter 13, "God's Plan ≠ God's Will," to better see how we should view and trust God's plans.

¶ See also chapter 22, "Testing, Testing," in the section on theology.

9

The God We Call Jesus

Looking for Fingerprints of Jesus

John 1:1–5 says, "In the beginning was the Word, and the Word was with God, and the Word was God. The same was in the beginning with God. All things were made by him; and without him was not any thing made that was made. In him was life; and the life was the light of men. And the light shineth in darkness; and the darkness comprehended it not."

Wow! That passage from John has to be the absolute best example of making a long story short. It states that "in the beginning" Jesus was not only there *with* God but that He *is* God. We're also told that Jesus was a principal—if not the only—physical participant in the creation of all things. Paul made a direct reference to this in Ephesians 3:9 when he wrote, "And to make all men see what is the fellowship of the mystery, which from the beginning of the world hath been hid in God, who created all things by Jesus Christ."

John explained that Jesus held life. Not only did Jesus-as-God breathe that life into Adam, but because of that life, Jesus-as-God knew that He also held knowledge about living that He needed to impart to humankind. Jesus-as-Jesus came to the earth and dispensed that knowledge by teaching and by example. The problem was this: when Jesus shone His light into the darkness of humankind, humankind did not—at least to the extent that they should have—comprehend what Jesus was trying to "show and tell." The darkness still exists, even more than two thousand years later.

Paul painted the same story with a broader brush in the first chapter of the book of Colossians. Notice that verse 16 speaks specifically about Jesus creating our world.

Another passage, Psalm 33:6, gives us a short but descriptive look at the creation: "By the word of the LORD were the heavens made; and all the host of them by the breath of his mouth."

Many people, not wanting to rock the boat, say that this is God the Father speaking the world into existence. We will see in this chapter that the "Word of the Lord" is God the Son. Yes, God created the universe, but it was God using a name other than God Almighty.

So John, in those five verses of his gospel account, and Paul both covered literally thousands of years of the history of humankind in very short passages.

My Question

If we believe the Word of God, we have to say that Jesus (God the Son) was with God before time existed. That might make us wonder what Jesus did after He had busied Himself with the creation of the universe.

The question is this: if we see God the Father as working with humanity along the way through the ages, was God the Son (the God we know as Jesus) simply taking a nap? Would any personage who had literally created everything simply walk away, saying, "Check ya later" or "Don't call us; we'll call you"?

This part of God's story is not glaringly plain, but with study, it is quite discernible. People might leave this discussion alone to avoid argument, but we are here to make sure that the true student of God hears and then—with prayer—gains a stronger personal faith in God, the Word, and the Scripture.

Jesus Had Other Names?

If we look, we can see the fingerprints of Jesus all over the Old Testament, not only in prophecies about Him but in His actual works. Let's look at His other names, keeping in mind that the names of the Old Testament were always a form of description.

Also, remember that throughout the history of God's people, names were changed to better describe a person or his change of status. Two examples that jump to mind are Abram to Abraham and Jacob to Israel.

The Word

This name for Jesus was partially addressed above. It is not the earliest of His names mentioned in the Bible, but it is scriptural proof that the Son of God existed before the universe was created. John 1:1 (see the opening of this chapter) tells us that God the Son is called "the Word."

The first mention of God the Son as the Word is in Genesis 15:1. The only other mention in Genesis of the Word of the Lord visiting is seen in verse 4 of the same passage. Take special note in this passage of the use of the first person as the Word addressed Abram. The Word also told Abram in verse 7, "I am the LORD that brought thee out of Ur of the Chaldees, to give thee this land to inherit it."

We know from John 1:1 that the Word is God the Son. Note specifically that, while speaking to Abram, the Word stated in no uncertain terms that He was the Lord who had been leading Abram and making covenants. The Word was not just speaking *for* God; He *was* God!

This is hardly the only mention of the Word. The Old Testament is replete with stories of the Word coming to various priests, prophets, and kings throughout the history of God's people. I'll not list them here (see appendix), but there are literally at least 112 verses of the Old Testament in a majority of books that say, "the Word of the Lord came unto [Solomon, Elijah, Isaiah, Jeremiah, Ezekiel, etc.], saying …"

If it helps, whenever you read the name translated "the Word of the Lord," replace it with the name *Jesus*. Or even better, call Him *Michael*.

Michael

Isn't that an angel's name? In the Bible, it is the name of nine Israelites and an archangel. We would be more correct to say "*the* archangel."

In an apparent attempt at fairness, the Roman church's "powers that be" declared Michael, Gabriel, and Lucifer all to be archangels. As we noted in the introduction, we accept the Bible as the only Holy Scripture.

Therefore, we see and accept the fact that only Michael is identified by the title of archangel, and that title is *the* archangel (Jude v. 9). Besides that, eternity being what we know it to be, there will only be one archangel "for all time."

Michael is mentioned by name only five times in the Bible. However, these mentions occurred during what we would consider momentous moments. We'll touch on them here.

He is mentioned in Daniel 10:13 when the angel Gabriel had a little trouble with Cyrus and remained with him until Michael came to assist. Gabriel was then free to go and help Daniel interpret dreams.

In Daniel 10:21, Gabriel said that he had to return to fight the prince of Persia (one of the Devil's angels) because the prince of Greece (another of the Devil's angels) was coming. Gabriel said he would explain the meanings of the dreams, but then had to go. Michael was the one who instructed Gabriel on what to do. Obviously, Gabriel was not the archangel.

Gabriel continued to show Daniel the progression of kingdoms up through the Roman Empire, and then he showed the near end of God's anger with His people, and the near end of God's patience with His people's enemies. Gabriel told Daniel in Daniel 12:1: "At that time shall *Michael* stand up, the great prince which standeth for the children of thy people: and there shall be a time of trouble, such as never was since there was a nation even to that same time: and at that time thy people shall be delivered, every one that shall be found written in the book" (emphasis added).

In the ninth verse of Jude, Michael is shown to be soft-spoken even in battle, and he relies on the power of God the Father to accomplish the Father's goals. There has never been a better earthly example of meekness and dependence on God than that of Jesus of Nazareth.

In Revelation 12:7, Michael is mentioned as the leader of the angels fighting the "dragon" and his angels. This was the war in which Satan was defeated and cast down out of heaven to the earth.

Remembering that names in the Hebrew were descriptions as much as identification, let's look at the name *Michael*. Think of the titles that we often give to people in our own day and time, e.g., caregiver, groundskeeper, paratrooper, paralegal, workaholic, and so on. Word combinations have been used through the millennia as descriptions and names at the same time.

Michael is actually a combination of three Hebrew words. *Mi-Ki-El* is pronounced in the Hebrew as "mee-ky-ale'." The first word is "Mi" (pronounced "mee"), meaning "who or whom." The second word is "Ki" (pronounced like "pie"), meaning "that [is] surely, or doubtless." The third word is "El," meaning "God." It becomes obvious that the translated name that we now spell as *Michael* has the original meaning of "[the] One that [is] surely God."

It is only through our humanization of the word that it has come to mean "one who is like God." We can't presume to be God, so we must—if we use the name for a human—use it with the more diluted, human definition of "one who is like God."

The name *Michael* (as used in the books of Daniel, Jude, and Revelation), when purely translated, means "one that is God."

The name makes perfect sense when you look at what he was doing. Michael was doing things that we would think only God would or could do. Michael personally fought the Devil and his angels with His own army of angels.

Gabriel's fight with the prince of Persia could not be broken off until Michael arrived to join the fray. Gabriel prophesied to Daniel that Michael, the "one that is God," was to stand up for "the children of thy people" and that the people would be delivered at that time. This sounds like the Messiah, doesn't it?

Some say that only an angel can be an archangel. This is not so. The word *archangel* is another compound, descriptive word. Notice that in the two times the word *archangel* is used in the Bible (both Greek), the first word is *archo*, meaning one time "to rule over" and the other time "to reign over." The second word, on both occasions, is *aggelos*, meaning "angels."

We can now see that Michael, "one that is God," is *the* archangel, the one who rules or reigns over the angels. This is why the author of Hebrews repeats David (Psalm 8) and makes such a point in Hebrews 2:7 and 9 of God making Him "a little lower than the angels."

Melchizedek

Abram went north toward Dan to retrieve his kidnapped brother and nephew Lot, along with other people who had been taken and goods that had been pillaged from Sodom and Gomorrah. The story is in the fourteenth chapter of Genesis. On the return trip, the King of Sodom—and others who had run from the original fight—met Abram's party at a geographical point near what is now Jerusalem.

Take note that Melchizedek, the king of Salem, brought bread and wine to the meeting. This must have been a large amount of food and drink, but that is not the point of this study. The question has often been asked: who was this Melchizedek fellow?

Melchizedek is identified in two separate scriptural accounts in the Old Testament and a third time in the book of Hebrews of the New Testament—each time, amazingly, about a thousand years apart.

The first accounting was just mentioned. In Genesis 14, Melchizedek was identified as the King of Salem. Salem was the earliest recorded name for the city (area) that was to become "Jeru-Salem." Jebus was another name used in the time of David, but that's another story.

Melchizedek was also identified as "priest of the Most High God." This might be a "so what" passage except that Melchizedek, as priest of the Most High God, blessed Abram to assure the kings who were present that Abram was God's choice. Make note, as did the author of Hebrews, that the "father of all nations" was blessed by one greater than he. "And without all contradiction the less is blessed of the better" (Hebrews 7:7).

Melchizedek, another compound word name, is pronounced in Hebrew as "mal-kee-tseh'-dek." The first word is *malki*, which is translated "king" over 2,500 times in the Old Testament. The second word is *tsedek*, which is translated "right" or "righteous." By this, we see that *Melchizedek* translates to "king of the righteous."

The second account of Melchizedek is in Psalm 110:4. This psalm is an interesting study. The first verse reads, "The LORD said unto my Lord, Sit thou at my right hand, until I make thine enemies thy footstool." Look again at Psalm 8, and note that "Lord-ship" translates from the Hebrew in such a way as to say, "God the Father said unto God the Son." You'll also note that Jesus was recorded repeating David's words in Mark 12:36 to the temple scribes *as proof of His authority.*

A study of the entire Psalm shows us that in verses 1 through 4, God was speaking to His Son. Not only was God making a new covenant with Mi-Ki-El, but God was also reaffirming the covenant that had made Mi-Ki-El, the "priest forever," as Melchizedek. Verses 5 through 7 show the prophet praising God for what Jesus, as the Son of Man, would do a thousand years later.

The third account comes from the unknown author of Hebrews, who gives us a very good picture of the New Testament priesthood in chapters 5 through 7 of that book. The point of his discussion was to show us that the Levite priesthood was of man and the law. Neither the law nor that priesthood showed people *the way*. Both were fallible because they were introduced for humanity and were applied by humanity. Only the infallible can establish and deliver perfection. Hebrews 7:19 ties the thought together: "For the law made nothing perfect, but the bringing in of a better hope did; by the which we draw nigh unto God."

The point of the name *Melchizedek* is best explained in Hebrews 7:1–3: "For this Melchisedec, king of Salem, priest of the most high God, who met Abraham returning from the slaughter of the kings, and blessed him; to whom also Abraham gave a tenth part of all; first being by interpretation King of righteousness, and after that also King of Salem, which is, King of peace; without father, without mother, without descent, having neither beginning of days, nor end of life; but made like unto the Son of God; abideth a priest continually."

Can anyone claim the titles of Hebrews 7:2 save the Christ? Can anyone claim the genealogy of Hebrews 7:3 save the Christ?

A great many scholars have "cast their lot" with the idea that Melchizedek was Shem, the son of Noah. By that very description, they refute Hebrews 7:3. If we say "son of Noah," we are saying that Melchizedek had a traceable genealogy. The Bible says otherwise; we just read it. Shem also had a beginning of life and an end of life. If we are to believe the Bible, Melchizedek does not.

Some people have taken issue with the part of Hebrews 7:3 that says, "But made like unto the Son of God." They say that being "made like" shows it to be another person. This is not so. This is simply Old English versus modern English.

Verse 3 alludes to Jesus' physical birth by Mary. Note that Jesus was not said to be the Son of God until after God told Gabriel to tell Mary that Jesus would be called the Son of God. It's as simple as that.

By the way, some people use this passage, among others, to attempt to prove that God the Son did not exist until God created Him. That, of course, is simply untrue. We have gone through quite a few of the other names for Jesus, proving otherwise.

The Angel of the LORD or Angel of God

There are forty-eight total occurrences of the identification of *the* angel of the LORD. Another eight are of *an* angel of the LORD. These are also listed in the appendix. One can see that this is Mi-Ki-El by the personal language and the angel's frequent use of the first person. He identifies Himself at length in Genesis 3 from the burning bush. Of course, the situations in which He appears also seem to be more "God-worthy" situations—situations where a "regular ol' angel" just wouldn't have the same *effect, ability, or authority.*

Manoah, who prayed for a son (Samson), asked the angel's name in Judges 13:17. The King James Version says that the angel replied, "It is secret." This is another translation issue. "The angel of the LORD" replied with the Hebrew words *hu peli*, which most often means "it is wonderful (full of wonder or incomprehensible)." This would be just a passing note if not for the fact that in Isaiah 9:6, Isaiah applied that exact wording to what no one disputes as a description of Jesus. "For unto us a child is born, unto us a son is given: and the government shall be upon his shoulder: and *his name shall be called Wonderful*, Counsellor, the mighty God, the everlasting Father, the Prince of Peace" (emphasis added).

There are only five Old Testament occurrences of "*the* angel of God" and five more of "*an* angel of God." Again, you can find a list in the appendix. He spoke in the first person to the point of saying, "I am the God of Bethel" in Genesis 31:13. He obviously did God-like things too.

No-Name Occasions

We're told that at the time of Abraham's test in Genesis 22, God came to Abraham, and moments later in the same passage, the angel of the LORD called to Abraham. Given the other Scriptures, I feel that this is Mi-Ki-El again at this most important event.

Jacob wrestled with "a man" in Genesis 34, beginning in verse 24. I have no doubt that this too was Mi-Ki-El in that He had "other things to do" (verse 26). The angel changed Jacob's name to Israel. This name translates to "persevere with God" or "struggled with God." Can there be any doubt as to who this "man" was that wrestled with Jacob?

The three men in the fiery furnace of Daniel 3 were joined by someone whom Nebuchadnezzar described this way: "The form of the fourth is like the Son of God." This, of course, was an absolutely accurate identification of Mi-Ki-El once more.

The Christ

I interject this here, knowing that we all know this to be another name of Jesus. However, to be accurate, we must realize that Jesus' last name is not *Christ*. Let's put it in human terms. Saying "this is the doctor, Bob Smith" is the same as saying "this is Bob Smith, the doctor."

Properly, I do not say "Jesus Christ" without understanding that we are giving a description as well as His name. His name, among others, was Jesus of Nazareth, the Christ–or the Christ, Jesus of Nazareth.

The word *Christ* literally translates to "anointed." We must understand that we are saying "Jesus, the anointed" when we speak the name of Jesus, the Christ, just as we also know that we think only of Jesus when we speak of "the Christ."

Jesus, the Man

Silly as it may seem, there are those who deny the very existence of Jesus, the Christ. Do notice, as we mentioned previously, that Christ is not the last name of Jesus but one of many descriptive titles, e.g., Jesus of Nazareth, Jesus son of Joseph, Jesus the Nazarene (never Nazirite). To deny Jesus is to deny the logical conclusion that must be drawn when one even lightly studies the history of the period.

The Name *Jesus* Used Logically

World history, both secular and religious, recounts the existence of Jesus. Jesus' character is also unquestioned. No one anywhere paints Jesus as a "bad person." The works of Jesus are unchallenged, even to this day. There are eyewitness recordings of all the works of Jesus that are listed in the Bible. Even those who despised Jesus could only accuse Him of getting His power from Beelzebub and such. They could not deny the events.

Jesus' identity was confirmed by God, who said, "This is my beloved son." Jesus identified Himself as "the way." Eye witnesses observed Jesus on the Mount of Transfiguration.

The Name *Jesus* Used Historically

Virtually everyone who studies the period will mention Josephus. Titus Flavius Josephus was born, we're told, in AD 37, and he died around AD 100. Josephus was a journalist and a witness to a good amount of apostolic history. He also witnessed and recorded other major events, such as the sack of Jerusalem. Josephus claimed to be a Pharisee—obviously a Jew—who grew up in and around Jerusalem.

Large parts of the writings of Josephus were actually historic, firsthand journals. He was commander of the Galilean army in AD 66 when Vespasian attacked. The list of the credentials of Josephus goes on and on. His history is viewed without skepticism.

However, Josephus was not the only one recording the occurrences of the day. Around AD 111, the Roman historian and senator Tacitus referred to Christ, His execution by Pilate, and the existence of early Christians in

Rome in his final work, *Annals*, (completed around AD 116) in book 15, chapter 44. Scholars generally consider Tacitus' reference to the execution of Jesus by Pilate to be both authentic and of historical value, as he was an independent Roman source.

You can find more, if you wish. I'll stop here, and unless you are more scholar—or perhaps skeptic—than most people, this should suffice to prove that Jesus, the Christ, was a genuine part of world history.

The Son of God: Human?

Jesus came to earth as a human. He grew up knowing that He was special and that He was "on a mission," but He was human. Jesus knew that He was to be both proof and example of a perfect human life.

Does it sound like I'm saying that Jesus was not God while He was on this earth? Good. If you think about it seriously, thinking anything else would discredit His greatest-of-all accomplishment.

No one can dispute that Jesus was godly and wholly righteous. How much more in tune with God was He than Abraham (the father of all nations), Moses (the bringer of the law), or David (a man after God's own heart)? There were two other men who lived lives so "in tune" with God that they didn't "see death": Enoch and Elijah. But even they did not know the "soul of God" to the point of saying, "The Father and I are one."

The reason that Jesus was so capable of living the perfect life was that He had a complete and ready recollection of the Word (John 1:1), He spent hours each and every day in prayerful, continual communion with God—and perhaps He even remembered what heaven was like.

The simplest question would be this: if Jesus was God, why did He pray *to God* like a human would? Here is where the *ad hoc* hypotheses kick in at full strength, and all sorts of speculations appear.

"In the beginning there was the Word." Jesus, by another name, existed before time. He became human in order to be completely human, not *partly* human. Think on this for a moment. How can any body of any kind be partly one thing and yet wholly another? In the spiritual realm, that may be possible, but we have seen that while in the earthly realm, God bound Himself by the earthly rules of time and physics.

We try to explain Jesus by saying that He was 100 percent God and 100 percent man. I suppose that's a vain attempt to prove that He was so much better than we are—or an attempt to excuse our humanness. We must realize that when we try to think on the things of God, we're probably never going to be absolutely correct. We must desist in attempting to squeeze God into our finite understanding of infinite thought. Romans 11:33 says, "O the depth of the riches both of the wisdom and knowledge of God! How unsearchable are his judgments, and his ways past finding out!"

However, when we look at what God the Son had to do, our thoughts must return to our human, earthly world. His purpose was heavenly, but His "job" was earthly. Jesus had a purpose in our human, earthly world. We see that He had to become human in order for God's law of atonement* to be satisfied.

There is no way that we can discount the life and death of Jesus, the Christ. We can, however, broaden our scope for a moment to realize that other men—before and after the Christ—have endured hideous and evil torture. Some of these men have lived to tell the tale, while others were fortunate to have died in the process. We have even retold the stories of some for their inspirational value, e.g., Spartacus, William Wallace (*Braveheart*), and so on.

This is where most people say, "It's not for us to understand," and then they start backing up quietly. It's pretty easy to understand this, unless you intentionally make yourself unable to do so.

Jesus, by the act of the Holy Spirit, became a human. Jesus, as a soul, came to earth, just like any of the rest of us. Think on this: all of us are souls with a body, *not* bodies with a soul. Jesus was born human, having human wants and needs. However, Jesus *never forgot why He was here*, and He *never forgot who He was*. Do you somehow think that the mother of Jesus didn't tell Him the wonderful story of His own birth? That she didn't remind Jesus every day of His childhood of His calling and His heavenly Father?

Remember the farmer in chapter 7? God had to become one of us in order to show us how to live. Jesus talked about faith being like a "grain of mustard seed" (Matthew17:20). He talked about expelling evil spirits only after spending much more prayer and time with God than the disciples had spent (beginning in Mark 19:14). In these and all the other examples Jesus

* Sacrifice and atonement are discussed at length in part 2.

gave us, He was speaking of things that any believer can do. There was nothing supernatural in Jesus—except, of course, that He had the Holy Spirit, which is freely available to all of us. There is absolutely no doubt that Jesus was literally *filled with the Holy Spirit.* Jesus spent time with God in prayer at all hours of the day and night. Jesus called on the power of God to perform all the miracles He did, because He (Jesus) was only human. Jesus—just like all of us—started out sinless. The important thing is that *He remained so.*

The point is that Jesus never forgot that He was the Son of God, made flesh by God the Holy Spirit, though He never claimed that birthright by boasting but by action. Think on this: Jesus never forgot who He was, and neither should we. That's what makes Him our firstborn brother: *He never forgot.* One of the most common apologies known to man is "I forgot myself for a moment."

Remember that Jesus was teaching us. Jesus did not come to give us a show, which it would have been if He were a god. Jesus came to give us an example. Yes, He did all that He did with the manifested power of God. Remember that Jesus literally spent most of His life in prayer and communion with God the Father for that power—just as any human must do to gain the very real power and indwelling of the Holy Spirit.

Jesus got a tremendous spiritual refill at the transfiguration. When we talk about Moses later,[†] you'll see that Jesus was not the first to receive such a boost—not to mention the angel in the garden. But if you or I were facing something as momentous as the crucifixion and sacrifice that Jesus faced, I'm sure that God would help us as well, in a bigger and better way than most people receive, if we were deemed worthy.

Son of Man or Son of God?

Jesus was very big on third-person identification. When speaking of Himself, Jesus invariably referred to Himself as the Son of Man. He continually reinforced the fact that He was as human as the next guy.

You may or may not have noticed that there is nothing physical that can be tied directly to Jesus. This is not by accident. Can you imagine what an

---

[†] See chapter 29, "God's Glory."

autograph of Jesus would be worth? Can you imagine how many people would die or be killed for such a thing?

Jesus spoke in consideration of that thought as well. His continual use of the third person allowed the lessons to be delivered, even as the source spoke like any other human. Again, this was not by accident. The lesson was what Jesus wanted us to remember. Jesus repeatedly told us to let people see the light, not the candle.

In fact, the phrase "I am the Son of God" occurs only once in the Bible. In that single time when Jesus used it, it was used as a participle phrase in John 10:36 (citing Psalm 82) when He said (paraphrased), "You say that I said that 'I am the Son of God.'" He only said it to remind His persecutors that they were being two-faced. Jesus made no claims—and certainly no boasts—because He didn't have to. Jesus was the living example of the word *meek.*

Just as we all do, Jesus spoke of His Father, God. However, Jesus was never recorded as making a direct claim to being either God or the Son of God. Jesus called Himself "Son of Man." It was everyone else who called Him "Son of God."

Jesus worked the power of God the Father into many passages where He was quoted. When speaking of the Holy Spirit, Jesus said, "All things that the Father hath are mine: therefore said I, that he shall take of mine, and shall shew it unto you" (John 16:15). When speaking to Philip, Jesus said, "Believest thou not that I am in the Father, and the Father in me? the words that I speak unto you I speak not of myself: but the Father that dwelleth in me, *he doeth the works*" (John 14:10, emphasis added).

Our confession of faith in believing that Jesus "is the Christ, the son of the living God" is one of the first steps of our salvation. Jesus said to Peter in Matthew 16:17, "For flesh and blood hath not revealed it unto thee, but my Father which is in heaven."

You'll notice that even then Jesus made no mention of Himself other than to use the words "flesh and blood," meaning "no human," including Himself.

Jesus was all about the message. Jesus thought, as we all should, only of spreading the message of God's goodness and benevolence.[‡]

---

‡ See also chapter 20, "Evangelism = The Christian Life."

10

The God We Call the Holy Spirit

God Gets His Hands Dirty

Although we can see how much God the Son has done throughout and before our own history, we have to describe the Holy Spirit as the workhorse of the Godhead. Below is a charted representation of Scripture references rather than a prose description as proof.

Creates—Gen. 1:2; Job 33:4	Leads—Rom. 8:14
Consummates baptism—Matt. 3:11; Mark 1:8; Acts 1:5; 1 Cor. 12:13	Witness of our salvation—Rom. 8:15–16
Anoints for service—Luke 4:18	Supports our frailties—Rom. 8:26
Empowers believers—Luke 24:49	Completes our prayers—Rom. 8:26
Believers are born of—John 3:3–6	Tunes God's ear toward us—Rom. 8:27
Teaches, brings remembrance—John 14:26	Inspires for the Word—1 Cor. 2:4
Testifies of Jesus—John 15:26	Gives discernment—1 Cor. 2:13–14

Convicts of sin—John 16:9

Witnesses of Jesus—John 16:10

Judges works of Satan—John 16:11

Guides to truth—John 16:13

Glorifies Jesus—John 16:14

Reveals believers—John 16:14; 1 Cor. 12:3

Empowers—Acts 1:8; 4:31

Calls and commissions—Acts 20:28

Liberates—Rom. 8:2

Indwells believers—Rom. 8:9

Manifests gifts—1 Cor. 12:7–11

Builds character—Gal. 5:22–23

Guides our life and path—Gal. 5:25

Seals for redemption—Eph. 1:13–14; 4:30

Strengthens—Eph. 3:16

Inspires prayer—Eph. 6:18; Jude v. 20

Delivers the Word and joy—1 Thess. 1:5–6

Renews the "old man"—Titus 3:5

Sanctifies—1 Pet. 1:2

Authors Scripture—2 Pet. 1:20–21

The Holy Spirit Is God

The above listing is not to say that the Holy Spirit is an underling who does the bidding of God Almighty. We see that the things God does *universally* are mostly, if not always, implemented by God the Holy Spirit.

We can see that the works of the Holy Spirit are the works of God. The Spirit's equality in the Godhead is exemplified in the following chart:

His Names	Attributes	Symbols	Sins Against	In Christ's Life
God Acts 5:3–4	Eternal Heb. 9:14	Dove Luke 3:22	Blasphemy Matt. 12:31	Conceived of Matt. 1:18, 20
Lord 2 Cor. 3:18	Power of God Luke 1:35	Sound of wind Acts 2:2	Resistance (unbelief) Acts 7:51	Baptism by Matt. 3:16

Spirit 1 Cor. 2:10	Omnipresent Psalm 139:7	Fire Acts 2:3	Insult Heb. 10:29	Led by Luke 4:1
Spirit of God 1 Cor. 3:16	Plans and wills 1 Cor. 12:11	*****	Lies to Acts 5:3	Empowered by Luke 4:14
Spirit of Truth John 15:26	Gives love Rom. 15:30	*****	Grieving Eph. 4:30	Anointed by Luke 4:18
Eternal Spirit Heb. 9:14	Speaks Acts 8:29; 13:2	*****	Quenching 1 Thess. 5:19	Sent by Luke 14:18

Please note that our listing of the attributes and descriptions of the Holy Spirit in this charted format is intended to compile study points for the convenience of the reader. Charts often seem to make the reader feel that the information is lessened by brevity.

This study has in no way attempted to lessen the impact of the presentation of the works or power of the Holy Spirit. Neither do we wish the reader to think that the works and power of the Holy Spirit need no further study.

To the contrary, in this chapter we have put to you the enormity of an in-depth study of God the Holy Spirit. Further study and understanding of the Holy Spirit will help you to ask for His continued presence.

The Original "Great Communicator"

The desire of this author is to exalt the attributes and works of the Holy Spirit to a new level of comprehension. The Holy Spirit is more important to our spiritual life than most Christians have ever perceived. Christians have lived and died having only thought of the Spirit when they sang about Him in church.

In the previous Scripture references, we've shown a spectrum of descriptions of the Holy Spirit from the New Testament. This is where we find most of our instruction as to the Holy Spirit's identity. In the Old Testament, to put it simply, God was God. It is through the writings of the New Testament that our understanding is increased. The Holy Spirit, being the workhorse of the Godhead, was obviously at work throughout Old Testament history as well.

David wrote, "The Spirit of the LORD spoke by me, and His word was on my tongue" (2 Samuel 23:2). In Mark 12:36, Jesus confirmed that David had spoken "by the Holy Ghost." Jesus was speaking of Psalm 110 at the time.

The Old Testament is stuffed with references to prophets and this or that "man of God." In each instance was some form of godly communication. Remember that the Holy Spirit is the spiritual interpreter, translating our communications to God and God's communications to us. We're told in 2 Peter 1:20–21, "Knowing this first, that no prophecy of the scripture is of any private interpretation. For the prophecy came not in old time by the will of humanity: but holy men of God spake *as they were* moved by the Holy Ghost" (emphasis added).

Upon examination, we can certainly see the innumerable instances of humankind's guidance by the inspiration and indwelling of the Holy Spirit. Many are recorded for our example and study, while many are known only to God.

The Fruits of the Spirit

Not only is "the gift of the Holy Spirit" bestowed upon us at baptism (Acts 2:38), but He also comes bearing gifts.

If you truly accept the Spirit and allow Him to work in your life, the tree (the Spirit) that God planted in you will begin producing fruit. In Galatians 5:22–23 (NIV), Paul told us of these fruits in a succinct and complete list: "But the fruit of the Spirit is love, joy, peace, patience, kindness, goodness, faithfulness, gentleness and self-control. Against such things there is no law."

In his letter to the Ephesians, Paul told them—and us—that we, when we are saved, leave darkness behind. In Ephesians 5:8–9, Paul said, "For ye were sometimes darkness, but now are ye light in the Lord: walk as children of light: (For the *fruit of the Spirit* is in all [God's] goodness and righteousness and truth)" (emphasis added).

If we are living in God's goodness, righteousness, and truth, then we will be manifesting the fruit of the Spirit. The attributes of the fruit of the Spirit will grow in you as you grow in Christ. As you will see in this continued study, doing right is *never* wrong. Paul says it in other words above: "Against such things there is no law."

11

FATHER, SON, AND HOLY GHOST

Splinter religions have been formed simply because their founders, e.g., Joseph Smith, C. T. Russell, and others, could not wrap their minds around the very simple concept of God being in three persons.

Trinity is a title, and as these splinter religions stand ready to point out, it is not found in the Bible. Some say that Theophilus of Antioch used the word first; others say it was Tertullian.

God is three personages—separate, but one—and descriptions abound. The point is that for eternity, God the Father, God the Son, and God the Holy Spirit exist as one. Each has His own "job," so to speak, but all are one as God over all. They, each and all, existed spiritually before time, and they will—as will each of us—exist spiritually after the end of time. A man-made description—extremely oversimplified—says that God is a committee of three that always agrees.

The truest point that can be made about the Holy Trinity is that our God would not be the same if He did not exist as He does. No other god of any of the man-made religions comes close, in functions or feelings. Our God is everlasting proof that you can't improve on perfection.

PART IV

Theology in Practice

This is the first of two major sections concerning theology and the practice and/or study of Christianity.

Part IV is basically concerned with the genuine practice of Christianity. Many people believe that being saved is all there is to it. They are correct only as far as "being saved" is concerned. Getting into heaven is another story.

The purpose of this part of our study is to view, reprove, reinforce, enlighten, and correct the tenets of Christian theology. There are things in this section that the reader may never have given thought to or considered in a particular light. Certainly, some information may change a person's mind or way of thinking.

We will show that the studies of this section are important, if not vital, to one's true faith and genuine salvation. The study will focus on the following:

- what is prayer, how to pray, what to pray, and what God hears
- the difference between God's plan and God's will

- the truth and error about being chosen, election, calling, appointment, and predestination
- sin: legalism vs. truth, and righteousness vs. relativism and pragmatism
- baptism and "buffet-style" salvation
- judgment
- the Lord's Supper
- benevolence and love
- evangelism and the Christian life

12

Prayer: Is This Thing On?

Why Study Prayer?

"The effectual fervent prayer of a righteous man availeth much" (James 5:16). That one statement puts forth a certain criteria for prayer—that is, *prayer that works*. To be sure, there are many who pray and look toward heaven like a comedian who didn't get a laugh. The comedian taps the microphone and asks, "Is this thing on?"

If prayer works, why are there so many unanswered prayers? Does God pick and choose? God hears all prayers, right? If I can simply "ask and it shall be given to [me]," why hasn't anything changed in my life? Do I have to be in church? Do I have to be saved?

To be sure, almost as many questions have been asked about prayer as the number of prayers that have been prayed. This chapter is full of realization and insight, for there are a tremendous number of misconceptions about:

- When to pray
- How God listens
- How to pray
- Prayer itself
- What constitutes a proper prayer that will get results
- Whether prayer is considered worship
- Whether prayer is necessary

We will answer many questions and, hopefully, enlighten those who seek the answers—and perhaps even those who thought they knew already. We will address these issues to the point that we might right some wrong thinking and learn how to better communicate with God, our Father.

There are many reasons for prayer. You may want to pray for someone or with someone. You may want to pray for forgiveness for yourself or your enemies. You may want to pray for your health or the health of another. You may want to pray for material help for yourself or someone else. You can see that the reasons for prayer are as varied as the number of people praying those prayers.

There are many parts to a complete study of prayer. I have attempted to cover them in what should be enough detail to help any reader to discern the truth. Prayer is central to both worship and faith, and it must be included here.

The Big Picture

In with the New

Jesus didn't teach any of His disciples or even His apostles how to preach. However, He took pains to teach them, and us, how to pray. Think on that.

Only two times in the Old Testament is God is called *Father.* Isaiah did it in Isaiah 63:16 and 64:8, referring to Him in a prayer as the father of all humanity. Malachi spoke *of* God as Father—our creator, the father of the universe—in Malachi 2:10. Neither of these instances addressed God as "Father" in the way a son would speak to his father. Rather, they spoke of God as Americans might speak of George Washington in referring to him as the "father of our country."

These are the only two occasions where God is mentioned as Father even indirectly in the King James Version of the Old Testament. I'll not even attempt a count of the times God is represented to us as a *parental* father in the New Testament.

Also, notice that prayer was only mentioned occasionally in the Old Testament, because communication with God was through patriarchs, kings, and prophets.

We, however, live under the new covenant. The Scripture of the New Testament is full of instruction on prayer and proper communication with God on an individual basis. We'll go deeper into these points, but for now, think on the fact that we—under the new covenant—are to consider God as our Father rather than as an unapproachable and distant deity.

This is one of the few changes between the old and new covenants, but oh, how wonderful are these few changes!

Hello, God. Can We Talk?

Many people have varied ideas of what is the most important thing in the practice of their faith. To be sure, benevolence is important. We even study benevolence later in this section. Many people say that the Lord's Supper is important. It is; and it is also studied in this section. Many say that public "church" is important. The assembling of the saints is very important, but it's not the point of worship to the true believer.

Let's divide our worship and our life in general into two parts. The points of the previous paragraph are very important—to the point of being vital—to our physical work and worship. However, prayer is the central point of our *spiritual* work and worship.

Do you get it? There are two worlds in which the Christian abides: the physical world and the spiritual world.

Prayer is central to our spiritual well-being. Prayer is central to our spiritual growth. Prayer is given to us by God Himself as our *only* true means of communicating with Him about anything and everything. Paul told us in Philippians 4:6, "Be careful for nothing [don't be anxious, apprehensive or uneasy—basically, don't fret and worry]; but in every thing by prayer and supplication with thanksgiving let your requests be made known unto God."

Types of Prayer

Am I saying that there are different types of prayer? The answer is: *absolutely.*

It genuinely does help to categorize prayers when we study the subject of prayer, which we all should do. Some people have broken the categories of prayer into two parts: personal and intercessory. That's a little broad for our study here, but it is still accurate. We'll dig deeper.

The categories of prayer are:

- Praise: admission of sovereignty
- Thanksgiving, love, and adoration
- Penitence, supplication, and remorse
- Petitions of all sorts
- Intercessions for every reason

One can look up each type in a dictionary and perhaps glean a little from it. However, we will be studying the categories of prayer while we study the act of prayer itself.

Praise

While we are granted the special privilege of speaking directly to God, we must never forget who we're talking to. In Matthew 10:28, Jesus said, "Fear not them which kill the body, but are not able to kill the soul: but rather fear him which is able to destroy both soul and body in hell."

Note that the word *fear*—in a great many uses in the King James New Testament, including this instance—better translates to the word *respect.* Is there any among us who does not believe that God is due proper respect? Think of it this way: "I fear (am afraid of) falling because I fear (respect) the truth of gravity."

God deserves our praise, but even more, He deserves the true respect due the sovereign God of all creation. Not only does He deserve it, but He expects it. Have you ever greeted a doctor by a first name? You will be corrected, instantly, to use the title that took him or her so long to earn.

Why would we fail to greet the Creator of all things and the granter of life itself with less than the proper acknowledgment of His sovereignty?

Thanksgiving

Philippians 4:6 says, "Be careful for nothing [do not be anxious about anything]; but in every thing by prayer and supplication *with thanksgiving* let your requests be made known unto God" (emphasis added).

It's as simple as that.

But how can we express our thanks to someone who has furnished everything for us, including life, without expressing our love in return for the love of God? In fact, we need to realize that even our love comes first from God. We are only returning what He has originally given us. In 1 John 4:19, it is very simply explained: "We love Him, because He first loved us."

The thought has deeper meaning when you think of this: if we have *anything* good to give, it's because God *first* gave it to us.

Any romantic will tell you that a continued expression of the recognition of love turns into *adoration*. There will be times when the thought of God's love leaves one speechless, and there's nothing left to do but express the adoration that the thought produces.

Penitence

God gave us the law by which humanity could know when, in the course of daily life, we were going "off the path."* Under the old covenant, people made the proper sacrifice for breaking a particular law, and that was that. Penitence, except for the conscience of the righteous person, rarely entered the process. It was legalistic, and many people of our time still believe this is proper.

With the new covenant, which is sealed with the blood of Jesus, we no longer look to what's wrong (think "electric fence"). We now have the example of what is right (think "middle of the road"). This change of covenants is the ultimate demonstration of God's love.

---

* See part II, chapter 6, "Judaism: The Practice," for a deeper discussion of "guardrails."

When we do not do right, our conscience shows that we know it, and we become penitent. We feel sorry and regretful for what we have done or not done.

At that point, the saved believer can ask for forgiveness. This is *supplication*. By definition, supplication is the act of asking—or perhaps more accurately, begging—for something. In our case here, supplication is the act of manifesting penitence by asking or begging for pardon or forgiveness.

Remorse is more applicable to guilt. A nonbeliever who has come to an understanding of what is right is "convicted" by his conscience and feels guilty. By definition, remorse is deep regret or a sense of guilt for some wrongdoing. Except at the point of salvation, a true believer should never feel remorse. The penitent believer who asks forgiveness—and is repentant—need never feel guilty.

Guilt is actually a product from Satan. It is designed to keep us from feeling free to do the work of God. The feeling of "I'm not worthy" is predominant in the guilt process. In modern terminology, we say that guilt is "baggage." If you are carrying "baggage," your hands are full, and you aren't free to do anything else.

Petition

This category requires the least explanation. The dictionary definition of *petition* is "to make or present a formal request to an authority with respect to a particular cause."

This is more like a blanket that covers most all of prayer. We petition our authority, our God, with any and all requests, most of which are discussed above.

Intercession

This is the prayer that most people, as well as this study, believe to be the prayer of the "sweetest savor of Christ" to God's nostrils. This speaks of the savor of sacrifice shown many times in the Old Testament. Paul wrote about it in 2 Corinthians 2:15, speaking of Christians thusly: "For we are unto God a sweet savour of Christ."

God enjoys the sweet savor of proper sacrifice. He expresses it over and over in the Old Testament. The main thought here is that when we are saved, God sees the Christ rather than us. In John 14:13–14, Jesus said, "Whatsoever ye shall ask in my name, that will I do, that the Father may be glorified in the Son. If ye shall ask any thing in my name, I will do it."

When we ask in Jesus' name, the "savor of Christ" anoints our prayer. God not only sees the Christ, but He "smells" the Christ as well.

Jesus, with rare and understandable exception, did not pray for Himself. Yes, Jesus prayed, "Let this cup pass from me," but He was praying that God would find an alternative plan, not asking for help. Jesus prayed for the progress of God's will and kingdom, for the sick, sometimes for the power to raise the dead, and, invariably, for His disciples. The Christ remains our intercessor even today as our one High Priest.

Intercessory prayer, praying for others, makes us most like the Christ. All other human attributes pale when compared to putting someone else's needs before our own. This is the truest definition of love.

The Perfect Prayer

Is there a perfect prayer? Perhaps the best way of looking at this particular question is to think of fitting a square peg into a round hole. There are two ways to think of the "square peg" scenario.

The first is to realize that the prayer must fit the situation. Praying for rain during a thunderstorm is useless. Praying for yourself while you see others in need is only appropriate if you're asking for the ability to help them.

In other words, praying for your heart's desire is only appropriate if your heart's desire is within God's will.

Another thing to realize is that even a square peg will fit into a round hole if the peg is compact enough. There may be gaps around the edges, but the peg will go through the hole. A prayer will be heard if it is singularly focused within the plans of God—even if it does not completely fill the needs of the moment. A prayer for a specific thing is appropriate if there is an important and specific need.

The second point is to realize that even a round peg will not fit in a round hole if it is too large to fit. This is not to say that lengthy time in prayer is inappropriate. To the contrary, God appreciates the believer who spends time in prayer. However, there is a difference between *being in prayer with God* and *speaking a prayer to God.* We discuss that difference in depth in the upcoming chapter called "Location, Location, Location."

The overall thought here is that a person speaking a bloated prayer, by which he hopes to be heard for his many words, is less likely to be heard than the penitent sinner uttering the single and simple request, "Please, help me."

Attitude Is Everything

We cannot improve on the story Jesus told of the Pharisee and the publican recorded for us in Luke 18:9–14 (NIV).

> To some who were confident of their own righteousness and looked down on everybody else, Jesus told this parable: "Two men went up to the temple to pray, one a Pharisee and the other a tax collector. The Pharisee stood up and prayed about himself: 'God, I thank you that I am not like other men—robbers, evildoers, adulterers—or even like this tax collector. I fast twice a week and give a tenth of all I get.' But the tax collector stood at a distance. He would not even look up to heaven, but beat his breast and said, 'God, have mercy on me, a sinner.' I tell you that this man, rather than the other, went home justified before God. For everyone who exalts himself will be humbled, and he who humbles himself will be exalted."

The Lord's Prayer

The disciples saw that Jesus prayed often. Just as those disciples did, we need to take note of all of the examples and teachings of Jesus. But of all the examples that Jesus gave us, prayer is the most important.

What we call the Lord's Prayer is actually listed twice in the Gospels. The first occurrence is the one we recite most often and was delivered by Jesus in the Sermon on the Mount in Matthew 6:9–13: "After this manner therefore pray ye: Our Father which art in heaven, Hallowed be thy name. Thy kingdom come. Thy will be done in earth [in this earthly world], as it is in heaven. Give us this day our daily bread. And forgive us our debts, as we forgive our debtors. And lead us not into temptation, but deliver us from evil: For thine is the kingdom, and the power, and the glory, for ever. Amen."

The second occurrence is purported to be somewhere between the eighteenth and nineteenth chapters of Matthew, chronologically, and is recorded in Luke 11:1–4: "And it came to pass, that, as he was praying in a certain place, when he ceased, one of his disciples said unto him, Lord, teach us to pray, as John also taught his disciples. And he said unto them, When ye pray, say, Our Father which art in heaven, Hallowed be thy name. Thy kingdom come. Thy will be done, as in heaven, so in earth. Give us day by day our daily bread. And forgive us our sins; for we also forgive every one that is indebted to us. And lead us not into temptation; but deliver us from evil."

The two times Jesus gave us an example of how to pray, He used, literally, the same words. Let's see why.

Parts of the Whole

Our Father. We discussed this earlier. We, under the new covenant, speak to God as our Father. In this day and age, we seem to take this for granted. Realizing that God wants us to think of Him as our Father is worthy of our praise, in and of itself! If we truly see God as our Father, we will see Him as *familiar*. The word *familiar* has taken on a definition beyond its original meaning: "of the family." For us to think of God as family is God's deepest desire. Those with children know the feeling. As we discussed earlier,

God's will is "that all should come to repentance." God's will is that we all live with Him eternally. Stop for a moment. While wrapping your mind around this thought, praise God for this single, most wonderful blessing.

Notice also that our modern definition of *familiar* is "often encountered or seen." The word convicts us when we put it in this fashion.

Which art in heaven. God is sovereign over all. God is in heaven, dispensing the Holy Spirit, His power, and His blessings to the saved who ask of Him.

Hallowed be thy name. *Hallowed*, by definition, means "sanctified, consecrated, highly venerated, and/or sacrosanct." These are a lot of big words that mean that God's name is sacred. In the Holy Scriptures, God has assumed—and humanity has given Him—many names, all of which describe deity, holiness, and power. God said not to use His name in vain, because it is powerful even when only spoken.

God deserves that we remind ourselves—and Him—that we hold His name to be much more than just a way to address Him.

Thy kingdom come. Many people argue that this has already occurred. When they say this, they mean that God's church has been established. In that sense, they are correct.

Jesus told His disciples, in the explanation of the parable of the sower and the seed (Matthew 13:3-23), that the heart is the center of understanding. Jesus explained that understanding is the key to the growth of the kingdom. At its root, this is the true purpose of this work.

Jesus told us that many have ears to hear, eyes to see, and hearts for understanding. However, for whatever reason, these same people hear but do not listen, and they close their eyes so they do not see. They actually do not have the right heart for allowing the seed of the word to grow.

Thy kingdom come applies as much or more to our personal hearts as to anything in heaven or on earth. Our prayer for the Spirit and understanding should be never-ending.

Another thought is this: Don't we pray to God that the final day of judgment will come quickly? Why? We pray for this so that we can see this earthly kingdom done away with and can live with God in the spiritual realm—God's complete spiritual kingdom yet to come.

Thy will be done in earth as it is in heaven. We should always pray that we are in tune with God's plans. Without fail, we should ask for guidance to remain within those plans. Obviously, God's will is followed in heaven. We should desire no less than the blessing of God's righteous will on earth. Even further, we should be praying about our heartfelt desire to be a part of it.

Press "pause." As an aside, let's notice what we have seen so far in this example given by Jesus. This prayer contains nothing about self, nothing about "me." This is vital to understanding proper prayer. This prayer talks about

- Thy name
- Thy kingdom
- Thy will

Yes, God is our Father. Yes, God is familiar. However, we must continually acknowledge that God is above all and we are nothing without Him and His kingdom and His plans for us.

Give us this day our daily bread. Two thoughts are present here:

- God supplies all. We should remember always that the first thing He gives us is our very life! We ask for God's continued blessing so we can do even more to further His kingdom.
- The record in Luke says, "Give us day by day." Note that there's no mention of tomorrow. Greed has no place in the Christian life, especially in prayer.

And forgive us our debts as we forgive our debtors. It's as simple as it says. You can't have one without the other. An old saying fits here: "To forgive and not forget is to have not forgiven." Wounds heal, but scars often remain. A scar can do one of two things: remind you of the one who wounded you and the injury itself, or remind you to avoid being wounded like that again as you go on with your life. The latter is the way of the Christian.

And lead us not into temptation, but deliver us from evil. Always ask God to give you guidance and to strengthen your armor (Ephesians 6:10–18).

For thine is the kingdom, and the power, and the glory, forever. Amen. Remind God that you know that we do not operate from our own power. We are in His kingdom, and our life is but a loan. God's glory is His alone.

Ten Elements of the Lord's Prayer

The *Book of Lists* shows it this way:

- a personal relationship with God: "our Father"
- faith: "which art in heaven"
- worship: "hallowed be thy name"
- expectation: "thy kingdom come"
- submission: "thy will be done in earth, as it is in heaven"
- petition: "give us this day our daily bread"
- confession: "and forgive us our debts"
- compassion: "as we forgive our debtors"
- dependence: "and lead us not into temptation, but deliver us from evil"
- acknowledgment: "for thine is the kingdom, and the power, and the glory forever"

All of this demonstrates the depth of what we call the Lord's Prayer. We must realize, above all, that Jesus gave us this example so we could comply with His teaching: "After this manner therefore pray ye …" (Matthew 6:9). This is a very complete example of prayer, but yours will most certainly be worded differently. Praying this example alone only proves that you can memorize Scripture.

When you pray, remember the proper elements of prayer, but talk to our Father in the name of Jesus, our High Priest, and your prayer will be heard—*if* you have followed the plan of salvation God laid out for us. See part I of this book, and if you have not followed the simple steps of salvation, do nothing else until you do.

Does God Hear All Prayers?

I've often said, "God answers every prayer, and sometimes the answer is no." This is true of the believer's prayer. However, this says nothing about God *hearing* every prayer.

And there's the rub. At this point, most people question the wording: "You said 'the believer's prayer.' What about the sinner's prayer? Just what do you mean?"

The short answer is this: *God does not hear the prayer of the unsaved sinner.* I word it that way because we can never deny that we are all sinners. One of the most quoted verses of the New Testament is Romans 3:23: "For all have sinned, and come short of the glory of God."

For purposes of this discussion, I'll use the word *unsaved* to be more specific. If you wish, you can think of the unsaved as nonbelievers. If you have any question about my meaning, I refer you to part I of this book. Conversely, when I speak of "sinners," I'll be referring to every human on the planet.

How many times have we heard some TV or radio evangelist say something to this effect: "Repeat this prayer after me, and you will be saved," or "God loves all of us; pray for your needs, and they will be filled," or the old favorite, "Lay your hands on the radio and pray with me for your salvation (healing, and so on)."

I will tell you flatly—and with the support of the Scripture that follows—that these statements and others like them hold out false hope for the spiritually lost. Here, deep in the middle of this work is, perhaps, one of this study's more important discourses.

What can the unsaved pray for? *It is an exercise in futility for the unsaved to pray.* If you think that God hears the prayers of the unsaved, you are wrong.

This is where we find what some might call a "fine line" of difference. We discuss it at length a little later in this section. While there is no difference in the eyes of God concerning the unsaved, there is a difference between an unsaved nonbeliever and an unsaved believer.

Both the saved and unsaved need to take note of some particular Scripture concerning prayer. The following verses refer to sinners of all types, not just the unsaved. I use the *New International Version* here to ensure that "the pill is swallowed."

> "We know that God does not listen to sinners. He listens to the godly man who does his will" (John 9:31). "The LORD is far from the wicked but he hears the prayer of the righteous" (Proverbs 15:29). "The face of the LORD is against those who do evil, to cut off the memory of them from the earth" (Psalm 34:16). "If I had cherished sin in my heart, the Lord would not have listened" (Psalm 66:18). "If anyone turns a deaf ear to the law, even his prayers are detestable" (Proverbs 28:9).

Prayer must be made in faith. Since people without faith cannot pray in faith, the radio preacher is wrong. It is just as wrong to think that one is saved the moment he or she believes in Christ as the Savior. We have seen that *belief leads to faith.* Even if one were saved at the point of faith, one cannot pray for salvation *at the point of believing* without praying before he or she has faith.

We must pray to God for salvation as we repent. If we are saved at the point of faith, then we don't need to pray for salvation. If we must pray in faith, then we must have faith in order to pray for salvation. One certainly cannot pray in faith without the Word. We already spoke of being unable to pray for faith. "Consequently, faith comes from hearing the message, and the message is heard through the word of Christ" (Romans 10:17).

The point is that if one has not been taught the gospel of God, he or she certainly cannot have the faith required to be saved.

The Error of Christian Belief

The largest error of the Christian world is to believe that God comes to humanity and simply grants salvation. We often hear of "unconditional love" and "amazing grace." We discuss this at length in part I of this book. Here is a refresher to drive home the point of acceptable prayer.

In Hebrews 11:6, we read, "And without faith it is impossible to please God, because anyone who comes to him must believe that he exists and that he rewards those who earnestly seek him."

God's hand is outstretched, and his invitation is always open, but we must come to him, not the other way around. We must grab His "lifeline." It's true that God has granted us the free gift of salvation. However, God has offered that salvation to us in the form of the new covenant.

The old covenant was given to Abraham in Genesis 17. This was the covenant of circumcision, which was given at the same time God changed Abram's name to Abraham. God's covenant was that He agreed to be the God of Abraham *if* Abraham and his seed would keep the terms of the agreement.

God saw that the covenant with Abraham was flawed on the human side, in that there was no true forgiveness because humankind continued to fail to keep the terms of the covenant. The imperfection was not with the covenant but with humankind. We were supposed to grow in our faith so that we would have to make fewer and fewer sacrifices, but instead we kept shrinking (slinking) away from God.

In Jeremiah 31:31–34, God promised the new covenant.

> Behold, the days come, saith the LORD, that I will make a new covenant with the house of Israel, and with the house of Judah: Not according to the covenant that I made with their fathers in the day that I took them by the hand to bring them out of the land of Egypt; which my covenant they brake, although I was an husband unto them, saith the LORD: But this shall be the covenant that I will make with the house of Israel; After those days, saith the LORD, I will put my law in their inward parts, and write it in their hearts; and will be their God, and they shall be my people. And they shall teach no more every man his neighbour, and every man his brother, saying, Know the LORD: for they shall all know me, from the least of them unto the greatest of them, saith the LORD: for I will forgive their iniquity, and I will remember their sin no more.

We studied more deeply the subject of God's logic in part II of this book.

Our error today is that we use buzzwords like *grace* and *faith* both indiscriminately and selectively. We all continue to say, "Grace is unmerited favor," and many people believe that God does it all and we do nothing except to "grab a bucket and catch the rain."

Please note this important thought: God's unconditional love and protection is available to us only after we have met His condition of joining into the covenant relationship with Him. This includes our ability to communicate with Him.

Humanity has continually sought loopholes. It's our God-given instinct to find the best way. However, when God said that there is only *one* way to come to Him, who are we to construe any other meaning from His holy Word? There are those, even today, who believe that if enough people say something, it must be true. Adherents to major religions are progressing through life with a false sense of security concerning their salvation.

We must keep our side of the bargain. We must abide by the terms of the covenant, or we are not a part of it.

What about the point of salvation?

The unsaved sinner's prayer is not heard, even at the point of salvation. The point of salvation is the part of God's plan of salvation that literally converts the unsaved sinner to a saved sinner. Yes, even the saved are still sinners. It's just that the saved sinner can claim the blood of the sacrifice of Jesus *and pray in Jesus' name* to be forgiven (see part I). The point of "confessing Jesus before men" is that it brings the unsaved sinner to the presence of at least one saved sinner. This allows those who are already saved to pray an intercessory prayer on behalf of the person repenting. That's a big deal, so stop and digest it.

This is the major realization that those who speak of the "sinner's prayer" are missing. Reciting any version of any "sinner's prayer" certainly won't save anyone. Also, note here that all the biblical points people give for the authorization of a "sinner's prayer" for salvation are either from before the new covenant (before the resurrection of Jesus) or are taken from writings to saved believers in existing churches. In either case, it's misapplication of context.

At the point of confession, anything resembling the "sinner's prayer" is acceptable, because it is actually a confession of sin and a confession of faith rather than an actual prayer. We must remember, however, that all of this is an exercise in futility unless the person is about to be baptized and is making that confession before a believing witness or witnesses who are interceding by prayer.

After that point of confession, God's grace-filled mercy kicks in. The unsaved sinner is buffered from God's hatred of sin by God's mercy, which is brought to bear by the interceding prayers of the believer(s) in attendance. God hears the intercession and then, *and only then*, reviews the repentant petition of the unsaved soul. The person is baptized, showing that he or she is following Jesus to the grave and rising again. Then the person's sins are "washed away," and the person's soul is saved—but not at any point before.

The point not to be missed here is that no one can be saved without a believing witness who is ready to pray intercession for and baptize the penitent, repenting, and unsaved sinner.

There are those who say, "Pray this prayer and be saved, and then go find a Bible-believing church and be baptized as an outward show of your inward faith." These people are literally saying that the "sinner's prayer" saves the soul of the unsaved sinner, which absolves the penitent of further responsibility—not unlike Pilate when he "washed his hands."

One can readily see the problem with this scenario. There are probably millions of people (alive and dead) who just haven't gotten around to getting baptized, and they are lost because of it—even as they believe that their souls are saved. Please realize that these people are not saved, because (as we showed in part I) they haven't "cashed their check."

What About Cornelius?

Most people who disagree with this discussion are waiting for me to take a breath so they can ask, "Why did God hear the prayer of Cornelius?" In Acts 10:1–2, we're told: "There was a certain man in Caesarea called Cornelius, a centurion of the band called the Italian band, A devout man, and one that feared God with all his house, which gave much alms to the people, and prayed to God alway."

In John 9:41, Jesus gave an explanation to the Pharisees with a single sentence: "Jesus said unto them, If ye were blind, ye should have no sin: but now ye say, We see; therefore your sin remaineth."

We've been over this, but it bears repeating. Jesus was saying that anyone who has not heard the gospel of Jesus (the "blind") but lives a right life by faith in God is saved by that faith, just as in Hebrews 11. However, Jesus also told the Pharisees that if they claimed to "see," or to "know God," but did not recognize Jesus as the Messiah and do as He said, they could not be forgiven. They were lost.

Do not let this thought get past you. To believe that Jesus is the Messiah is to do as He commanded. If you do not follow the examples and teachings of Jesus, you are saying that Jesus is *not* the Messiah. It's as simple as that.

In the case of Cornelius, we are speaking of "the blind" in verse 41 above. Some people say that Cornelius could have been written about in Hebrews 11. This would certainly be true of him—but not of his family. This was after that world-changing event of the resurrection of the Christ.

The blind man Jesus healed on the Sabbath (John 9) explained it, and we can do no better here. In verse 31, the blind man told the Pharisees, "Now we know that God heareth not sinners: but if any man be a worshipper of God, and doeth his will, him he heareth."

Peter repeated the thought in Acts 10:34–35. "Then Peter opened his mouth, and said, Of a truth I perceive that God is no respecter of persons: But in every nation he that feareth him, and worketh righteousness [lives rightly], is accepted with him."

This was the situation with Cornelius. We read about it in Acts 10:2. Cornelius was devout and "prayed always." God answered the prayer of this "worshipper of God" with a visit from Peter. Cornelius *then* heard the gospel of the Christ from Peter. The Holy Spirit descended upon all who were there, and Peter baptized Cornelius, his family, and his near friends.

The point is that Cornelius was living a right life—outside the gospel of Jesus. However, to bring Cornelius into line with the new covenant, God sent Peter to allow God to save not only Cornelius but his family and "near friends" by a belief in the gospel. There are many who have been (and no doubt will be) saved by faith, having never heard the gospel of Jesus.

The story of Cornelius is an "apples and oranges" story. It just doesn't match up with the applications that people try to make it fit. Some people say that an unbeliever's prayer was heard. That is wrong. Cornelius *was* a believer. Like the "rich young ruler," Cornelius wanted to know how to better please God, not only for his own salvation but for the salvation of his family and friends.

Some people say that Cornelius was saved before Peter preached to him and the company gathered. That is wrong. As we just said, Cornelius was a believer. He may even have been justified by his personal faith in God, but his household and friends were not. Cornelius was *not* saved, in the New Testament sense, before Peter got there.

We've said it before, even in this chapter: God will judge those who have not heard the gospel of Jesus using a different yardstick than He uses on those of us who have heard the gospel. The point of the story of Cornelius is that God made sure that Cornelius and his household heard the Word so they *could* be saved. That's the part of "seek and ye shall find" in Matthew 7:7, which people often don't understand or apply correctly.

We see that Cornelius, as with any other person who believes and is seeking the Lord, was shown how to find salvation. He was not saved by his prayers. He was saved by hearing, believing, and complying with God's plan of salvation. The prayers of Cornelius were continuous. His prayer was heard, obviously, because he was seeking to please God.

We cannot say that Cornelius was an unbeliever simply because he was a Gentile, which the Jews of that time did. We cannot say that Cornelius, in the New Testament sense, was saved before hearing the gospel, because it just wasn't so. Simply put, the story of Cornelius does not fit anywhere near a study of the "unsaved prayer" or the "sinner's prayer."

What About the Macedonian?

In Acts 16:9, Paul, who was in Troas, received a vision of a Macedonian who seemed to cry out to him. "And a vision appeared to Paul in the night; There stood a man of Macedonia, and prayed him, saying, Come over into Macedonia, and help us."

Paul went straightaway to Philippi.

Note that many see the change in personal pronouns in verse 10 as an indicator of Luke joining Paul in Troas. If Luke was "the Macedonian," we certainly understand why the prayer was heard. If "the Macedonian" *was* a dream, we can also see why the prayer was heard—if we look at the faith of Lydia. On the Sabbath, Paul went to the riverside where worshippers gathered. In Acts 16:14, we read, "And a certain woman named Lydia, a seller of purple, of the city of Thyatira, *which worshipped God*, heard us: whose heart the Lord opened, that she attended unto the things which were spoken of Paul."

The prayers of the worshipper(s) of God were, and still are, answered by someone preaching the gospel to them that they might be saved—just as it was with Cornelius.

As a sidebar, consider this. We know that there were no practicing Jews in Philippi, because the worshippers were not in a temple (or synagogue, as we now know them). It takes eleven Jewish men to establish a synagogue. We can say that this area of Europe was "virgin territory" as far as the gospel—and therefore, even the Word of God—was concerned. No wonder Paul had such a warm spot in his heart for the Philippians. This was perhaps the first church in Europe.

We End as We Began

The day-to-day prayer of petition of the unsaved is not heard. Of course, there is no such thing as a prayer of the true nonbeliever. A very great problem lies with the many people out there who have been told that they are saved and who believe that they are saved while they are not. These people are the ones who wonder why they pray and "nothing happens." These people have been told a lie by those who think their own way to salvation—even though it is different from God's—is good enough or even better. The blood of the lost will be found on those teachers' hands (Ezekiel 33:6).

The prayer of the unsaved person who believes and is seeking the truth is heard only in that the person will be led to salvation. Even this work you are reading may be the result of some person's prayer (yours?) to find the truth. Who knows? Cornelius prayed for God's leadership and got it. Lydia prayed for God's leadership and got it. Notice in the Scripture that they celebrated only after being baptized and thereby becoming saved.

A point that is often overlooked here is that when Cornelius was presented with the gospel of the Christ and the plan of salvation, he both accepted and complied. He had the option of thinking that his own way was good enough, just as you or I do. However, Cornelius accepted the truth and became a baptized believer, a true follower of Jesus. We can say the same of Lydia.

Only after being saved could Cornelius, Lydia, and their saved "households of faith" pray successful prayers of petition for their daily lives. Our lives and prayers are no different.

Location, Location, Location

Am I now saying that *where* we pray is important as well? I answer with an emphatic yes!

Jesus told the woman at the well, "Woman, believe me, the hour cometh, when ye shall neither in this mountain, nor yet at Jerusalem, worship the Father."

Yes, I said that location is important, but you will soon see that by saying *where* to pray, we are really saying *how* to pray.

Jesus had left Judah to go to Galilee, and He had to travel through Samaria along the journey. He stopped at Jacob's Well and rested, while the disciples went to get some meat. A Samaritan woman came to draw water, and Jesus asked her to give Him a drink.

Jesus proved yet again that the Lord uses those who are least expected to "spread the word." This woman of a half-breed people, who were treated like lepers by the "real" Jews, became an evangelist of Jesus Himself. It's an interesting story. Read it in John 4:1–41.

The point we take for this discussion is the statement of Jesus in John 4:23: "But the hour cometh, and now is, when the true worshippers shall worship the Father in spirit and in truth: for the Father seeketh such to worship him."

Most every preacher out there stops reading before the last part of the verse. However, that last part is the part that should make us all open our ears: "For the Father seeketh such to worship him." Remember that; we'll come back for it.

During that conversation in John 4, part of the discussion was about the racism of the time. Then the woman said in verse 20, "Our fathers worshipped in this mountain; and ye say, that in Jerusalem is the place where men ought to worship." She was pointing out that the Samaritans worshipped on Mt. Gerizim but that the Jews said the only proper place was the temple on Mt. Moriah (Jerusalem). To this, Jesus replied, "Woman, believe me, the hour cometh, when ye shall neither in this mountain, nor yet at Jerusalem, worship the Father. Ye worship ye know not what: we know what we worship: for salvation is of the Jews.[*] But the hour cometh, *and now is*, when the true worshippers shall worship the Father in spirit and in

---

* See part II, "God's Logic."

truth: for the Father seeketh such to worship him. God is a Spirit: and they that worship him must worship him in spirit and in truth" (John 4:21–24, emphasis added).

A note of historical background is warranted in discussing the story of Jesus' conversation with the Samaritan woman at Jacob's well. The biggest point is that Jesus continued to prove that He had come not for the saved but for the lost. He *spoke* with a Samaritan. Traditionally, that, in and of itself, was considered sinful or at least a crime. That Jesus wanted her to give Him a drink from *her* cup would have made Him "unclean" according to the tradition of the Jews. Of course, this didn't bother Jesus. He proved many things without a word of explanation.

The Samaritans, as mentioned, worshipped on Mount Gerizim, and they do so to this day. Because of their "adultery" with the surrounding non-Hebrew people, Samaritans were considered to be no longer a part of the "chosen people"—an attitude that had begun centuries before this encounter.

After the encounter at the well, the woman left her water bottle (an important possession in the desert) and went into town, telling the people that she had met the Messiah. The people came to see this man. Isn't it interesting that the "Gentile" people were the ones most prepared to "see if it was so"? The people of Sychar asked Jesus to stay so they could hear more. Jesus stayed for two more days while they sat at His feet, "and many more believed because of his own word" (John 4:41).

An interesting point here—and one that often seems to be pervasive among the followers of God—is that the people outside the Word seemed more interested in knowing the Word than those of us who are in "possession" of it.

The Samaritans worshipped with only the Pentateuch, or the first five books of the Bible. They called these books the Torah. They might have heard of the writings of Isaiah and others, but the Torah was their only "scripture."

The Jews, of course, had all the books of the Old Testament. They should have been much more ready to receive Christ, but it seemed to be the other way around. We've already talked about the problems Jesus had with the temple leaders.

Jesus often said something to this effect: "He that has ears, let him hear." The most important thing in this study that you should realize about your true, effectual worship—and you should carve it on your heart—is this: Jesus said, "But the hour cometh, and now is, when the true worshippers shall worship the Father in spirit and in truth: for the Father seeketh such to worship him. God is a Spirit: and they that worship him must worship him in spirit and in truth" (John 4:23–24).

Don't let this get past you. This would be a good time for you to pause and pray for understanding. What Jesus said is vital to our understanding, but it will help for us to remember a couple of things. Jesus spoke of His body as a temple when He said that the temple would be destroyed and rebuilt in three days (John 2:21). Paul told the Corinthians in 1 Corinthians 6:19, "Your body is the temple of the Holy Ghost which is in you, which ye have of God, and ye are not your own."

We Must Still Worship at the Temple

Remember when we called Christianity the "new and improved Judaism"? The more one understands, the more one can see that this is true. Remember that even sacrifice is still required, either that of Jesus or ourselves. Actually both are required, as we will see.

Let's pull the above points together. The Samaritans worshipped at Mt. Gerizim, and the Jews worshipped at Mt. Moriah (the threshing floor David bought that was transformed into the "temple mount"). Jesus said that neither location was a destination for worship anymore. Jesus said, "But the hour cometh, and is now." The word *now* makes it plain.

So where is the temple now? Paul told us, as we read above. Remember our discussion in the previous segment about the kingdom being in the heart? We've also seen that there is no salvation without the Spirit. Well, Paul points out that our bodies are, individually, "temples of the Holy Spirit," because the Spirit comes to us at the point of salvation and afterward gains an even greater portion when we pray.

We carry the temple with us? Yes, if we realize that our soul carries our body around. But *how* we worship in our temple is the most important thing.

Jesus said that "the true worshippers shall worship the Father in spirit and in truth" (John 4:23). Most people take this to mean that our public worship should be sincere, that we should worship rightly. To that we add "of course." However, our study here seeks meaning, and this passage contains far deeper meaning than what can be viewed from the surface. Let's take three things from this passage.

First, notice the specifics of what Jesus said. Jesus used the phrase *true worshipper*, and that same true worshipper shall worship the father "in spirit and in truth."

Second, notice that Jesus sought to clarify and repeat His point by saying, "God is a Spirit: and they that worship him must worship him in spirit and in truth."

Third, notice the middle of this passage. It is the glue that will bind our understanding together. Jesus said, "For the Father seeketh such to worship him." Look at that again. The Lord God is seeking those individuals who will worship Him in spirit and in truth.

Here's the point. Look back to when Jesus said this: "But thou, when thou prayest, enter into thy closet, and when thou hast shut thy door, pray to thy Father which is in secret; and thy Father which seeth in secret shall reward thee openly" (Matthew 6:6).

The location we seek for our temple to worship God "in spirit and in truth" is our closet! The location where God waits, "seeking such to worship him" in spirit and in truth, is in our closet!

Here, most of us think about praying at church, and rightfully so—*if* we are thinking we should do as the writer of Hebrews tells us in Hebrews 10:25: "Not forsaking the assembling of ourselves together, as the manner of some is; but exhorting one another: and so much the more, as ye see the day approaching."

In terms of prayer, a focused, single prayer from a number of believers—simultaneously and reverently—demands to be heard. The prayer of the assembly—if it's more than a ritual—is powerful.

We should—no, *must*—meet together, exhort one another, build each other up, partake of the Lord's Supper together, sing praises to God, study the Word, and, of course, pray in the name of Jesus, our High Priest. This is our communal strength. This is our chance to edify and rectify ourselves and others.

Are we saying that we don't worship in church? You can call it worship, if you want to. Indeed, prayer is a form of worship. However, allow me to show you the apostle Paul's view in Romans 12:1: "I beseech you therefore, brethren, by the mercies of God, that ye present your bodies a living sacrifice, holy, acceptable unto God, which is your reasonable service."

Think about what Paul said. This begs the question, "When do we sacrifice at the assembly of the church?" We do many things when we assemble with the saints, but our sacrifice is a personal one. We must go into our own temple—alone with the God who is waiting for us—and give our sacrifice of our selves to Him. We still sacrifice, as before and always, *at the temple.*

> We receive from the Lord every day the fruits of his mercy. Let us render ourselves; all we are, all we have, all we can do: and after all, what return is it for such very rich receivings? It is acceptable to God: a reasonable service, which we are able and ready to give a reason for, and which we understand.
>
> Conversion and sanctification are the renewing of the mind; a change, not of the substance, but of the qualities of the soul. The progress of sanctification, dying to sin more and more, and living to righteousness more and more, is the carrying on of this renewing work, till it is perfected in glory ...
>
> The work of the Holy Ghost first begins in the understanding, and is carried on to the will, affections, and conversation, till there is a change of the whole man into the likeness of God, in knowledge, righteousness, and true holiness. Thus, to be godly, is to give up ourselves to God. (*Matthew Henry Commentary*)

Paul's exhortation says, "Which is your reasonable service." This phrase has also been translated to mean "which is your spiritual service of worship" (NASB).

Remember that Jesus said that the *true worshipper* will worship *in spirit and in truth.* We commune with the Spirit, with God, in the closet. We should all feel a real need to assemble with the saints, but how much more—and more often—we should be looking forward to stepping into the Holy of Holies with Jesus at our side to commune with God on a one-to-one basis. This is worship on the highest and most intimate scale.

Your "closet" can be anywhere that is private and quiet. Turn away all distractions and, if you can, get on your knees (I use a pillow), bow your head, prostrate your being, and begin. You'll be through when you feel you are. Hold your Bible or even lay your forehead on it. Feel a genuine nearness with the Word.

How you go to God in prayer is up to you. Just remember that there is a world of difference between *being in prayer* and *saying a prayer.* Let me expand upon that vital point. *Being in prayer* is a place, a state of mind, a true communion with God where conversation is often silent and truly infinite. *Saying a prayer* is mouthing a finite number of words, however eloquent. It is never silent, and it is usually meant to be heard by others. Both have their place, but the former is infinitely more valuable to your individual soul and your true worship "in spirit and in truth."

Do Not Delay

God is waiting for you in your private place. He said so. Remember above all else that "the Father seeketh such to worship him." If you have not made time for private, quiet prayer time, you are missing out on the true beauty and the deepest meaning of worship. Worse yet, you are depriving God of your personal sacrifice.

Remember these words from the lips of Jesus: "For the Father *seeketh such* to worship him." If you are actually looking for Him, God is actually looking for you—and waiting for you in your closet. James 4:8a says, "Draw nigh to God, and he will draw nigh to you."

What Should I Pray For?

Once more, I wish to reiterate the point of being saved. My point here is that if the reader is not saved, as we discussed in part I, reading this section on prayer is only an exercise. Clarification is in the previous chapter, "Does God Hear All Prayers?"

I'm Not Worthy

An old phrase used by many students is, "The more I learn, the more I realize there is to learn." This is very true of the saved person who is striving for righteousness. The better we get at living a right life, the more aware we are that we often do what's wrong. In Romans 7:15 (NIV), Paul said, "I do not understand what I do. For what I want to do I do not do, but what I hate I do."

Paul was speaking from his own spiritual growth experience. With the increase of "right" in himself, it was easier for him to catch himself not living up to the righteous life he continued to envision. It's actually paradoxical in all our lives. We all want to get closer to God, but the closer we come to God—and the bright light of His purity—the easier it is to see our faults.

In the eighth chapter of the book of Romans, Paul spoke about the tribulations that newborn saints face. He made sure at the outset that we understood that we are not under the condemnation of the law but that we are—when we walk in the Spirit—free of the law's bondage. We are under the "law of the Spirit of life in Christ Jesus … that the righteousness of the law might be fulfilled in us, who walk not after the flesh, but after the Spirit."

This is the beauty of the new covenant. The truth of Jesus has set us free of any form of legalism to let us live a life worthy of the children of God.

For a born-again believer to say "I'm not worthy" is a confession that the person does not understand what it is to be a saved soul. Paul reinforces the point in Romans 8:15: "For ye have not received the spirit of bondage again to fear; but ye have received the Spirit of adoption, whereby we cry, Abba, Father." We are God's adopted children, and *we may call Him Father*."

This point gives us the power—courage, if you will—to come to our Father with our petitions in prayer. Paul also makes a point that few truly realize. Because of our adoption, we are joint heirs with the Christ. This means that we are a little higher than the angels of heaven. The Christ is truly our brother by adoption—not figuratively but literally. This thought alone should empower us to greater strength.

However, Paul also addressed the point of our tribulations. Continuing in Romans 8, he reminded us that any trials at present "are not worthy to be compared to the glory that shall be revealed in us." This is our hope. This is the real reason that the saved "groan within ourselves, waiting for the adoption, to wit, the redemption of our body" (verse 23).

In verse 24, Paul expounded further, saying that "we are saved by hope." The definition of *hope* is "a desire based on a reasonable expectation." This means that hope rises from expectation. We know this to be true, and we expect to be redeemed at the judgment. It sounds a lot like faith, doesn't it? One might turn to Hebrews 11:1 for another description: "Now faith is the substance of things hoped for, the evidence of things not seen."

Many see God as a sadistic being in heaven, who is waiting for the pleasure of punishing us when we do not do exactly what He has commanded. This thought is the greatest opposite of the one true God. As children of God, we can expect that God will do all He has promised. We all need to see God as our Father, who delights in rewarding our ongoing efforts toward right behavior.

I Don't Know What to Say

Remember what we discussed previously. There is a world of difference between *saying* a prayer *to* God and *being* in prayer *with* God. Understand a couple of things, here. In Romans 8:26–28, Paul reminded us again of our hope. "Likewise the Spirit also helpeth our infirmities: for we know not what we should pray for as we ought: but the Spirit itself maketh intercession for us with groanings which cannot be uttered. And he [God] that searcheth the hearts knoweth what is the mind of the Spirit, because he maketh intercession for the saints [us] according to the will of God. And we know that all things work together for good to them that love God, to them who are the called according to his purpose."

Jesus spoke of prayer in Matthew 6:7–8, just before he said, "Pray like this." "But when ye pray, use not vain repetitions, as the heathen [nonbelievers, Jew and Gentile] do: for they think that they shall be heard for their much speaking. Be not ye therefore like unto them: for your Father knoweth what things ye have need of, before ye ask him."

Prayer is designed by God Himself to be a communion. The dictionary defines *communion* as "the sharing or exchanging of intimate thoughts and feelings, especially when the exchange is on a mental or spiritual level."

Any businessman will tell you that you should be prepared for a meeting. This is no less true of prayer. If you have a number of things that you want to include in your meeting with God, by all means, bring notes.

However, the point of all this is that you don't need a script! Don't go to your closet with a prepared speech. Don't think that the words have to be "just right." Don't believe that God won't understand; if you are saved, the Holy Spirit, the interpreter, is in your heart. Jesus, from His own lips, said that God knows what things you need—before you ask.

If God Knows Already, Why Pray at All?

Remember that your closet is where you manifest your most true worship. No one else is listening; no one else hears, save God alone. God wants to know that *you* know that He is the "fount of every blessing." God wants to know that you want to be with Him. He wants to hear your praise. He wants to hear what you think is important.

He wants to speak to you! Yes, if—and only if—your heart is open, God can, and will, place His thoughts and plans there. God will not "open the lid" to your heart, but if you open it to Him, He will fill it full!

Prayer is not a place to present a laundry list to God. Prayer is a place for communion with God. Please note that we're thinking of prayer as more of a *place* than a *thing*. If you haven't already, start now to think of *being* in prayer rather than simply *saying* a prayer. This doesn't mean that you can't present personal desires to God. In fact, prayer is the only place where it is appropriate. Prayer is a place of praise, supplication, and communion. The point is that prayer should never be thought of as sitting in the lap of

Santa Claus but as more of a cozy, fireside chat with your oldest and dearest friend, your Father in heaven.

Having confirmed that, let's look at what the Scripture directs us to pray for.

Pray for the Spirit and the Understanding

Paul talks of understanding in 1 Corinthians 14:15: "I will pray with the spirit, and I will pray with the understanding also." Both the Old Testament and the New Testament have numerous mentions of the Spirit and the understanding used, with both physical and spiritual connotations.

The Spirit is invariably the Spirit of God, very often called by a proper name, the Holy Spirit. The "gift of the Holy Spirit" is not a fixed amount of the Spirit dispensed to you at baptism. You receive the Spirit as a gift. How much depends on you and your prayer life. In Luke 11:13, Jesus tells us, "If ye then, being evil, know how to give good gifts unto your children: how much more shall your heavenly Father give the Holy Spirit to them that ask him?"

The understanding only comes from the Spirit. To understand that statement, one must have *the* understanding that comes only from the Spirit of God. *Understanding* is having a heart for God and knowing the heart of God.

The Spirit and the understanding, when mentioned in the Bible, are almost invariably mentioned in the same breath. Wisdom is often spoken of with this biblical pairing.

Pray for Knowledge and Wisdom

Wisdom is often described as "the application of knowledge." Solomon, son of David, prayed for wisdom and has long been touted to be the wisest man who ever lived.

Paul said that he was pleased to hear that the church in Colossi had been established. In Colossians 1:9–10, he added, "For this cause we also, since the day we heard it, do not cease to pray for you, and to desire that ye might be filled with the knowledge of his will in all wisdom and spiritual understanding; That ye might walk worthy of the Lord unto all pleasing, being fruitful in every good work, and increasing in the knowledge of God."

Note that Paul explained why he prayed—as we should also pray—for the four things we've listed so far. The *knowledge* of God and His will most certainly will lead to "all *wisdom* and *spiritual understanding*." With that *knowledge* of God, we can walk "worthy of the Lord" and be "fruitful in every good work." Paul also indicates, as we did earlier, that "knowledge leads to deeper knowledge."

Pray for Forgiveness and Strength

It's a shame to say that most Christians simply say, "Forgive us of our sins," and expect that to suffice. Perhaps that's okay for a public church service, but not for a true worshipper's personal prayer. Remember this phrase: "God knows, but He wants to know that *you* know."

Weakness is human. Pray for places in your life where you are weak. Pray for strength to overcome those weaknesses. Asking for forgiveness of sin is the same as treating a runny nose or a sore throat when the actual problem is that you have a cold. Pray for strength to overcome the problems of your life, even as you pray for forgiveness of the indications that both you and God see as symptoms of those problems.

Pray for Power

Since the church in Thessaloniki was manifesting the love of God, Paul said in 2 Thessalonians 1:11, "We pray always for you, that our God would count you worthy of this calling, and fulfil all the good pleasure of his goodness, and the work of faith with power."

Faith, the reason we come to pray, is often linked with power. Power and strength are—and are not—synonymous. I'm reminded of a basic premise of karate. You heard it in the movie, *Karate Kid*. When asked "Why do you learn karate?," the student replied, "So I don't have to use it."

The point of having power is that if you know you have it, your confidence to act rightly is strengthened. With God's power, we have nothing to fear. God's power gives us the ability to do all the things that we know are right without ever wondering "what if ...?"

God's power *is*. Think of a bully who leaves the weak boy alone because the bully knows that the boy who looks like easy prey has a big brother who will put anyone in the hospital who "messes with my little brother." We have a direct example. Our firstborn "big brother" is Jesus, the Christ. Demons tremble upon just hearing His name!

If we have a firm faith in God's power, the powers of darkness—and even Satan, the ruler of this earth—will give way and give a wide berth to avoid interfering with our works of faith. Pray for a stronger faith in God's power every time you say, "Our Father in heaven." If you have a firm faith in God's power, you will see fewer stumbling blocks. Fewer obstacles will obstruct your works of faith. Living a Christian life becomes the easiest (and best) way to live.

Pray for Faith

We just mentioned this above. Pray for greater faith. Pray for blessings that prove God's power. The caveat here, though, is that you'd better be ready to have your faith tested. The only way that you know the strength of anything is to test it—and, of course, prove it. (By the way, that goes for patience too.)

You say you already have faith? In James 2:19 (NIV), James said, "You believe that there is one God. Good! Even the demons believe that—and shudder." James went on to talk about faith being manifested by, as Paul said, "good works, which God hath before ordained that we should walk in them" (Ephesians 2:10). This is very important, but that study is not germane here.

What applies here is the simple fact that believing in God is not enough. Perhaps the man who came to Jesus in Mark 9 was more insightful than all of us. We mentioned a story about belief in part I. Here's the story again, expanded in a different direction.

Mark told us in Mark 9 that Jesus returned to the disciples in town after the transfiguration. He saw some disciples defending themselves against some temple scribes and other people who had seen them fail to cast a demon out of a boy. Jesus basically asked, "What's going on?"

A man told of the terrible things that the demon had done to his son in what appeared to be an effort to simply kill the boy. The man said, "And

I spake to thy disciples that they should cast him out; and they could not" (v. 18).

Jesus actually rebuked his disciples, saying, "O faithless generation, how long shall I be with you? how long shall I suffer you? bring him unto me " (v. 19). Jesus was saying that after all the time they'd had together, the disciples should have had more faith. Jesus basically told them that He was not going to be with them forever, so they were going to have to be stronger in their faith in the power of God.

The disciples brought the boy to Jesus, and when the demon saw Him, it threw a fit and took the boy with it. The boy's father told Jesus about the things the demon had done and then said, "If you can do anything, take pity on us and help us" (v. 22).

If it had not been Jesus, one might say that He seemed insulted, for He instantly answered the man: "If I can?" (NIV) Then He said, "Everything is possible for him that believes" (v. 23).

In verse 24, the man, probably dropping to his knees to cry and beg for his son, immediately answered Jesus with this most profound plea: "I do believe, Lord. Help me overcome my unbelief!"

Then Jesus rebuked the demon, and it left the boy.

The point of this story, as it applies to us in this study, becomes clear a bit later. Jesus and the disciples went into the house, and the disciples asked, "Why couldn't we cast out this demon?" Apparently, they had done these things previously and had been successful. Jesus told them that there were levels of strength in the spiritual world. He said, "This kind can only come out by prayer and fasting."

The point Jesus made—and the point we make here—is that one must continue in a prayer worship to garner the strength to truly overcome *all* the demons of Satan. Of course, this makes it obvious that long, deep prayer worship is needed to do battle with Satan himself.

Your strength of faith is obviously relative. You are a vessel, as we're told many times in Scripture. You must continue to fill your heart with greater faith, and force unbelief to spill out and leave you.

A larger point to digest is to realize that while "God is faithful, who will not allow you to be tempted [tested] beyond what you are able" (1 Corinthians 10:13), temptation is not the only fight you will see. If you truly grow in faith, you will want to do more, and Satan will throw stronger adversaries and circumstances at you, since your faith is stronger.

If you're thinking, then, that it is safer not to grow in faith, you should do a separate study of the parable of the talents, told by Jesus and recorded for us in Matthew 25:14–30. The short version is this: "God doesn't abide benchwarmers."

Pray for Others

Intercessory prayer, as mentioned previously, is the prayer that "goes to the head of the line." Praying for others is one of the greatest things you can do for God's spiritual world, and it is the most beneficial for you personally.

The one point I've made over and over about God's way of thinking is one of the simplest points, and Jesus told it to us in the parable of the talents in Matthew 25:14–30. Basically, Jesus said that if you don't use what you have, you certainly don't need any more of it. If you don't give your love away, the only love you'll receive will be in the form of pity. If you give anything you have—within the will of God—you will get more. If you do not use what you are given, you're to be considered lazy and wasteful and unworthy of *any* reward—even the presence of God.

In Luke 6:38, Jesus told us how to give. He said, "Give, and it shall be given unto you; good measure, pressed down, and shaken together, and running over, shall men give into your bosom. For with the same measure that ye mete withal it shall be measured to you again."

Pray for the sick; the traveler; your family and friends; government leaders of city, state, and country; leaders and members of the church; and the unsaved. The list is endless.

God's love has been given to you. Be doubly sure that you share it with others in your prayers.

Pray for Yourself

I will give you no direction for your personal prayer except the direction above. Don't pray for a Cadillac when a bicycle will do just fine. You'll find that judgments come as a result of prayer. God moves, within His will, to the expressed wishes of those who pray in the name of Jesus. Don't even attempt to abuse the privilege.

What You Pray as Opposed to *How* You Pray

In a previous section on the types of prayer, we talked about the parable of the Pharisee and the publican, told by Jesus. We reiterate here that attitude is everything.

Jesus said, in both Matthew 9:13 and 12:7, "I will have mercy, not sacrifice." This means that a right life—a life of faith that is proven by love, selflessness, and mercy toward our fellow man—is what God seeks. God does not desire lip service. In fact, Jesus spoke to the temple leaders, repeating Isaiah 29:13 when He said in Matthew 15:7–9, "Ye hypocrites, well did Esaias prophesy of you, saying, This people draweth nigh unto me with their mouth, and honoureth me with their lips; but their heart is far from me. But in vain they do worship me, teaching for doctrines the commandments of men."

By the way, have you ever noticed that Jesus spoke very few *new* things without noting them as "a new commandment" or some such? After all, Jesus—in the beginning—was the *Word.* The Word was what Jesus spoke. We sometimes have trouble remembering the fact that, in Jesus' time, there was no such thing as New Testament Scripture. A deeper study of the words of Jesus shows that He quoted nearly every book of the Old Testament.

The understanding was in the hearts of the "seekers of God" long before Jesus walked the earth. David understood this and wrote in Psalm 51:16–17, "For thou desirest not sacrifice; else would I give it: thou delightest not in burnt offering. The sacrifices of [to] God are a broken spirit. A broken and a contrite heart, O God, thou wilt not despise."

This thought was not just an understanding limited to Bible scholars or the faithful. Hosea pronounced the judgment of God on Israel in Hosea 6:6. God Himself said to all the people, "I desired mercy, and not sacrifice; and the knowledge of God more than burnt offerings."

The point here is that God sees your spirit and knows your heart. We've discussed this before, but we genuinely must remember that any form of ritual "worship" is wasted on God. This principle is no more important anywhere than in one's prayer life!

Perhaps the most effective prayer—and certainly the most worshipful—is the prayer of a broken, contrite heart that is prostrate before God and simply cries, "Help me."

When Should I Pray?

We've already seen that we should worship "in spirit and in truth" in our "closet." Doesn't that cover it?

All Times Are the Right Times

The church at Thessaloniki was very young when Paul had to leave. Idol worship was very strong, and persecution was, apparently, fierce. The leaders of any "revolution" were always targeted. Paul wrote to the Thessalonians to encourage them to remain in the faith. Given that, we see that these writings are especially pertinent to those just beginning their Christian life, but they do apply to all of us. When Paul addressed prayer, it was in the middle of a small list of "practical precepts" in 1 Thessalonians 5:16–22:

- Rejoice evermore.
- *Pray without ceasing.*
- In every thing give thanks: for this is the will of God in Christ Jesus concerning you.
- Quench not the Spirit.
- Despise not prophesyings.
- Prove all things; hold fast that which is good.
- Abstain from all appearance of evil.

In another instance, Paul didn't express any real doctrinal problems in his writing to the church in Ephesus. It appears that when Paul wrote to the Ephesians, it was to get them to expand their understanding, to inspire them to greater work for the glory of God. However, Paul was not remiss in addressing the basics.

In Ephesians 6:18, Paul had just discussed the "armor of God" and was ending his letter when he said that they should be "*praying always* with all prayer and supplication in the Spirit, and watching thereunto [the day of judgment] with all perseverance and supplication for all saints."

I'm Not a Monk

When we speak in terms of "pray without ceasing" or "praying always," most people instantly retort, "I'm not a monk. No person can be in prayer twenty-four hours a day." This reply is true, on both counts. But it's only true when we think of the true, worshipful prayer "in the closet."

I have no recollection of where, or even when, I heard it, but this is the most succinct explanation I've ever heard concerning this point: "When you open your eyes in the morning, you say, 'Our Father in heaven,' and when you've laid your head on the pillow and are just about to close your eyes, you say, 'Amen.'"

I'm reminded of a funny (in an un-funny way) morning prayer:

> Dear Lord,
> So far I've done all right.
> I haven't gossiped, haven't lost my temper,
> haven't been greedy, grumpy, nasty, selfish, or overindulgent.
> I'm really glad about that.
> But in a few minutes, God,
> I'm going to get out of bed.
> And from then on,
> I'm going to need a lot more help.

The idea of continual prayer, as well as worshipful prayer, is one of practice. Live your daily life in a continual conversation with God. If you start your day with a prayer that ends with "to be continued," you'll come to think of your words as conversation, realizing that everything you say can and will be heard by God.

When you're in a hurry and you get an unexpected green light, say, "Thank you, Lord." Rather than cussing a red light, say, "Thank you, Lord, for giving me a chance to practice my patience." The other day, a friend on Facebook said, "Lord, thank you for the spilled coffee. My keyboard needed cleaning, and I really shouldn't have had another cup of coffee."

When you catch that jar that would have made such a mess, thank God. If you drop a tool beside your foot instead of on your toe, thank God for showing you in time to move your foot. When you need help with any little problem, ask God for help. I could go on and on.

The point is that you are asking—actually inviting—God to be a larger part of your life. God is so happy with his children who show that they want to be with Him. How often do you wish for advice or wisdom? God stands willing and able to help. And what about those little things that you might think God doesn't have time for? You'll start to see that even those little things are important to the Father who is approached by a loving child.

Your language will start to clean up considerably. You'll curse at something or someone, and then stop to tell God (because you now believe He stands ready to help), "No, please don't, Lord, I didn't mean that. I'm sorry." You'll come, more and more, to the real and intimate relationship that we all need and that God desires.

When you look at the radar and ask God for protection from the storm, you'll realize when you've made it through okay. When you thank God for the protection from the storm, God knows that you know that He was the one who waved that cloud to the side.

Ultimately, you will come to truly believe that "coincidence is merely God wishing to remain anonymous." You will come to realize that there really *is* an angel on your shoulder, an "angel of the Lord," directed to your aid by the Holy Spirit, which you continually ask for in your private prayers.

The Rewards of Continual Prayer

You'll begin to realize that God is closer than you ever thought possible. This life is not without God's promise.

Matthew 7:7 has been my favorite verse since childhood. It begins a passage that points out the rewards of a continual conversation with God. Matthew 7:7–11 (NIV) is nearing the end of what is called the Sermon on the Mount. Jesus emphasized the point of prayer when he said, "Ask and it will be given to you; seek and you will find; knock and the door will be opened to you. For everyone who asks receives; he who seeks finds; and to him who knocks, the door will be opened. Which of you, if his son asks for bread, will give him a stone? Or if he asks for a fish, will give him a snake? If you, then, though you are evil, know how to give good gifts to your children, how much more will your Father in heaven give good gifts to those who ask him!"

The point of continual prayer is continual communion. It's not wrong to consider it an ongoing conversation with God. God is a very good listener, and He can do something about what's bothering you.

You'll feel God's presence more and more. You'll find a "peace that surpasses understanding." Things will simply start "going your way"—as long as your way is the way of the Lord.

How Should I Pray?

We are adopted brothers of Jesus. In terms of Christianity, Jesus is our High Priest. We went into detail about this earlier in part II. However, at that time we did not discuss why this is so important to us. Hebrews 4:15 explains in precise detail: "For we have not an high priest which cannot be touched with the feeling of our infirmities; but was in all points tempted like as we are, yet without sin."

Jesus understands. In our modern times, one can hear Jesus saying, "Yup, been there, seen it all, was crucified in the T-shirt." Jesus saw temptations that we should all hope we never see. Jesus can relate to every possible human problem, because He was human too.

The high priest was the intercessor for the people. It was that way long before Jesus walked the earth. How much greater is our intercessor—our High Priest—than any before. Jesus is the High Priest of His own order, the order of Melchizedek.* Read Genesis 14:18 and Psalm 110:4 to see that Jesus, by the Godhead's plan, was "groomed" to be our High Priest long before AD 33.

We'll repeat Hebrews 7:1–3 here. "For this Melchisedec, king of Salem, priest of the most high God, who met Abraham returning from the slaughter of the kings, and blessed him; To whom also Abraham gave a tenth part of all; first being by interpretation King of righteousness, and after that also King of Salem, which is, King of peace; Without father, without mother, without descent, having neither beginning of days, nor end of life; but made like unto the Son of God; abideth a priest continually."

Realize that, by our adoption to the family of God, we are brothers of the Christ. We are truly above the angels of heaven. Recognizing this *kinship* and the fact that Jesus is our High Priest and intercessor, we can approach the throne of God in the Holy of Holies of our personal temple with boldness reserved for only "members of the family." Hebrews 4:16 says, "Let us therefore come boldly unto the throne of grace, that we may obtain mercy, and find grace to help in time of need."

It's put another way and explained a little more in Hebrews 10:19–22: "Having therefore, brethren, boldness to enter into the holiest by the blood

---

* For detailed explanation, refer to the discussion about Melchizedek in chapter 9.

of Jesus, By *a new and living way*, which he hath consecrated for us, *through the veil*, that is to say, his flesh; And having an high priest over the house of God; Let us draw near with a true heart in full assurance of faith, having our hearts sprinkled from an evil conscience, and our bodies washed with pure water" (emphasis added).

The writer says "boldly," because human high priests were only allowed behind the veil of the tabernacle and temple once a year on the Day of Atonement. One needs to remember the very real significance of the moment of Jesus' death as told in Matthew 27:51. In verse 50, we're told that Jesus "yielded up the ghost." The next verse (v. 51) follows with a simultaneous occurrence: "And, behold, the veil of the temple was rent in twain from the top to the bottom; and the earth did quake, and the rocks rent."

The veil was very thick curtain; Jewish tradition says it was "a hand's breadth thick." Note that at the moment of Jesus' death, the veil was "torn in two" from top to bottom. That doesn't sound too important, except that the veil, as thick as it was, was sixty feet tall! Only God Himself could accomplish this feat.

At the point of Jesus' death, God showed that the veil no longer separated us from Him. We had a new High Priest and a better way to approach God. Because of the sacrifice of Jesus, we can go "through the veil" on any occasion of prayer, as long as we go with our brother, the High Priest Melchizedek (Jesus) by praying in the name of Jesus. Jesus told us in John 14:13–14, "And whatsoever ye shall ask in my name, that will I do, that the Father may be glorified in the Son. If ye shall ask any thing in my name, I will do it."

When we realize that the Christ, our brother, is our High Priest, the word *boldly* means that we can approach the throne *without fear*.

Attitude Is Everything

Boldness also can mean that one has more than a casual desire to get what is requested. Immediately following His example prayer recorded in Luke 11:2–4, Jesus gave us a tremendous amount of information on how to pray effectively.

Remember that hospitality is one of the biggest requirements of a right life throughout the history of the "chosen people." The desert was an inhospitable place. With that in mind, Jesus related a story in verses 5–8 (NIV).

> Then he said to them, "Suppose one of you has a friend, and he goes to him at midnight and says, 'Friend, lend me three loaves of bread, because a friend of mine on a journey has come to me, and I have nothing to set before him.' Then the one inside answers, 'Don't bother me. The door is already locked, and my children are with me in bed. I can't get up and give you anything.' I tell you, though he will not get up and give him the bread because he is his friend, yet because of the man's boldness he will get up and give him as much as he needs."

We've read this before in Matthew, but here in Luke, Jesus continued with instruction and logic in verses 9–13:

> So I say to you: Ask and it will be given to you; seek and you will find; knock and the door will be opened to you. For everyone who asks receives; he who seeks finds; and to him who knocks, the door will be opened. Which of you fathers, if your son asks for a fish, will give him a snake instead? Or if he asks for an egg, will give him a scorpion? If you then, though you are evil, know how to give good gifts to your children, how much more will your Father in heaven give the Holy Spirit to those who ask him!

We glean three points from this passage.

First, buried deep in this passage is one of the major points that Jesus was making. "Because of his boldness," the man got what he wanted. As Jesus noted, the man did not get what he wanted because he knew the other man. He didn't get what he wanted because the man inside felt obligated. The man got the loaves simply because he was bold enough to go asking in the middle of the night. The man inside knew that no one would go in search of bread in the middle of the night unless he was in earnest.

So, when Jesus says to ask, to seek, and to knock, He is not indicating meek actions. These things are to be done boldly. These are action words. *Asking*, *seeking*, and *knocking* are not separate actions but a combination of actions. If we are asking within God's will and are diligently seeking, we must knock—boldly. This is not arrogance. This is proof of earnestness.

While it is not related to *how* to pray, the second point is one that has been bantered about in many pulpits: God is much better at everything than we are. Logically, this applies to God's ability to answer prayer.

The third point is also unrelated to *how* to pray, but it is too important to "leave on the table." This point—which often seems to get passed up, both intentionally and unintentionally—is that Jesus is talking specifically about the Holy Spirit in this instance. I say it this way because I believe that this passage also applies to prayer in general. Notice that Jesus specifically tells us to ask for the Holy Spirit! That's because Jesus saw the Holy Spirit as involved in every aspect of our lives.

Most people, including believers, think that the Holy Spirit is a "thing" that we can't describe. Many believe that you "get" the Holy Spirit at baptism, and that's that. Many believe that you get a "dose" of the Holy Spirit at baptism, and that's all anybody ever receives or needs. Most just leave a discussion of the Holy Spirit alone and say, "It's not for us to understand."

We've discussed most of this already in chapters 10 and 11, but we haven't discussed the Holy Spirit in light of our ability to ask for His help. In a previous chapter, we discussed the question of what we should pray for. Let's look at that question with the Holy Spirit in mind.

- *the Spirit and understanding*: the Holy Spirit is shown hand-in-hand with understanding.
- *knowledge and wisdom*: Wisdom is applied knowledge. Knowledge, on the wholesale level especially, comes from God. The Holy Spirit guides us to and through knowledge so that we may apply it wisely—with His guidance.
- *forgiveness and strength*: God grants forgiveness by and through our mediator, the Christ. But where is the strength of God on this earth? It is in God, the Holy Spirit, alone, under the authority that was given to the Christ by God Almighty.
- *power*: The power of God lies in His strength and sovereignty. Do you get it? It's in His *strength (previous).*
- *faith*: We understand that faith comes by hearing. Let me take you past that to increasing faith. After we begin our journey of faith,

we must continually ask for all the things we have mentioned previously in this list in order for our faith to increase. All of these, as we've seen, are products of the work of God the Holy Spirit.

- *others and yourself*: We must pray for an increase of the Holy Spirit in ourselves so we can grow in our service and in our prayer life. An increase of the Holy Spirit will give us more of the knowledge of God and His will, so that we will think more of others than ourselves. Salvation is only the first step of our God-fearing and God-serving journey through our "born-again" life.

Let's look again at Jesus' words in Luke 11:13. This time, let's look at what Jesus thought was important enough for us to ask *expressly* for. "If ye then, being evil, know how to give good gifts unto your children: *how much more shall your heavenly Father give the Holy Spirit to them that ask him*?" (emphasis added).

But wait: there's more! They say that on TV all the time. It's true, here. Jesus made yet another point about how to pray in Luke 18:1–8. He told His disciples a parable to show them that they should always pray and not give up.

> In a certain town there was a judge who neither feared God nor cared about men. And there was a widow in that town who kept coming to him with the plea, 'Grant me justice against my adversary.' "For some time he refused. But finally he said to himself, 'Even though I don't fear God or care about men, yet because this widow keeps bothering me, I will see that she gets justice, so that she won't eventually wear me out with her coming!'" And the Lord said, "Listen to what the unjust judge says. And will not God bring about justice for his chosen ones, who cry out to him day and night? Will he keep putting them off? I tell you, he will see that they get justice, and quickly. However, when the Son of Man comes, will he find faith on the earth?" (Luke 18:1–8 NIV)

Of course, the lesson here is *persistence*. If your Bible has topical headings, it probably labeled this passage as the "Parable of the Importunate Widow." The word *importunate* is defined as "persistent, especially to the point of annoyance or intrusion."

Just as Luke stated in verse 1 of this passage, we should always pray and not give up. Note verse 8: "However, when the Son of Man comes, will he find faith on the earth?" This question is an important one. Will there be—is there—a persevering faith, the kind of faith that continues in belief and loyalty to the point that prayer is an integral part of daily life?

You Can Change God's Mind

Another point to remember is that God does change His mind. No, it is not heresy to say that God changes His mind, thereby saying that God changes His plans. We have various records throughout the Bible of God either being persuaded by intercession to change His mind, or simply changing His mind on His own.

An actual event that was recorded for us by both Matthew and Mark is the story of the Canaanite woman. Mark noted that she was a Syrophoenician. This is only one of two times that anyone is referred to as Canaanite in the New Testament. "Canaan" did not exist in New Testament times. Matthew was probably using the term in much the way a southerner uses the word *Yankee* to refer to someone who is not from the south, i.e., an outsider.

Remember that Matthew was a Jew who was writing to the Jews about a Jew, whereas Mark was directing his writing to the Romans. Matthew was speaking about the woman, while Mark told us where she was from. The records are in Matthew 15:21–28 and Mark 7:24–30. We'll use Matthew for the text.

> Leaving that place, Jesus withdrew to the region of Tyre and Sidon. A Canaanite woman from that vicinity came to him, crying out, "Lord, Son of David, have mercy on me! My daughter is suffering terribly from demon-possession." Jesus did not answer a word. So his disciples came to him and urged him, "Send her away, for she keeps crying out after us." He answered, "I was sent only to the lost sheep of Israel." The woman came and knelt before him. "Lord, help me!" she said. He replied, "It is not right to take the children's bread and toss it to their dogs." "Yes, Lord," she said, "but even the dogs eat the crumbs that fall from their masters' table." Then

> Jesus answered, "Woman, you have great faith! Your request is granted." And her daughter was healed from that very hour.

Mark's rendition of this story is even harder to understand than this one. This passage in Matthew almost explains what Jesus meant, but most people just read this passage and merely skirt any misunderstood part. By now, you must realize that we are not going to do that.

Remember, Jesus was a Jew. All Jews, and Hebrews before that, have seen themselves as "a separate people," to the point that we would call it racist in today's time. Notice, in verse 22, that Jesus would not even speak to the woman. Verses 26 and 27 are usually where people are thrown off. Jesus was ministering to the Jews. The "Greek" (non-Jewish) people were "not invited" at this point in time. The "children" Jesus spoke of were the Jews. Jesus, speaking as a Jew, said that it was not right to give the gifts that were reserved for the Jews to other non-Jewish people.

But the woman was *persistent*. The disciples said, "She keeps crying out to us." She was begging Jesus for His healing. She was a mother seeking help for her child. Her point was that all she wanted was a crumb off the loaf reserved for the Jews. Jesus was "badgered" into delivering His healing to this woman on behalf of her child.

A very real point is that Jesus, obviously, had not sealed the new covenant at this point. This woman was another person who was not mentioned in Hebrews 11. Before the new covenant, God rewarded the faithful, no matter what "race" they belonged to. Jesus tested the woman with His statement of being sent to the "lost sheep of Israel." If she had gone away and accepted His "put-down," there is little doubt that her daughter would not have been healed.

She passed the test. Jesus said, "Woman, you have great faith! Your request is granted."

Jesus changed his mind! God still rewards faith wherever He sees it.

Atrophy

Atrophy is defined as a wasting or decrease in size, owing to disease, injury, or lack of use. That makes atrophy the largest detractor of your Christian prayer life! Your soul may have been diseased by sin or injured by another person. But injury should never keep you from your Christian life. Forgiveness cures those ills. Lack of use is simply a lack of exercise, for whatever reason.

You must exercise your prayer life regularly. *Regularly* does not mean listening to a prayer in church. *Regularly* means regular, earnest, "in your closet" time in prayer with God.

How to Pray: A Summary[†]

1. Boldly and without fear, approach the throne in the name of our High Priest, Jesus. We must be bold with our requests. We must realize that there is a major difference between humility and timidity. We will be humble toward God because He is the Almighty. But we must not be timid. Timidity is an indication of insecurity. If we are insecure in our relationship with our LORD, God, He may tell us to come back later when we're more certain of ourselves and our spiritual relationship. Earnestly state your petition, like the man asking for bread in the middle of the night.

2. Persistently pray your request. We must be persistent with our requests. Yes, God hears every believer's prayer, but He wants to know that you are serious. He knows what you need, but do you know what you need? A one-time request only says, "I want." Persistent prayer says, "I'm serious." You may see that you didn't need one thing but rather something else. God may lead you that way during prayer. Only if you are persistent with your prayer requests can you begin to see your true needs.

3. Pray without ceasing. Persistence not only applies to a single request but to your prayer life on the whole. If we are persistent in prayer, we also examine ourselves regularly. We perform our own form of therapy. We continue to recognize our shortcomings, and we help God by helping ourselves. With God's answer (the Holy Spirit) to our persistent prayer, we will overcome our shortcomings and gain victory after victory.

[†] See also the section entitled "Types of Prayer" in this chapter.

4. Pray with faith. God wants to see that we truly believe that He is the source of blessing. The Canaanite woman truly believed that Jesus was the Christ, and she was rewarded for it. If we manifest our faith in prayer with God, we will be rewarded as well.

5. Praying without fear is the only way to get God to change His mind. God doesn't abide "wishy-washy." Our Father will even change His mind if we manifest our faith in such a way that He knows that it will not be in vain. God needs to know that He can have faith in us as well. God may have decided that things should occur in a certain fashion. With bold and persistent prayer, even if your prayers disagree with God's plans, God may change His mind. We may, with our bold and persistent prayer, keep God from bringing His wrath upon our wicked and perverse society. He may allow our country to stand long enough for us to change things.

6. Praying without fear means praying out of love. Love is not timid; ask any parent. We mentioned that timidity manifests insecurity. If we truly believe that we are in the presence of God, how in the world can we feel any more secure? Prayer is the one place where we should feel love more than any other. We need to return that love to God and further manifest it by our love for others. Isaiah 30:18 tells us, "Yet the LORD longs to be gracious to you; he rises to show you compassion. For the LORD is a God of justice. Blessed are all who wait for him!"

God stands ready—even more than we do for our own children to bestow His grace and blessing. We have but to ask.

13

God's Plan ≠ God's Will

Semantics May Help

"If you will …" That's a nice, polite way to begin a request. "If it be your will …" is also nice. Notice, however, that these simple phrases are actually shortened versions of "if you are willing" and "if it be that you are willing," respectively.

To be willing to do something is totally different from having a desire to do something. It is even more different from having a predetermined, long-range "rule" about always doing something or never doing something.

The short version is that "God's will" can be the immutable purpose or decision of God, i.e., the unchanging will of God, or it can be a simple contraction of "God is willing."

When we read or say "if it be God's will" (depending on context), the phrase can mean (1) "if it is the immutable purpose, determination, or decision of God" or (2) "if it will be that God is willing."

These two variations are, obviously, very different. The first is what most people mean (or think they mean) when they say things like "it must have been God's will" or "if it be God's will." The second is more like God answering a prayer request or such.

Let's look at God's plan juxtaposed with God's will.

God's Plan(s)

For clarity, I will state here what many people will consider obvious. I'd venture to say, though, that just as many people will not have seen the idea put so simply: *God's plans are continually working toward the fulfillment of God's will.*

Forming a plan is the first step in turning intention into reality. Let's look at that from a spiritual aspect with a question: are all plans, either God's or humanity's, always carried out as originally set forth without fail? How many plans have you made, whether dependent on other people or not, that simply did not happen? Well, God's plans, in that they involve humans, very often do not come out as originally intended.

God will see that His plans succeed, with or without the original cast members. God said in Isaiah 46:10 that His plans would go forth because He was "declaring the end from the beginning, and from ancient times the things that are not yet done, saying, My counsel shall stand, and I will do all my pleasure."

I liken God's plans to the song by The Impressions: "People Get Ready" (1965). The lyrics go like this:

> People get ready, there's a train a-coming.
> You don't need no baggage; you just get on board.
> All you need is faith to hear the diesels humming.
> Don't need no ticket. You just thank the Lord.
>
> People get ready for the train to Jordan,
> Picking up passengers from coast to coast.
> Faith is the key. Open the doors and board them.
> There's room for all among those loved the most.
>
> There ain't no room for the hopeless sinner
> Who would hurt all mankind just to save his own (believe me now).
> Have pity on those whose chances are thinner,
> 'Cause there's no hiding place from the kingdom's throne.

So, people get ready for the train a-coming.
You don't need no baggage; you just get on board.
All you need is faith to hear the diesels humming.
Don't need no ticket. You just thank the Lord.

That song is so much more accurate than most people see. I continue to liken God's plans to a train for many reasons, one of which is that a train is often considered unstoppable. Certainly God's plans are unstoppable. Another reason is that after the train leaves the station, no one can board it. Highlight this: there may be another train for you, hopefully, but you will never be on "the one that just left."

From other studies herein, we see that God has plans for the future. However, the decision about which persons will fulfill those plans is more often up to us. If we are not willing to "get on board," there's also a plan for that—one that doesn't include us.

God's Will

We stated above that a plan is the first step for turning intention into reality. In that statement, we find the most succinct definition of God's will: God's will = God's intention.

Lest there be any misunderstanding, let's establish that, in this segment, we are studying God's will and that God's will is defined as an unchanging decision, purpose, or determination of God. The theological question is not only "what is God's will?" but also "how is God's will applied to our lives?"

There are actually three levels of God's will that may (or may not) apply directly to our lives:

1. God's fixed or sovereign will (intention)
2. God's will (intention) of sanctification for us as humans
3. God's will (intention) for each of us as individuals

Let's look at these separately.

God's Sovereign Will

God is over all. God created everything. God holds sovereign power over everything. If you do not believe this fact, please, for the sake of your immortal soul, rethink your position and refer to part I about salvation.

Visualize creation. God thought He would form a place for us to live. God's Word brought the heavens and the earth into existence. Imagine the laws of physics that appeared as God said, "I want this" and "I want that." God wanted Earth to sit in a particular place, so "pop." Then, pop-pop, pop-pop, pop-pop-pop, … up popped all the planets, stars, black holes, and laws of physics that we have yet to understand, for they were required to keep Earth exactly where God wanted it.

I'll make a long story short: God created even the ancillary periphery of the universe *for us*. The universe stays in place because God wanted Earth to stay in place. Obviously, we humans cannot change anything, in heaven or on earth, that God positioned especially to do whatever job it does. Nor can we change or even alter the universal laws of physics that appeared as God decided on what He wanted. This is God's *sovereign* will. God is over all. To say that some things never change is, in the strictest sense, to speak directly of God's sovereign will. To those who say that we have the technology to change these things, I simply point out the Tower of Babel.

God's Will of Sanctification: His Moral Will

This is the "will of God" that we read of in 1 Thessalonians 4:3 where Paul wrote, "For this is the will of God, even your sanctification." Peter wrote, "The Lord is … not willing that any should perish, but that all come to everlasting life" (2 Peter 3:9).

You see, God's desire, directive, decision, purpose, and focus is that we all live with Him for eternity. God wants us to take care of His creation, to care for those harmed both physically and spiritually by sin, and to manifest God's love through benevolence and community. God's will, in this regard, is that we be stewards of His love, that we manifest His love and bring others to the knowledge of God so that none "should perish." God's will is a will of upright human character and the obligatory morality that comes with it. This is God's will of sanctification, His moral will.

We have a complete and thorough guide for us in this regard. We have God's Word in the Holy Bible and the examples of Jesus. We have the Holy Spirit as further witness.

God's Will for Us as Individuals

This is where we realize the inequality sign (≠) of the equation. God's plan does not equal God's will.

We know that various people and religions believe that God has had a plan for our lives from the time of our birth.* Others hold to the idea that God has had plans for individual lives since the beginning of time.

God's plans are in place† and are being revised, by Him, moment by moment. God can only desire that we will all come to be a part of them in order to be with Him.

God will help us through life if we become a part of His adopted family. We read in Psalm 119:173, "Let thine hand help me; for I have chosen thy precepts." However, God holds no individual plan for you and me other than this: to be a party to God's will, we must voluntarily manifest our faith and become a part of God's family. Then, and only then, will we become party to God's plans.

To put it another way, we cannot know what God's plans are or what God has planned for us except that we first have the Holy Spirit indwelling our temple (ourselves, our personal "Holy of Holies"). Only then will we be able to interpret the happenings in our life as the indicators of our path.

Let's Play Chess

Think of human chess masters. These fellows have the ability to "foresee" twenty-five or more moves in advance! This ability allows them to both

---

* See chapter 14, "Chosen, Elected, Called, Appointed, Predestined" for greater detail.

† See also the section about the "omni" words in chapter 8.

move their own players strategically and also predict with some degree of accuracy what the opponent will do. In an abstract sense, it appears that they can predict the future.

The chess master will look at the board and "see" what he must do if the opponent moves a bishop. He also "sees" what he must do if the opponent moves this pawn or that pawn. The chess master has thought about what he must do if the opponent moves either knight, and so on.

The chess master "sees" what he must do if his opponent "zigs," but also if he "zags." If the opponent does something that a spectator might see as unexpected, the chess master has already thought of it and can move his pieces accordingly to facilitate his plan to capture the opponent's king, which is his ultimate goal.

Chess masters the world over often prove their prowess and ability by playing tens or even hundreds of opponents simultaneously. Some have even done it blindfolded and play using only their memory!

In Sofia, Bulgaria, in 2009, Kiril Georgiev, a chess grandmaster, played a total of 360 games simultaneously (winning 284, drawing 70, and losing 6) during a marathon that lasted fourteen hours and eight minutes—setting the world record for the most simultaneous chess games played up to that time.

On February 8–9, 2011, Iranian grandmaster Ehsan Ghaem-Maghami made the *Guinness Book of World Records* for playing the most simultaneous chess games. He played for twenty-five hours against 604 players, winning 580 (97.35 percent) of the games, drawing 16, and losing 8.

What a wonderful God is ours that He created humans and instilled all of us with wonderful innate abilities such as these. However, these are just people. We may think of their minds as, perhaps, superhuman, but they are merely practiced, and their abilities are honed to a sharpness little known to most of us.

The point is that God's abilities are boundless. How much more a chess master is God than a person? God formulates plans on such a scale and plane that we might fear madness if we even attempted seriously to comprehend the magnitude of them.

This is where we realize that God has the future firmly in His grasp—not because He can see the future, but because He has planned for every possible eventuality of the acts of humanity and sin, both good and bad. No matter what happens, if we are within God's moral will, we are "under

His wing" (Matthew 23:37; Luke 13:34). Our comfort is not in knowing that God sees the future, because He does not.‡ Our greater comfort is in the realization that God *determines* the future for His faithful followers by planning for it and bringing His plans to fruition.

In Isaiah 46:10–11, we have the truth of God from His own lips: "Declaring the end from the beginning, and from ancient times the things that are not yet done, saying, My counsel [plans] shall stand, and I will do all my pleasure: Calling a ravenous bird from the east, the man that executes my counsel [plan] from a far country: yea, I have spoken it, I will also bring it to pass; I have purposed it, I will also do it."

God said, "Declaring the end from the beginning, and from ancient times the things that are not yet done." God is saying, "I've got a plan, and I can tell you how things will end because of it. I will make it happen."

In Practicality

When thinking about human proof of God's plans, there pops into my mind the story of Joseph. There is no doubt that God could see that the house of Jacob needed to regroup and strengthen, because that was precisely what happened. God saw the good heart of Joseph and formulated various plans on how to get him to Egypt where there was plenty of food and land that could support the Hebrews. The land of Canaan was not conducive to forming a nation at that time.

To be sure, God had formulated many plans for the "zigs and zags" of Joseph and his family. Whatever scenario might arise, God had a plan for it. He obviously had a plan for dealing with the brothers' jealousy.

Take note that God did not cause the brothers to be jealous. No evil comes from God. However, God plans for such eventualities, and "all things work for good for those that love the Lord"—in this case, Joseph.

There were only seventy people in the family of Jacob when they arrived in Egypt. When Moses led the Hebrews out of Egypt, they numbered in the millions (six hundred thousand men plus their family groups). God's plan to raise a great nation was successful because He had made His plan for Joseph come to pass.

---

‡ Reference previous endnotes.

The big thing to remember, in this study and in our own lives, is that if Joseph had faltered somewhere along the way, God would have implemented "plan B," and things would still have gone as God planned—except with another man, e.g., Saul and David.

When we read the story of Joseph after he was sold into slavery, we can see how God looked after Joseph. There were times when Joseph might even have looked up in prayer and said, "Really?" But the "proof is in the pudding." God brought Joseph out of the dungeon and into the palace. Joseph loved the Lord and proved it, and God never forgot him.

A Look at the World on Autopilot

God created a perfect world. God created a perfectly innocent man, who was just like a newborn child. "And Jesus called a little child unto him, and set him in the midst of them, And said, Verily I say unto you, Except ye be converted, and become as little children, ye shall not enter into the kingdom of heaven" (Matthew 18:2–3).

Satan got the innocent Eve to "eat the apple" while the innocent Adam looked on. Adam ate as well, and Satan had his first victory on the earth.

Remember that the purity of God will not allow Him to abide with any sin. Because of Satan's victory on the earth, God literally left the earth to him. Satan became, and still is, ruler of the *earthly realm*. This is the complete answer to the question of why bad things happen to good people.

We discuss this elsewhere, but suffice it to say that God left the earth on autopilot. The earth still holds its place in the universe in orbit around the sun. The rain still "falls on the just and the unjust." However, sin abounds on the earth because Satan is in charge of it.

Satan is "the prince of the power of the air" (Ephesians 2:2). In biblical times, "the air" was beneath heaven and was considered to be the realm of demons. Sin randomly wreaks havoc on the earth with the sole purpose of trying to cause humanity to curse God.

When sin entered the world, God turned His intentions toward bringing humans back to a sinless state—or at the very least, to a state of righteousness. God has demonstrated through history that He will protect those who believe in Him and have faith in that protection.

Did you hear that? God protects "His children." God does not protect the world! God is good, and by His covenant, He has given protection to those who desire to be "good" with Him. God protects those who are in the covenant with God. That was His agreement.

As has long been established, humanity's definition of "good" is not the same as God's definition. Bad things befall the people of the world who are not within the covenant and under the protection of God Almighty. God has limited Satan's free rein to those outside of God's protection. For a true understanding of this, see the story of Lot. This should bring an important thought to saved readers: it is up to *us* to bring the world to repentance so that Satan can be rendered impotent.

The point we have been making here is that the protection and blessings of God are only for those who abide within the covenant of God. God's *chosen people*[§] have always had extraordinary protection throughout history.

The rest of the world was (and is) relevant to God only when the chosen people have required discipline. You'll notice, however, that whenever an army smote the chosen people, even by God's plan, the attacking army was also punished for the action.

Simply put, *God will have no part with those who want no part with Him.* It's not that God doesn't know what's going on in the rest of the world. God fully expects us to do all we can to alleviate what sin brings to the world. Remember that God knows everything that can be known. The term "godly sorrow" applies here as much or more than anywhere else.

Please, please, note that this does not keep us from praying intercessory prayer for the world around us. Intercessory prayer probably pleases God more than anything else. In Matthew 5:44, Jesus said, "But I say unto you, Love your enemies, bless them that curse you, do good to them that hate you, and pray for them which despitefully use you, and persecute you."

Do you get it? Now, with new understanding, you can see what Paul meant (both talking about and being inspired by the Holy Spirit) in Romans 8:28 when he said, "And we know that all things work together for good to them that love God, *to them who are the called according to his purpose*."

---

§ Reference the section on the "change of the chosen" in chapter 7, "Judaism: New and Improved."

Conclusions of Comparison

It is evident that the title of this chapter is true: God's plan does not equal God's will. The point of comparison is to assure the believer and unbeliever alike that free will is real and that we hold our own salvation in our own hands.

God's will of sanctification is that we be moral, upright, and benevolent by following the examples and teachings of Jesus and by following the guidance of the Holy Spirit.

In no way is it appropriate to believe that God is going to "get on board" with us. God has no individual will for us until we get on board *with Him*. God's plans only include us if we agree with God and are willing to be a part of His grand design. It has been this way from the beginning and will remain so until the end.

Eat these words found in Ephesians 5:8–10: "For you were once darkness, but now you are light in the Lord. *Live as children of light* (for the fruit of the light consists in all goodness, righteousness, and truth) *and find out what pleases the Lord*" (emphasis added).

14

Chosen, Elected, Called, Appointed, Predestined

Aren't They All the Same?

This area of study, depending on your point of view, is either a very real salvation issue or not a salvation issue at all. This area of study has been picked over and picked apart until it resembles Swiss cheese. There are areas of overlap and areas of segregation. There are religious schisms and even religious chasms that have formed over the definitions, applications, and theory of the words of the title of this chapter.

I have intentionally placed this chapter to follow the previous "God's Plan ≠ God's Will." This area of study follows so closely on the heels of that chapter that one might consider it an extension rather than a separate area. Of course, one might apply that same thought to this entire work.

We will look at these words—*chosen*, *elected*, *called*, *appointed*, and *predestined*—both separately and collectively to determine what they mean as they apply to the Word of God. Once again, understanding is the vital element.

Why Is This Important?

Your receiving the gift of salvation makes you important to God. God has the ability to know each of us as individuals. However, God only provides loving nurture and care for those who desire to be with Him. Jesus said in Matthew 5:44–45, "But I say unto you, Love your enemies, bless them that curse you, do good to them that hate you, and pray for them which despitefully use you, and persecute you; That ye may be the children of your Father which is in heaven: for he maketh his sun to rise on the evil and on the good, and sendeth rain on the just and on the unjust."

Jesus tells us that we must strive to be like God, in that *He loves everyone equally* and blesses all of us (good and bad) with a rising sun and rain by which we can sustain our lives—whether or not we choose to follow Him. Jesus continued in verses 46–48, saying, "For if ye love them which love you, what reward have ye? do not even the publicans the same? And if ye salute your brethren only, what do ye more than others? do not even the publicans so? Be ye therefore perfect, even as your Father which is in heaven is perfect."

Jesus spoke of having the perfect love of God, of loving and blessing everyone—*everyone*—regardless of its return.

By our love, we will be different. By being different, we will be special. How better to make someone feel special than to call them "chosen"? Notice in Matthew 20:16 that Jesus explained the story of the workers in the vineyard by saying, "So the last shall be first, and the first last: for many be called, but few chosen."

By that statement, Jesus told us that the workers who did not answer the invitation to work did not get paid, but that those who did answer got paid an equal minimum wage, no matter when they started during the day. In other words, the first commitments were indistinguishable from the last, and vice versa. See the complete story in chapter 1 in the section entitled "It's My Money," Says Jesus."

Our purposes here will make us notice that Jesus said, "For many be called, but few chosen." Jesus noted that some did not come. These were among the "many" who had been called. The few who got a day's wage were the ones who came to the vineyard to work. These were "the called" who *answered* the call. These special men were the *chosen* of whom Jesus spoke.

See how it works? A worker became one of the *chosen* few by simply showing up and asking to work. Before the day of harvest began, the owner of the vineyard had chosen to pay each worker who showed up a denarius (a day's wage). The owner may have decided it even before the season, much less the day, but it is no matter. By extension, the workers who came had been chosen before that day to receive the day's wage, even though the landowner had no idea who, or how many, would come.

The same meaning comes from this same story when you substitute any of the words *elected*, *called*, or *appointed* in place of *chosen*.

As mentioned in the study of "God's Plan ≠ God's Will," God's will is that we all be "paid a day's wage"—that is, that we all come to eternal life, that we all be *chosen*. Remember this: God's plans are for the purpose of attaining God's will. It is up to us whether or not we are part of "the chosen." It is *not* decided for us.

Visualize a rock star who yells, "By being here tonight, you have been chosen to receive one of the best concerts ever seen or heard on this stage!" Were any in the audience handpicked by the performers? No. But everyone who had a ticket was "chosen" by the performer to receive that special performance. If you and I didn't get to see it, it's because we didn't attend.

One might hear questions like "What about the *elect*?," "What about the 144,000?," or "What about the *called*?

The problem is in the translation and—after the translation—in the interpretation. Isn't it always? The word *chosen* from the Greek actually implies *favorite* or *favored*. This makes the whole thing easier to understand. God does not plan on who is going to answer His invitation, but I can guarantee to you that only the ones who do will be *favored* with salvation.

Your salvation has not been decided in advance of your life (and death). Your personal decision to be saved (or not) is very much up to you alone.*†

The Overlap

We sometimes get confused when speaking of "the chosen" or "the elect," in that there sometimes develops a gray area of overlapping definitions. This is where God's plan versus God's will stands the greatest abuse. The biggest problem in this area is when someone has predestination in mind.

---

* See the in-depth discourse in chapter 8, specifically the section about omniscience under the heading "The 'Omni' Words." Also see chapter 13: "God's Plan ≠ God's Will."

† An in-depth discourse on God's salvation is in part I.

Predestination is a stumbling block for many people and a pillar for others. So, what is predestination?

More often than not, predestination is considered to be unconditional election. This is a major tenet of Calvinism and the Primitive Baptists, among others. *Unconditional election* is the belief that God selected (or elected) the saved souls before time began. Those holding this belief do no evangelism whatsoever, their reason being that the decision has already been made and evangelism is a waste of time.

An adapted form of unconditional election is, obviously, *conditional election*. Conditional election is basically Arminian at its outset. The argument is that Jesus died for all but that God foreknew who would/will answer that call to salvation, and that the Scripture calls these saved "the elect." Conditional election allows for evangelism, in that we may be "characters in the play," but even as such we will not, technically, affect the outcome that is thought to be already known by God.

Free Will and Predestination

Some may ask, "Where does *free will* fit into predestination?" The simple answer is that *free will* fits *nowhere* in the concept of predestination. If what you are going to do is known before you do it, even if it is known only to God, there is no decision involved.

Some say that if a person doesn't know what his or her decision will be, that decision is made by *free will*."

I submit to you that if *any* personage, God or human, knows exactly and precisely what you are going to do at any future moment, then the decision has been made before you arrive at that future moment, and *there is actually no decision to be made*. To speak of free will in this scenario verges on silliness.

Any variant on election or predestination from the standpoint of "God knows" is tantamount to putting a mouse into a straight length of pipe and calling it a maze. When we know where and even why (no choice) the mouse is coming out, there is no decision necessary on the part of the mouse concerning its destination. No matter how the mouse chooses to get there—whether it runs, rolls, walks, or crawls to the other end of the pipe—it comes out, just as we knew it ultimately would. The hardcore believer of predestination will tell you that God knows when it will come out as well.

Unlimited or Limited

Another way of qualifying a belief in predestination is an attempt to clarify the doctrine of election by comparing the thoughts about *unlimited atonement* and *limited atonement.*

First, the Holy Spirit is completely left out of this explanation. This belief makes it sound like the atonement of Jesus—the sacrifice of Jesus—is what saves us. While it is true that without the sacrifice of Jesus we would never be able to repay the debt of sin that we owe, it is not true that the sacrifice alone saves us.

One needs to realize that if we die without God's salvation, our sin debt has already been settled. That is, we will pay the debt with a life—our own. Our soul, however, reaps the spiritual judgment of our life.

Believing that Jesus is the Christ, the Son of the living God, is only one step in becoming the saved soul that we should all desire to be.

The "election" argument states that a person who believes that Jesus died for all (unlimited atonement) is saying that the atonement was weak, because it took the "power of man" to make it work when that human begged for forgiveness.

So, the "election" believer would say that it had to be a *limited* atonement if it were to be a true and "full-strength" atonement. Therefore, the pretzel logic of "election" and "limited atonement" concludes that only the elected souls receive atonement, without any human input to "dilute" its strength. This would further mean that God would have elected those who would receive the atonement of Jesus, long in advance of our even coming to this earth. (We've already discussed this above.)

With these distorted views of the gift of salvation and how a person is to receive and apply it, we have failed to see the simplicity of righteous living. We have attempted to put God inside the box of human understanding.

Humanity Can Put No Limits on Salvation

In reality, the atonement of Jesus did exactly what God had planned. Jesus was born to Mary, lived a perfect life as a human, and died, sinless, as the perfect, unblemished Lamb of God. God has never, from the beginning to this day, changed the way we sacrifice for sin. God did, however, change *what* we sacrifice.‡ We're told, "Present your bodies a living sacrifice, holy, acceptable unto God, which is your reasonable service" (Romans 12:1).

We can present ourselves as a living sacrifice in that we claim and confess the death of Jesus—which God considers proper atonement—and prove our belief by our own death to sin. We do this by following Jesus to be "buried" in the watery grave of baptism and to "rise" from that grave as a resurrected, new creature (2 Corinthians 5:17). We are raised to walk in newness of life (Romans 6:4).

The simple fact is that Jesus died *for all humankind*, and it is up to each of us to "turn on the tap" and drink the living water of life. The power of God cannot and will not be diminished by whether or not you or I decide to be saved.

It sounds rather silly to even think that we could diminish the power of God, doesn't it? It sounds just as silly to think that God rolled the dice on all of humanity, from beginning to end, before humanity began. People who believe this are probably the same ones who ask if God can create a rock so heavy that He can't move it.

The real truth of our wonderful, loving God is that His invitation is for everyone who will take it, and God's will is that everyone will accept that invitation (2 Peter 3:9).

Example and Thought

One man, believing God knows the future of all of us, said of Abraham, "God knew that Abraham would kill his son, but Abraham didn't. God didn't test Abraham, but simply proved to Abraham what God already knew." This is almost perfectly circular reasoning. I am not being flippant when I point out that the "Abraham scenario" proves what *Back to the*

‡ See part II, as well as chapter 12 on prayer, and specifically the section titled "Location, Location, Location."

Future and other such movies tell us: that every move in the past changes the future. Therefore, God would have "manufactured" the future by proving to Abraham that Abraham had the faith to kill his own son. No matter how you construe it, that is predestination. If God knew anything ahead of time, then it was not God doing it; rather, the future itself performed what we call the act of God.

The truth is that God tested Abram (Abraham) to see if such faith existed. Before God offered His own Son to be a human sacrifice, God wanted to know if humanity would do it for Him. The faith of Abraham saved us all.

Editorial Note

I'm sure there are some people who might actually feel comforted by predestination and other versions of "it's not up to me." For others, if that were true, it surely would bring a whole new (and even humanistic) impetus to the question, "Why am I here?"

I, personally, find far greater comfort in realizing that God doesn't know the future but that He plans for it. This indicates to us that if we become a part of God's plan, if we "get on the train," not only will we be "special" to God, but we will receive the protection and peace of mind that comes from knowing that God's train will not be derailed. It proves to me that God is proactive, not reactive. When you see that God doesn't react to the knowledge of the future but plans for what He desires the future to be, God's power is magnified beyond comprehension.

I am far more comforted by knowing that *God has plans for me* than by thinking something like "God knows what I'm going to do."

I, personally, do not have the strength or wisdom to make it on my own. I stumble. I am not perfect. God's plans are complete and always perfect. If I "zig," He's got a plan for that. If I "zag," He's got a plan for that. I know that if I am a saved soul, God's hand will guide me so that I can help Him complete His will. For the true believer, the Holy Spirit offers guidance and does the "heavy lifting."

Knowing that God has plans for the future comforts me far more than thinking that He can see the future and react to it. God will not be dictated to, even by something we call the future.

The larger point gleaned from this chapter is this: If you are not "working in the vineyard," you are not going to receive "a day's wage." It is *your* choice whether or not to "apply for the job"—that is, to "be chosen." It's your choice to answer or not answer the unchanging invitation that God continues to offer.

15

Sin: Do This, Don't Do That

In order to know if one thing or another is a sin, one must be able to answer a decisive question for oneself: what is sin?

I stated it that way because no one can make a detailed list of what is a sin for you. Yes, I'm saying that one thing may not be a sin for me, but that the same thing *will* be (or will appear to be) a sin for someone else. Paul explained all this a number of times in the Bible, but you will read the Scripture here, along with explanatory notes.

Another point to make here is that when we speak of sin, we are speaking in terms of one of three areas:

- the law
- the behavior of people outside the law and/or the gospel
- sin under God's new covenant

We've established that only good comes from God. That leaves us with another question: where did sin come from?

Adam, whose name literally means "man," was the second sinner. Eve was the first. In the grand scheme of things, who sinned first is of no consequence. We will speak of the first sin as the "sin of Adam," only because it has been referred to as such for thousands of years.

The point is this: When Adam took that bite out of that apple, sin was *invited* to crawl out of Satan's handbag to take up residence here on earth. Death existed, but sin raised it to prominence. Score one for Satan. Therefore, sin, for our purposes here, will be defined as *any thought or deed counter to God's nature, God's will, or God's direct commands*. We understand that God is pure and true. Ergo, anything that is not pure and true is, indeed, sin or sinful.

Original Sin

At this point, many will think of the *doctrine of original sin*. I speak of it as doctrine, because so many teach it as theology. When taught as doctrine, the doctrine of original sin takes one of two forms:

1. It adheres to the idea that the sin of Adam is literally transferred to us at birth, that we are born with sin.
2. It follows the interpretation of St. Augustine and others, who considered original sin to be more a "consequence of this first sin, the hereditary stain with which we are born on account of our origin or descent from Adam" (*Catholic Encyclopedia*).

According to those who believe either of these two things, this is where the practice of infant baptism gains its necessity. This doctrine of original sin finds all humankind to be born sinners, regardless of whether it was by the actual sin of Adam or the "stain" of the sin of Adam. I will gladly debate that all six of the Pelagian tenets* are true.

I'll not belabor a discussion of original sin or infant baptism in this chapter, except to quote the *Catholic Encyclopedia* once more as it speaks of the Pelagian Commentary of St. Paul: "But the commentary on St. Paul is silent on one chief point of doctrine, i.e., the significance of infant baptism, which supposed that the faithful were even then clearly conscious of the existence of original sin in children."

The *Catholic Encyclopedia* explains itself. Our reply is that Paul was tediously explicit when it came to doctrine. Paul, like Jesus, was "all about the message." Paul warned over and over against believing any doctrine other than the doctrine that he and those with him had presented. Paul never soft-pedaled any point of doctrine, and his instructions on all manner of worship and practice were so detailed as to leave no doubt.

Paul (and thereby Pelagius) never mentioned infant baptism because, as Paul said in Romans 10:17, "Faith comes by hearing," and infants

---

* The Pelagian tenets are listed, with argument, in the appendix.

innocently care about little more than the teat, having absolutely no regard for or understanding of an eternal soul.

No Void Exists

In Isaiah 45, God speaks of things relatively defined by other things. Relativity is used by humanity to define a number of things, e.g., that cold is the absence of heat, vacuum is the absence of pressure, darkness is the absence of light, black is the absence of color, and so on. In Isaiah 45:7, God said, "I form the light, and create darkness: I make peace, and create evil: I the LORD do all these things."

As we said before, nothing evil comes from God, but Satan certainly stands ready to fill in all the opposites of the goodness of our God. Satan, whose name literally means "accuser" or "adversary," existed before time. Satan had been adversarial to God even before God created the world. Satan was very prepared to tempt Eve and Adam. We're told in 1 Peter 5:8 that even to this day, Satan, "as a roaring lion, walketh about, seeking whom he may devour."

Our point here is that sin exists just as truly as God's love exists. Sin exists because it is the opposite of God's purity and goodness. Sin came to the world because humanity (Eve and Adam) did not resist temptation. However, on the day of judgment, the sins of Adam will be accounted for by Adam, and your sins and mine will be accounted for by ourselves alone.

Why Do Bad Things Happen to Good People?

As we just discussed, sin exists. That is to say that sin *is*, just as surely as God is God Almighty.

Sin knows no season. Sin knows only the boundaries that God has placed on Satan himself. If you know anything about the myths of vampires, think of sin as a vampire; it can only go into any place where it is *invited*. Eve and Adam invited sin into our earthly realm.

Sin and the evil it represents are as random as they are methodical. We mentioned that Satan is relentless in his efforts to "devour" humankind. Sin in the form of "bad things" is the easiest way that Satan can cause people to doubt and even curse God.

As concerns the question, "Why do bad things happen to good people?," we must define what is good. The human definition of *good* very often conflicts with the truest definition of *good*. Good, in a few ways, is "good enough" for most folks. Jesus told the rich young man in Matthew 9:17, "There is none good but one, that is God."

Even so, the question still stands. Why does God let these things happen? The answer is not that God doesn't care. However, God's sovereign will[†] is all that planet Earth has for protection. Earth will keep on spinning until God stops it.

Those early scientists who said that the earth was the center of the universe were not entirely incorrect. God put the entire universe in place *after* creating the earth (Genesis 1:1). We could liken it to building a hanging mobile for a child or making art.

To build a hanging mobile, one must add counterbalance here and there until the whole piece finds balance. In order for Earth to remain a "hospitable" place for people, it had to remain in a nearly circular orbit around a heat source. That heat source needed to remain relatively static for the orbit of Earth to remain constant. The gravitational pulls had to be such that more planets were needed to orbit that heat source as well. For that solar system to remain relatively static, galaxies of other stars and planets needed to exist, and for those galaxies to remain relatively static, a universe was needed. All of it was positioned in order to keep Earth a hospitable environment in which we could live.

However, this was not trial and error for God. As God's Word formed the creation, all the pieces of the universe came to be, along with all the laws of physics that were needed to keep things as He wanted. God didn't have to make the myriad calculations that would be required of humans.

Simply put, God "set the earth spinning," literally. For those who may be counting, that was the fourth day of creation.

God set our physical world in motion, and then He went about being a "friend to man." All God wanted from all of this was for man to be a "friend to God."

As we all know, Eve and then Adam quashed God's plans. They allowed sin into the world by succumbing to Satan's temptation. At that

---

† Refer to chapter 13, "God's Plan ≠ God's Will," and chapter 34, "The Covenant," for deeper discourse.

point, God turned His attention to humanity and left the earth to Satan. Satan has been the "prince of the power of the air" ever since. Like it or not, Satan is ruler of the earth. However, *Satan does not rule humanity unless humanity chooses to allow it.*

Yes, God is in control. However, it's God's sovereign will that keeps the earth spinning. It is so because God wanted it to be so. It will also stop when God so desires. To put it in human terms, "the rain falls on the just and the unjust." The point is that God is concerned with humanity. But humanity must be concerned with God in order for God to enter in and avert the ability of sin to harm humanity.[‡]

That's harsh, some say. In human terms, it seems so. The problem is that we humans have made it so. It is up to us to bring and spread God's love over the earth, and as we do, sin will find fewer and fewer places to roam and wreak havoc.

Those who have "turned toward the light" of God have always been blessed for doing so. Those who have not, do not fall under any covenant relationship and do not receive any form of what would be called "undue" protection. Sin lives on the earth, and God lives in the heart.

There Is No Laundry List

There was a time when the law was considered the leader toward righteousness. A deeper discourse on the function of the law is in chapter 6. The law didn't show us how to live; it showed us how *not* to live. The law pointed out all the things that were wrong, but God's people were left to their own devices—and their scriptural history—when it came to discerning what was right. A notable example is that only two out of the Ten Commandments did not contain, "Thou shalt not."

As we've discussed, the law was like guardrails on the highway. God intended for people to be basically good, and the law would keep people from "going off the road" at the dangerous spots. The problem was that people continually considered keeping the law to be more important than living a right life and worshipping God.

‡ See chapter 25, "Revelation," in the section entitled "One Large Misconception" for a prime example.

Humanity did not know where the "middle of the road" was, concerning righteousness. The law, then and now, points out where we have gone too far, but the law can never indicate the center between the guardrails or how to stay in that center area.

Jesus came to give us that example. Jesus taught goodness, benevolence, mercy, kindness, and all things opposite the "other side of the guardrails" of the law. Jesus did not dispute the law; after all, Jesus was *the Word* (John 1:1). Nor did Jesus, in any way, tell us to ignore the law. He did, however, teach us what God wanted all along: for us to walk the more narrow path of goodness (Matthew 7:14), which we call here "the middle of the road."

The law had one more failing. Paul explained it, as he also spoke of sin, in Romans 7. Adam Clarke put it this way: "In the law there was condemnation, but no cure."

Do we live by the law of the Old Testament? That's a question worded to confuse. Do we live by the law? Yes. Do we live under the old covenant? No. Jesus converted the entirety of the law into a simple, right-life instruction. We spoke of that at length in chapter 7, "Judaism: New and Improved."

Concerning statutory law, the point here is that God never changes. God is the same yesterday, today, and forever. If God never changes, His moral laws have not changed. We need to realize that God's rules for living together and caring for one another will always be in effect.

We can still read the law and know where the "guardrails" are. The law is a very good guide for the "young in the Lord," who need to learn, as toddlers do, that the stove is too hot to touch. We have to believe that if God didn't want us to know the law of Moses, there would be none who could repeat it—nor would it even be in the Bible.

When, Where, and What Is Sin?

We've been talking about sin itself, not individual sins. We see that sin simply exists. Where there is less light, there is more darkness. Where there is less good, there is more evil. Consider your life, and even your world, as a container. If you fill your life with goodness, you spill evil over the brim of your container and out of your life. Of course, if you begin to fill your container with darkness, light spills out and your world gets darker. In 1 John 1:7, John told us, "But if we walk in the light, as he is in the light, we have fellowship one with another, and the blood of Jesus Christ his Son cleanseth us from all sin."

There is no reason to look for a list of sins. There are many people in the world that use "legalism" as a rule and believe that if they simply "don't do this" or "don't do that" they will be okay with God. Certainly, as children—whether in life or in the church—we need to have rules as guides. Paul noted this in Galatians 5:24–25. However, our discussion here is about deeper faith.

Situation ethics is defined by the old hippie phrase: "If it feels good, do it!" Most everyone demonizes this phrase and considers the thought to be sinful. I, however, am telling you that *your ethics will define your situation*, rather than the other way around. Think on this. A Christian can say, "If it feels good, do it!," and, providing that the thought is accompanied by a clear conscience, he can consider it an accurate judge of right and wrong.

That "clear conscience" I mentioned is brought to bear in James 4:17. James was talking about not giving God credit even for life itself, and then he told those merchants who were planning on furthering their own interests, "To him that knoweth to do good, and doeth it not, to him it is sin." James was speaking to them about remembering the work of the church, but the statement is more far-reaching.

This is a lesson that applies to *all* situations and *all* people. If you know the right thing to do and don't do it, you have sinned in your own heart, and that's the part that God listens to. You actually condemn yourself. Within the law (between the guardrails), you yourself define sin.

Right and Wrong

So, do I make my own list of what is sin? If you are thinking that you can arbitrarily decide whether or not something is a sin and live with that, you are wrong. If you do not understand the following point, reread this segment until you do. *In and because of the new covenant, there is no longer a list of sin. There is only right and wrong, good and evil.*

The thought here is that I am speaking of saved Christians. A saved individual will have that clear conscience we speak of. The unsaved individual has no real, actual definition of sin; basically he has a "lack of conscience" concerning sin. Paul tells us in Titus 1:15, "Unto the pure all things are pure: but unto them that are defiled and unbelieving is nothing pure; but even their mind and conscience is defiled." Paul was talking about the Cretes when he said this. (It's why *boorish* and *cretin* are now synonymous.) But it applies to all of us. He's applying *situational ethics*.

The point here is that an unbeliever is living in the condemnation of the law. Without faith in God and/or the belief of the gospel, a person doesn't recognize sin as sin. Note that Paul wrote to Titus, "Even their mind and conscience is defiled." Defining sin to an unbeliever is an exercise in futility.

Jesus told us in John 3:18 that "he that believeth on him [son of man] is not condemned: but *he that believeth not is condemned already, because he hath not believed* in the name of the only begotten Son of God" (emphasis added).

Paul did a good job of explaining this in Romans 8, which begins with this statement: "There is therefore now no condemnation to them which are in Christ Jesus, who walk not after the flesh, but after the Spirit."

Paul was saying that the condemnation brought to us by the law and its guilt "missed the mark" in showing us how to live. Man never saw righteousness, only the law and its condemnation. Do not miss the fact that the passage also notes that judgment is already made for those who do not accept the invitation to follow Jesus.

Jesus came and gave us the righteous example so that—in our new life of walking after the Spirit in the footsteps of Jesus—we may live where there is neither condemnation of the law nor even a need of the law.

A Right Life, Simplified

The point is that the baptized believer is no longer married to the law but to God. So, what did Jesus have to say about what is important? Let's turn to Matthew 22:34. Jesus was asked, "Which is the greatest commandment?" To this, Jesus answered in verses 37–40, "Thou shalt love the Lord thy God with all thy heart, and with all thy soul, and with all thy mind. This is the first and great commandment. And the second is like unto it, Thou shalt love thy neighbor as thyself. On these two commandments hang all the law and the prophets."

Jesus was quoting Deuteronomy 11:13 and Leviticus 19:18. Jesus said that He had boiled "all the law and the prophets" down to these two commandments "1a" and "1b.".[§] I think that we can boil it down even more by saying, "Do the right thing."

If you are a saved believer, your conscience can, *and should be*, your guide. Jesus Himself, when He gave us "the golden rule" in Matthew 7:12, said it this way: "Therefore all things whatsoever ye would that men should do to you, do ye even so to them: *for this is the law and the prophets*" (emphasis added).

In other words, the only person without a conscience is a psychopath, according to the "shrinks." Even the unsaved know what's right, even if they have no "pangs of conscience" over not doing it. We learn what it is to share very early in our lives, and we know the "right thing to do." In 1 John 3:10, we're told how to recognize a child of God by pointing out what a child of God is *not*: "This is how we know who the children of God are and who the children of the devil are: Anyone who does not do what is right is not a child of God; nor is anyone who does not love his brother." Note that the Greek (New Testament) word for *sin* is *hamartia*, which comes from the root word *hamartano*. It is a sporting word that means "to miss the mark and not share in the prize."

Can you make your own list of sins? No, you don't get to decide. Your conscience has beat you to it. The problem is this: if you are not saved, whether or not you sin is totally unrelated to the future of your soul. I will repeat what Jesus said: "He that believeth on him is not condemned: but he that believeth not is condemned already, because he hath not believed in the name of the only begotten Son of God" (John 3:18).

In answer to the question "what is sin?," let's repeat James 4:17: "Therefore to him that knoweth to do good, and doeth it not, to him it is sin.

---

§ Ravi Zacharias, in *The Loss of Truth*, part 4 of 4.

Righteousness v. Relativism and Pragmatism

"Still a man hears what he wants to hear and disregards the rest" (*The Boxer*, by Paul Simon).

Doing the Right Thing

We just looked at how to define sin. Do you really know what the "right thing" is? Do you decide in advance or wait for the individual situation?

If you're looking for examples, Jesus continually showed us "the right thing" in both His speech and His actions. This was God's plan in sending us Jesus to begin with.*

Since we are made righteous through faith in Christ Jesus, as the truth of the Word of God declares, how do we live this out in our day-to-day lives when a philosophy of relativism is so strong in our society?

In our modern times, the seed of relativism was replanted in the 1960s and 70s. The "free love" movement was the source of *situational ethics*. The hippies are credited with saying, "If it feels good, do it." I interject this thought simply to point out that many of us, and many of those around us, who grew up with this thought process are literally "running things" today (May 15, 2013).

Take note that relativism is often confused with *pragmatism*. Pragmatism is proof with facts–*practicality*, if you will. The difference is real and should be noted when misuse occurs.

"Pragmatism is the only philosophy native to America. Pragmatism shuns any hope of discovering ultimate truth. It is skeptical with respect to objective principles of righteousness and defines truth as 'that which works.' In this philosophy, the end always justifies the means. The driving force behind decisions within the scope of pragmatism is the force of expediency, or adherence to self-serving means" (R.C. Sproul, *Principle versus Pragmatism*).

What does all this mean? A "truth" in pragmatism is "that which works." The *Pragmatic* says, what "works" for you is not necessarily what "works" for me. The premise of the thought is that "whatever works for

---

* See chapter 7, "Judaism: New and Improved."

you" is your truth. Your truth may be different from mine, but "live and let live."

A "truth" in Relativism is just simply whatever makes you feel good. "Whatever makes you feel good" in Relativism need not be based in any truth, at all.

The Yardstick

Pragmatism contains no emotion, hope, or spirituality. Pragmatism reminds me of "Joe Friday" of *Dragnet* saying, "Just the facts, ma'am." Yes, the pragmatic truth of a person's beliefs may be relative to their personal perception of truth, but any pragmatic idea is based on the idea that a truth exists.

A pragmatist uses a yardstick for life, but he or she first designs the yardstick to be used. The fact that other people have different yardsticks is irrelevant to the pragmatist's own views. The pragmatist feels comfortable after deciding, "This works for me."

Relativism doesn't care nearly as much about hope as it does about comfort. It paints with a much broader brush. Relativism can apply to virtually any type of situation—emotional, spiritual, practical, superfluous—with equal error.

A relativist may be said to use a yardstick for life, but that measurement is simply a "relative" comparison to others. It doesn't take much to find someone a relativist can disdain in order to prove that his way is better. The pity of relativists is that they have no rest. They must constantly revise their own standing if they wish to remain "morally superior."

Both pragmatism and relativism hold truth to be whatever a person believes it to be, but only relativism can totally ignore any truth (real or imagined) in its entirety. Pragmatism may be based on error, but it has roots. Relativism can be total fantasy and still offer comfort to the user. Both will be found in "philosophical" discussions about the nature of truth. The pragmatist may actually want to know the truth, while the relativist will only be looking to argue or put it down.

Righteousness has only one, never-changing yardstick for life. That yardstick is the example of Jesus, the Christ. Not everyone seeking righteousness is looking for truth. The truth of righteousness is established and is readily discernable. It cannot be "bent a little." Righteousness is the only way of life that has unchanging benchmarks. In 2 Corinthians 10:12 (NIV), we are told, "We do not dare to classify or compare ourselves with some who commend themselves. When they measure themselves by themselves and compare themselves with themselves, they are not wise."

Given these three choices, we can genuinely see that living a righteous life is, in the long run, far simpler and certainly requires less effort.

What *Is* the Right Thing?

One question nags at both the philosophies of relativism and pragmatism: if there is no such thing as truth, why do people the world over continue to search for it?

This is perhaps the largest single problem of our society today. One can never build a lasting relationship—physically, spiritually, or even in the making of true friends—when that person's core belief is in "that which works" or "that which feels good to me." No one can trust a person who shifts his position on core beliefs whenever the winds of life shift direction. Life itself becomes a listless wandering rather than a journey with purpose. Ultimately, *nothing to live up to leads to nothing to live for.*

This is the real reason people "seek the truth." Seekers are looking for an anchor to tie onto. They are seeking an answer to that age-old question: "Why am I here?"

We're told to be "the light of the world" in Matthew 5:14. How do we live as light? In John 8:12, Jesus said that we are to follow His example as the first "Light of the World." A light in this world of darkness will certainly be seen.

- Doing the right thing may not expedite your progress at work, at school, or in life, but it will gain you the respect of others (and self-respect), which will bring equal or greater progress in due time.
- People may not see you doing the right thing, because sometimes doing the right thing in the right way will not be visible. That is, it will not to be "seen of men."
- Doing the right thing may be deemed weak, unpopular, or even stupid by others, but *it's still the right thing.*

I tell you one truth that can never be refuted: doing the right thing is *never* wrong, and it will garner for a person the real respect of both God and humanity. Chapter 19, "Benevolence = Love," holds an even a deeper discourse on doing the right thing.

I also say this to you: people who do not respect a person for doing the right thing deserve neither your respect nor your company. This includes you. Do you respect yourself?

16

Baptism Doesn't Save You

Baptism doesn't save you … by itself.
Repentance doesn't save you … by itself.
The atoning sacrifice of Jesus doesn't save you … by itself.
Prayer—any prayer—doesn't save you … by itself.
God's gracious nature doesn't save you … by itself.

By the way, faith alone *can* save a soul, if and only if that faith has been proven and that person has never heard the New Testament gospel of Jesus (see Hebrews 11). If you're reading this, you do not qualify for this exception.*

If you have somehow failed to notice the numerous referrals to part I on salvation, you definitely started reading right here. If you have not read part I along with part II, you may not want to (and really should not) begin this study here. However, the truth is the truth, no matter where you begin to see it.

Let's Review

After the sin of Adam, God established blood sacrifice as the only sacrifice that would affect sin in any way. In Leviticus 17:11, God told us, "The life of the flesh is in the blood: and I have given it to you upon the altar to make

* Faith as salvation is discussed in Hebrews 11 and Romans 2 as well as other Scriptures. See also chapter 17, "Judgment: Doesn't Everybody Go to Heaven?"

an atonement for your souls: for it is the blood that maketh an atonement for the soul."

God established restitution as the requirement for true atonement. From the time when sin entered the world, God noted that the only true restitution for sinning would be the life of the sinner. God decided that animal sacrifice was enough to "roll forward" or "cover" the sins of the people on an annual basis, which is now called Yom Kippur by the Jews.

God established that atonement must be made *before* sins can be forgiven (forgotten). The application of *lex talionis* (an eye for an eye), when "ramped up" to the level of atonement for sin, means "a life for a life." God is literally saying to us, "You owe me a life as atonement for your sin."

God also established that He would only accept unblemished and perfect firstfruits for sacrifice. Because "all men have sinned" and no person with a human father is perfect, no person with a human father would ever be worthy as an atoning sacrifice.

There are those who may ask, "If a man's life is not equal to the debt of sin, who else will pay the debt?" Remember that God is the ultimate in fairness. It is not fair to make someone else pay your debt. God considers your debt satisfied if you give all you have—that is, your life.

What about before death? Well, if all you have to give is your own life (unsaved) as restitution for sin, you have no "living sacrifice" to give in service to God. At your death, your life is given as restitution. This means that at judgment, since you have only your life to give to God, you—or more correctly, your soul cannot be saved.

At judgment, a person's whole life must be given as atonement, unless that person can find a perfect person to sacrifice on his or her behalf. We all know who was the only perfect person to be sacrificed on this earth.

God came to realize that humanity was not going to get any better and that the sins of humanity (rolled forward and not forgiven) needed a plan of forgiveness. God formulated His plan for a "new and improved" Judaism by giving His own "firstfruits," His only Son, Jesus, as a human sacrifice that could be perfect: worthy of sacrifice and equal to atonement.

The faith of Abraham proved to God that humankind was worthy of the sacrifice, so God sent Jesus to earth to enact His plan for true atonement and forgiveness of sin.

Jesus came to earth as a human being and lived a sinless life. Jesus, buried after crucifixion, defeated death itself when God resurrected Him (without corruption) on the third day after His death. Jesus then rose from the grave, and the Holy Spirit bears witness of the event, even to this day.

Jesus, a perfect human sacrifice, made proper atonement for human sin. From that point forward, God has been able to forgive the sins of those who claim the blood of Jesus as propitiation for their own personal sins.

How Do We "Get Saved"?

As we've seen in part I, chapter 2:

1. You must hear the gospel that Jesus is the Christ, the Son of the living God (Romans 10:17). The story of Philip and the eunuch in Acts 8:26–39 shows us that a person must not only hear but must understand the gospel message.

2. You must believe that Jesus, the Christ, came to be our example and to die as the perfect sacrifice and propitiation (atonement) for our sins (1 John 4:10). Obviously, a person will believe the gospel of Jesus, or that person will not be saved.

3. You must repent of your sins (Acts 2:38). If you believe the gospel message, you'll also believe that you are a sinner and cannot be a true child of God without forgiveness of your sins. You must choose to turn your back on sin and desire to live a more right life. This is repentance.

4. You must confess that you believe (Matthew 10:32). Jesus said, "Whosoever therefore shall confess me before men, him will I confess also before my Father which is in heaven."

5. You must be baptized in the name of the Father, Son, and Holy Ghost for the remission of your sins (Matthew 28:19). This is very often called "an outward showing of an inward faith." It is that, but it is very much more to the person who truly understands the complete plan of salvation. There are those who believe that baptism is superfluous. They are wrong. Jesus told Peter, just before the crucifixion, "Where I go, you cannot follow Me now;

but you will follow later." What Jesus was alluding to was the fact that the new covenant had not yet been bound by His sacrifice, but after the sacrifice, Peter (and the rest of us) will follow *exactly* in His footsteps through baptism. We follow Jesus by dying to sin and the world (being "crucified with Christ" through repentance), going to the grave because of that death to the world (represented by the immersion of baptism), and rising from that grave, just as Jesus did, to a newness of life. At that point, God adds you to His Church, and your name is written in the Book of Life—but not before.

6. You must live as a new creature, spreading the gospel in your daily life by your example as a follower of Jesus, the Christ (Revelation 20:12). We continue to follow Jesus and keep His commandments. We're shown by the passage in Revelation that, in addition to our names being in the Book of Life, "other books [are] opened" that contain a record of our life after our baptism.

But You Said These Things Don't Save Us

Separately and individually, the parts of God's plan of salvation do not save a soul. As we mentioned at the outset of this chapter, we do not get "a la carte" choices when it comes to God's plan of salvation. A person can own all the parts of a car, but until it's put together, it's just a pile of parts.

God's *grace* is synonymous with God's mercy. We are all blessed, beyond our ability to comprehend, to have a God who is gracious enough to grant us salvation rather than just collect the debt of death we all owe. It is because of God's gracious mercy that we have a plan of salvation, but *God's grace is not salvation unto itself.*

The lynchpin of God's perfect plan of salvation is the *atonement* of the human sacrifice of Jesus. The death of Jesus on the tree of crucifixion (Deuteronomy 21:23; Galatians 3:13) gave us all a chance to offer sacrifice for our sins without dying to do it. Jesus atoned for all our sins. Jesus died once, for all. However, *the atonement of Jesus is not salvation unto itself.*

Belief is a basic requirement of salvation. Belief is obviously needed for one to feel the conviction of sin and to desire forgiveness. Belief becomes *faith* in larger and larger amounts as one's belief is bolstered. However, *neither belief nor faith is salvation unto itself.*[†]

Hairsplitters say that Paul says we are justified by faith in Galatians 5:24. Those are the words in that verse, yes. However, Paul is speaking of the necessity of the law as a tutor, and he continues in verse 25, saying that when we have faith, we don't need the law anymore. Why? Because in verse 26 he said, "[We] are all children of God by faith in Christ Jesus." Are we making the point that faith alone saves us? No. Read on.

In the very next verse, Paul told us that our faith will lead us to God's will and the commandments of Jesus. He states plainly in verses 27–29, "For as many of you as have been baptized into Christ have put on Christ. There is neither Jew nor Greek, there is neither bond nor free, there is neither male nor female: for ye are all one in Christ Jesus. And if ye be Christ's, then are ye Abraham's seed, and heirs according to the promise."

Now, in context, we see that we are justified by *manifested* faith, in that we "put on Christ" by following the commands of Jesus in following Him to His resurrection by the *complete* plan of salvation.

A contrite heart is a basic requirement of salvation. Without a contrite heart, true *repentance* cannot be manifested. However, *repentance is not salvation unto itself.*

Confession, in the plan of salvation, is twofold. First and foremost, Jesus told us to confess His name before men, and then He will confess our names before God. Second, confession of sin goes hand in hand with repentance. However, *confession is not salvation unto itself.*

Baptism is an absolute requirement of salvation. Baptism—immersion, not sprinkling—is a presentation to God, before men, that we are following Jesus to His burial in the watery grave and are rising from that grave to live a more Christlike life. Baptism completes the plan of salvation, but *baptism is not salvation unto itself.*

---

† See also the sections titled "Does God Hear All Prayers?" and "What About Cornelius" in chapter 12 for another discussion of faith—before and after the resurrection.

Is This the Only Way to Heaven?

In a word, yes. Look back and review the section of this chapter called "How Do We Get Saved?" The simple steps are plainly shown.

If you have read part I, chapter 2, and this chapter, and you are still holding to other teachings, you *must* read chapter 17, "Judgment: Doesn't Everybody Go to Heaven?"

17

Judgment: Doesn't Everybody Go to Heaven?

Everyone Is Invited

Do you remember the statement, "Many are called, but few are chosen"? We discussed it back in chapter 14. I won't reprint the Scripture here, but there are two parables that you need to read: the parable of the great supper in Luke 14:15–24, and the parable of the marriage of the king's son in Matthew 22:1–14.

Both of these are examples of God's behavior concerning those who "have better things to do" than answer His invitation to salvation. As we've seen earlier in chapter 14, your choice is not made for you. The *result* of your decision is predestined for you, but your decision is not! Stop and think on that a moment.

We see in those passages that while your choice may not be made for you, the *result* of your choice has long been predetermined. The difference is immeasurable.

Do Nothing or Make a Choice

Some people believe that if they put their heads in the sand (the old ostrich trick) that the decision will simply go away. The opportunity is often mistaken for the chance to choose. Just because no one is breaking down your door and asking you to "come and be saved" doesn't mean that you will no longer have to deal with it. This chapter speaks directly to that scenario.

Visualize a fork in the road. You must decide to take the path to follow Jesus, or you will be swept away by the crowd that seems to be rushing down the fork to the other path. *The absolute truth* of the "salvation decision" is that if you do not choose for yourself, the choice is made already. The door to your salvation must be opened by you and you alone. In John 3:18, Jesus told us, "He that believeth on him [Son of Man] is not condemned: but he that believeth not is condemned already, because he hath not believed in the name of the only begotten Son of God."

We see here, as we've seen previously, that without heeding God's gospel message, we automatically have chosen to remain unsaved. It requires our conscious effort and obedience to choose the path to salvation.*

Not My God

On a few occasions, I have heard people say, "That's not *my* God" or "That's not the God I worship." Know this: there is only one God Almighty. There are also those who claim that they have the same God but call Him by other names, or that they have different ideas about how to answer God's invitation to the feast. I pray that we will come together and that the truth will be known and shown to them as well.

Acts 17:22–31 is Paul's "sermon" to the men of Athens on Mars' Hill (Areopogus). Paul had seen the many shrines and temples with many statues of many "gods." There were so many that the Greeks had even made a statuary shrine to "The Unknown God" in case they'd missed one. Paul stood in the midst of the "brain trust" of Athens and told them about the god they did not know. It is both a great and simple "sermon," the type that seems to let the Holy Spirit do all the "heavy lifting." Some scoffed and some believed, just as they do today.

I have also known people who say that they don't have a god at all. It seems odd, but most of the people who don't rely on or even believe in God are people we humans consider to be well-educated people. Most of them do not realize until they approach their own death or that of a loved one that they "could be" wrong.

---

* Again, see part I on salvation.

Notice a truth here. A truth or fact is a truth or fact, in that it will stand without being relative to any other thing. That being given, *atheism* is not a truth. To be an atheist, one must acknowledge that there is a *theism* to be opposed to.

God stands without atheism, but atheism cannot exist without God.

We all need to realize that God's invitation is for us to become joint heirs with Jesus, the Christ. Yes, after becoming saved souls, we are adopted brothers of Jesus Himself. Just think about this for a moment. Since Jesus is the judge, we're brothers of the judge. Would you, could you condemn *true* brothers of your own?

I do have one more question for you, though. If you had given your life as Jesus did, would you accept anyone at your bench of judgment who brought you forged adoption paperwork? That is, if someone tried to fake it or not do things the way you'd asked them to before they came to see you, would you accept them as family? Neither will Jesus.

Attendance Is Not Optional

The problem with most folks is that they give their day of judgment less than proper respect. Judgment day is mandatory attendance for all. Every person who has lived since time began will be called to make an accounting of their life here on earth.

On judgment day, not only will there be no excuses, but every soul in attendance will have no doubt that Jesus is the Lord of Lords. We read about it in Romans 14:11–12: "For it is written, 'As I live', saith the Lord, 'every knee shall bow to me, and every tongue shall confess to God.' So then every one of us shall give account of himself to God."

We see more in Philippians 2:9–11: "Wherefore God also hath highly exalted him, and given him a name which is above every name: That at the name of Jesus every knee should bow, of things in heaven, and things in earth, and things under the earth; And that every tongue should confess that Jesus Christ is Lord, to the glory of God the Father."

But They Said All I Had to Do Was ...

- Pray this prayer.
- Pray to Mary.
- Pray to Allah.
- Be sprinkled, not immersed.
- Simply believe because everything else is "works," and baptism is optional.
- Be saved and live any way you want to. Do nothing to further the kingdom.

"Satan does not want the lost to sin. He wants them to be fine, well-educated, well-liked, moral, religious people. It is a better advertisement for him. He offers them a 'heavenly' way to go to hell" (Dr. A. R. Stanford, Handbook of Personal Evangelism).

Many, many people believe that Satan's effort is to make people sin. Satan's major thrust is to get people to worship! Yes, you heard me. Satan wants us to worship anything or anyone that is not God Almighty, or worse yet, to think we worship God when we practice what we call Christianity in ways other than prescribed by God's holy ordinance.

We've been through all this before. The entire list above, and anything other than God's original plan of salvation, will be a failed attempt. The simple truth is that if you wait until judgment day, you will have waited too long. The words of Ephesians 4:3–6 are too plain to be misunderstood: "Endeavoring to keep the unity of the Spirit in the bond of peace. There is *one* body, and *one* Spirit, even as ye are called in *one* hope of your calling; *One* Lord, *one* faith, *one* baptism, *One* God and Father of all, who is above all, and through all, and in you all" (emphasis added).

Jesus said in Matthew 7:21–23, "Not every one that saith unto me, Lord, Lord, shall enter into the kingdom of heaven; but he that doeth the will of my Father which is in heaven. Many will say to me in that day, Lord, Lord, have we not prophesied in thy name? and in thy name have cast out devils? and in thy name done many wonderful works? *And then will I profess unto them, I never knew you: depart from me, ye that work iniquity*" (emphasis added).

The Gates of Heaven

Visualize a ball game or any event for which you have to purchase a ticket for parking. On judgment day, if your name is written in the Book of Life, you get into the parking lot. If not, you won't even get in the parking lot. Your only reward is to realize that you may never be with God. That is hell, all by itself.

You will see "one more chance," however, before you enter the parking area's turn-around lane on your way to the gates of hell.

The "final check" is to see if a person's name is not in the Book of Life because that person never heard the gospel message of the new covenant. Of course, if you're reading this, it doesn't apply to you. However, if the final check *is* true, that person will be judged by the "law of conscience" and a right life. That person also "gets in the gate," as explained in Romans 2:13–15: "For not the hearers of the law are just before God, but the doers of the law shall be justified. For when the Gentiles, which have not the law, do by nature the things contained in the law, these, having not the law, are a law unto themselves: Which shew the work of the law written in their hearts, *their conscience also bearing witness*, and their thoughts the mean while accusing or else excusing one another" (emphasis added).

Paul continued and finished the thought in verses 28–29: "For he is not a Jew [keeper of the law], which is one outwardly; neither is that circumcision [a mark of salvation in the first covenant], which is outward in the flesh: But he is a Jew [believer], which is one inwardly; and circumcision [salvation] is that of the heart, *in the spirit*, and *not in the letter*; whose praise is not of men, but of God" (emphasis added).[†]

But if Jesus sees that your name is not in the Book of Life (not a baptized believer), and you *have* heard the gospel message, He has His reason for your name not being in the Book of Life. He will then say, as He said He would in Matthew, "I never knew you. Depart from me."

To the shame of believers and against our own account, the judgment seat is as close to heaven as a many people will ever be. To avoid the "at the gates" scenario, one must be saved in the way God designed salvation and none other.[‡]

---

† See also Hebrews 11.

‡ Again, see part I on salvation.

The Final Cut

If your name is in the Book of Life, or you have never heard the gospel, you totally miss the horror of being turned away at the gate. However, you still have to be judged worthy to enter the stadium. This would be the same as showing your ticket at the entrance of the stadium. This is where those folks who believe the "once saved, always saved" doctrine find their reward is not what they expected.

If you think about it, judgment by the law of conscience applies to all of us, no matter which covenant dispensation we've lived under—if, of course, we made the first cut.

I'll let Jesus tell the story from His own lips, as recorded in Matthew 25:31–46 (NIV).

> When the Son of Man comes in his glory, and all the angels with him, he will sit on his throne in heavenly glory. All the nations will be gathered before him, and he will separate the people one from another as a shepherd separates the sheep from the goats. He will put the sheep on his right and the goats on his left.
>
> Then the King will say to those on his right, "Come, you who are blessed by my Father; take your inheritance, the kingdom prepared for you since the creation of the world. For I was hungry and you gave me something to eat, I was thirsty and you gave me something to drink, I was a stranger and you invited me in, I needed clothes and you clothed me, I was sick and you looked after me, I was in prison and you came to visit me."
>
> Then the righteous will answer him, "Lord, when did we see you hungry and feed you, or thirsty and give you something to drink? When did we see you a stranger and invite you in, or needing clothes and clothe you? When did we see you sick or in prison and go to visit you?" The King will reply, "I tell you the truth, whatever you did for one of the least of these brothers of mine, you did for me."
>
> Then he will say to those on his left, "Depart from me, you who are cursed, into the eternal fire prepared for the devil and his angels. For I was hungry and you gave me nothing to eat, I was thirsty and you gave me nothing to drink, I was a stranger and you did not invite me in, I needed clothes and you did not clothe me, I was sick and in prison and you did not look after me."

> They also will answer, "Lord, when did we see you hungry or thirsty or a stranger or needing clothes or sick or in prison, and did not help you?" He will reply, "I tell you the truth, whatever you did not do for one of the least of these, you did not do for me." Then they will go away to eternal punishment, but the righteous to eternal life.

Jesus Held No Secrets

Jesus Himself said that benevolence will be His criteria for whether or not we get to spend eternity in heaven. We repeat what Jesus said in Matthew 7:21–23 (NIV): "Not everyone who says to me, 'Lord, Lord,' will enter the kingdom of heaven, but only he who does the will of my Father who is in heaven. Many will say to me on that day, 'Lord, Lord, did we not prophesy in your name, and in your name drive out demons and perform many miracles?' Then I will tell them plainly, 'I never knew you. Away from me, you evildoers!'"

We have to see this as Jesus "tipping His hand," as they say in poker. Jesus was showing us His cards! Jesus was telling us what we need to do to be with Him for all eternity. He's also telling us what's *not* going to work. Please note that simply going to church will not satisfy these criteria.

That's So Mean

What about forgiveness? What about love? I've heard people say that they don't want anything to do with "a mean God like that"—meaning a God who will actually judge on the day of judgment. We discussed these things at the outset of this chapter and elsewhere.

And what about forgiveness and love? These blessings and more are being offered at the very moment you're reading this. They are being offered until the moment you die. Of course, we don't know when that will be, so why take a chance? If you're reading this, I can't help but think that you believe. If you have not repented, confessed Jesus before men, and been baptized—by immersion—for the remission of your sins, do it now![§]

[§] Again, see part I on salvation.

18

The Lord's Supper: Communion

The Ws of the Passover

- who: the Jewish nation
- what: celebration and remembrance of the Lord God bringing the Hebrews out of Egypt
- when: fourteenth day of Nisan, first month of Hebrew calendar (early March to early April)
- where: anywhere, but all wish to be in Jerusalem in the modern seder
- why: detailed edict of God

Passover Symbolism

There is regular feast ritual, and there is Passover ritual.

The Passover seder (*seder* means "order") consists of what most people consider to be fifteen parts, done in the exact way and exact *order* that has been recognized for centuries. The problem with the seder is with the changes that have been made along the way. Over two thousand years ago, this was the same problem that Jesus had with the temple leaders and all the changes they had introduced to the law. (See the section titled "Jesus Changed Everything While Changing Little" in chapter 7.)

The most remarkable change to the seder (among many changes) has been the addition of an orange to the foods displayed at the seder table. While not accepted by many families, it has become common enough to mention. This was added in the 1980s to "protest" or call attention to the lack of women in the ceremony and the "snubbing" of gays by proper Judaism.

To make a long story short, the symbolism of the seder is a reminder to those celebrating the *Passover* about the angel of death during the last plague in Egypt. On the tenth of Nisan, each household was to select an unblemished lamb to be roasted on the fourteenth. The blood of the lamb of the first Passover was to be put on the doorpost and lintel of the Hebrews' doors. This signaled the angel of death to "pass over" that house as it was killing the firstborn children and animals of all of Egypt.

By way of note, God's plan was to have the angel of death "pass over" every house that had the blood of the lamb on the doorpost and lintel. One can easily believe that there were Egyptians close to the Hebrews who performed the act and were spared. However, any house that did not have this mark of obedience was not spared the tenth plague. It was a simple sequence of actions that proved their belief in God, but it had to be obeyed to show an outward sign of faith. See? God never changes.

The Feast of the Passover seder contains, as did most every meal, the "breaking of bread." In the fourth step of the seder, one matzah is taken from the three at the table and is broken. The larger "half" is literally hidden for later in the ceremony. This piece is now called the *afikomen*. More on this later.

There are four cups of wine in the ceremony. The *first* cup is blessed with the *Kiddush* (literally translated "sanctification") and is sipped by all attending as the first step of the seder. Wine was the customary drink of every meal in the time of Jesus. The Kiddush signifies that the occurrence was a holiday or Shabbat. At Passover, this is the "cup of sanctification."

In *maggid*, the fifth step of the seder—after hiding the afikomen—is the telling of the Exodus story. After announcing that the *matzot* (plural of *matzah*) is the "bread of affliction," the *second* cup of wine is poured but not drunk. After pouring, the story is told—at length. The leader of the seder splashes wine into a broken vessel (long story), and the wine that is left is the "wine of joy." The cup is filled again. After more story and the eating of the bitter herbs, etc., all bless God and drink the second cup—while reclining on the left elbow, of course. The maggid (fifth step) may be many hours in completion. This cup is the "cup of judgment and deliverance."

After the *Rachtzah*, the *Motzi*, the *Matzah*, the *Maror*, and the *Korech* are performed, the Passover meal (feast) of roasted lamb (now often brisket) is eaten, and the afikomen is found and returned. If you wondered, the drinking of wine during the meal does not count as any of the four cups.

The *third* cup of wine, the "cup of redemption," is poured after the afikomen is blessed and divided among all present. The feast (dinner) is over when the afikomen is passed, and there is absolutely not another bite or drink (gluttonous Greek history). After a long string of after-meal blessings and another blessing for the wine, the third cup is drunk. This is why the third cup is never misunderstood if it is called the "cup of blessing" (1 Corinthians 10:16).

The *fourth* cup of wine (now called the "cup of praise or restoration") is poured. This is the cup poured for Elias (Elijah). While the cup is being poured, someone opens the door as an open invitation to the prophet. This is followed by another string of blessings and the blessing for the wine. Then the fourth cup is drunk.

There are those who leave the cup for Elijah and do not drink it, for they still feel that Elijah has yet to come again to announce the Messiah.

At this point, the Passover Feast is over, but many stay for continued blessings and even more stories of the Exodus.

Jesus Was a Jew

The Last Supper of Jesus was His twentieth as a man (over thirteen years old). He and His disciples were well versed in the seder of the Passover. There can be no doubt that everyone with Jesus was participating in the Passover Feast with the same frame of mind that they always had. Many times, Jesus marveled at the lack of spirituality of His disciples. There is little doubt that the disciples had gathered to simply celebrate the beginning of another new year.

Jesus, however, knew what was coming. He also knew of the cup "from which only He could drink," the cup being the upcoming crucifixion.

There were too many parallels between the Passover and the new covenant to think that this was just a good opportunity for Jesus to introduce His new covenant. This subject alone is another complete study. I, personally, see the Passover Feast as prophetic of this Last Supper event from its outset.

God's new covenant, heralded by Jesus during the ceremony celebrating the old covenant, was to be sealed with the same commemorative emblems as the first Passover.

Again, the more things change, the more they stay the same.

Jesus Instituted the New Covenant

Jesus went into action when virtually all the Passover seder had been completed. The aficomen that was hidden was returned to Him. We have to believe that Jesus was the leader of the seder on this and other Passovers.

As was the tradition, the aficomen was hidden, but it was found and returned to Jesus. The aficomen would represent the Messiah, who was hidden for a while but was found and made public. The symbolism is obvious.

Previously in the ministry of Jesus—for instance, after He quizzed the disciples, saying, "Who do you say that I am?" in Matthew 16—Jesus had told the disciples to not tell anyone who he was. In the incident mentioned, verse 20 says, "Then charged he his disciples that they should tell no man that he was Jesus the Christ." The time was not yet right.

At the time of the Last Supper, however, God's plan was upon them. Jesus took the aficomen, the bread that was hidden. Matthew 26:26 says, "As they were eating [as they were finishing the food], Jesus took bread, and blessed it, and brake it, and gave it to the disciples, and said, Take, eat; this is my body." At His Last Supper, Jesus changed the significance of the bread. It had been, until then, the "bread of haste." Jesus changed its meaning to symbolize His broken body, which He gave on the cross.

After a blessing or two more, in verses 27–29, "He [Jesus] took the cup [the third cup], and gave thanks, and gave it to them, saying, Drink ye all of it [signifying the blessings were finished]; For this is my blood of *the new testament*, which is shed for many for the remission of sins. But I say unto you, I will not drink henceforth of this fruit of the vine, until that day when I drink it new with you in my Father's kingdom" (emphasis added).

The wine of the Passover seder signified the blood of the sacrificial lamb. John the Baptist identified Jesus when he first saw Him, and again the next day, by saying in John 1, "Behold, the lamb of God!"

At His Last Supper, Jesus didn't actually change the meaning of the wine; He changed the wine's source. The wine is still the blood of the sacrificial lamb, but the Lamb of the new covenant is the Christ [the anointed]. The Lord's Supper, as we know it today, was established.

At that point in the seder, we read, "And when they had sung an hymn, they went out into the mount of Olives" (Matthew 26:30).

Realize that Jesus abandoned the Passover ceremony without completing the traditional seder, without including the fourth cup. Without saying a word, Jesus gave confirmation that Elias had come already (Matthew 11:14; 17:11–12).

Communion

There's a reason that many believers partaking of the Lord's Supper call it *Communion*.

It should be just that. In fact, Paul, after reminding his readers of the story we just related, told the church at Corinth, "For as often as ye eat this bread, and drink this cup, ye do shew the Lord's death till he come. Wherefore whosoever shall eat this bread, and drink this cup of the Lord, unworthily, shall be guilty of the body and blood of the Lord. But let a man examine himself, and so let him eat of that bread, and drink of that cup. For he that eateth and drinketh unworthily, eateth and drinketh damnation to himself, not discerning the Lord's body" (1 Corinthians 11:26–29).

Many Christians believe that *unworthily* means that a person has sin or ill will in his heart. We hear things like, "We should examine ourselves to make ourselves worthy." While it is quite right to wish to be a righteous partaker of the Holy Communion, this was not what Paul meant.

What Paul meant by *unworthily* was that the person was "not discerning the Lord's body" (v. 29). In other words, if you are partaking of the Lord's Supper and are not taking the emblems to represent the broken body and blood of Jesus, you are not partaking in a worthy manner. Realize, that if you are merely "going through the motions," *you are not partaking in a worthy manner.* It's not that the sky will fall, but you are not partaking of the Lord's Supper.

Think on this: a person who does not discern the body and blood of the Christ is either observing the Passover or is simply eating some bread and sipping some wine. In either case, he is returning to the life previous to salvation and the institution of the Lord's Supper. Therefore, he is *removing himself from the ranks of the saved,* if we are to believe Paul. In discerning the body and blood of Jesus, one might even better invite Jesus to "please, come more into me" while partaking of the emblems.

"Take, Eat"

There is a major and yet often overlooked detail of what Jesus meant when He said, "Take, eat." The contemporaries of Jesus knew better than we do what His words meant, I think. The Hebrew and Aramaic languages, among others, often used the word *eat* to mean "study thoroughly, absorb deeply, or feel greatly." None of these instances have anything to do with food and everything to do with Communion. A modern parallel might be to say, "You are what you eat."

In the instructions of Leviticus, many directives were given about the priesthood. In Leviticus 21, specific instructions were given about a priest with blemishes. A long list of possible blemishes and/or birth defects is listed in verses 18–20. A Levite with a blemish was not to do public service but was still to study as a priest. Leviticus 21:22 says, "He shall *eat the bread of his God, both* of the most holy, and of the holy" (emphasis added).

The psalmist spoke of God's having turned His face and allowed woe to come to the people. Psalm 80:5 says, "Thou feedest them with the bread of tears; and givest them tears to drink in great measure." Proverbs 4:14–19 tells us to shun the ways of the wicked. One reason is found in verse 17: "For they eat the bread of wickedness, and drink the wine of violence."

When Jesus said, "Take, eat," He was telling us to internalize His *self.* Jesus was saying that by partaking of the bread and the wine that we should be taking Jesus into our selves - into our hearts and souls. With every Communion, Jesus is to be a larger part of our very being. Put another way, every time we partake, we should feel that we are adding Jesus to our own soul. Jesus referred to Himself as "the bread of life" in John 6:16 and elsewhere in the same passage. This, of course, means that Jesus is our sustenance, and we need no more than Him.

The Lord's Supper is a communion with God. Many see this as a ritual to show others that we are remembering Jesus and His sacrifice. Others say we use it as a time of introspection. While these reasons are true, given the realization above, they pale as being much less than the real reason we are to partake of this Holy Communion. Jesus said, "Take, eat." Think on these things.

The Modern Lord's Supper

We see, from Paul's language, that the Lord's Supper—the commemoration, remembrance, and internalization of Jesus until He comes again—was practiced often at Christian gatherings and with an actual meal. Paul corrected that practice by telling the Corinthians—and us—to wait for a specified time rather than treating the remembrance as trivial and self-serving. He said in 1 Corinthians 11:21, "For in eating every one taketh before other his own supper: and one is hungry, and another is drunken."

In modern times, we have removed this temptation to eat or drink too much or without others by making the Lord's Supper a separate action that cannot be taken as a "come and go" luncheon.

When Is the Lord's Supper to Be Practiced?

There are many who believe that the Lord's Supper is an action that can only be performed in a church building—and even there, only on specific days. Some say that it can only occur on a Sunday, while others say it should be quarterly or even only once a year.

With one simple question, I propose to you that there is nothing wrong with a respectful commemoration of the sacrifice of Christ on any other day of the week in any place "where two or three are gathered together" (Matthew 18:20). The question is this: is the Christ only the Christ on Sunday? Both common sense and Paul tell us that we should treat the occasion with proper dignity and reason. However, with proper respect accorded to the service, it can be done anywhere at any time.

There are those who believe that the Lord's Supper may be practiced only "on occasion" or irregularly. Some say that it should be practiced only at the Passover time, as the first one was. These folks cite Paul in the passage to the Corinthians (1 Corinthians 11:26), where he said, "For as often as ye eat this bread, and drink this cup." They believe that Paul was saying that the schedule was up to us.

Note that Paul was not saying "whenever you decide to do this." Paul was saying "every time you do this" Paul already knew that the Corinthians were meeting on the first day of the week, or he would have pointed that out. In fact, Paul said in 1 Corinthians 11:2, "Now I praise you, brethren, that ye remember me in all things, and keep the ordinances, as I delivered them to you."

Paul actually praised the way the Corinthians were keeping the apostles' doctrine. He was only pointing out error in their practice of the Lord's Supper, not error with their schedule.

First of all, how can one truly remember the sacrifice of the Christ when one does not practice the very action (the Lord's Supper) presented by the Christ Himself? To say that it's not necessary is to say it is frivolous. Can you believe that an institution of the Christ is frivolous in any way?

Second, we are to continue in the "apostles' doctrine" as did the first century church. The first-century church met as an assembly on the first day of the week, as well as elsewhere in lesser groups in peoples' homes and such during the week. In Acts 2:42, we're told about the early church: "And they continued steadfastly in the apostles' doctrine and fellowship, and in breaking of bread, and in prayers."

Luke recorded a visit to Troas in Acts 20:7: "And upon the first day of the week, when the disciples came together to *break bread*, Paul preached unto them, ready to depart on the morrow; and continued his speech until midnight" (emphasis added).

Paul told the church at Corinth in 1 Corinthians 16:2, "Upon the first day of the week let every one of you lay by him in store, as God hath prospered him, that there be no gatherings when I come."

It's more than obvious that the "apostles' doctrine" was to meet on the first day of the week and *break bread*. Paul said that the situation also made the assembling a good time for the church's collection.

Not only was Paul in agreement with meeting on the first day of the week, but he added another facet (collection) to the meeting as well. This more than indicates Paul's approval. Any student of the Bible will tell you that Paul did not falter in his teachings. If something was not right, Paul made sure to point out the error in no uncertain terms. (Talk to the Corinthians; they'll tell you.)

The point is that we've been told that partaking of the Lord's Supper is to be practiced on the first day of the week, *at the very least.*

Pulling It All Together

The Lord's Supper is not to be taken lightly. It is much more than a simple memorial ritual. It truly is a point of communion with Jesus, the Christ. *We get a physical chance to internalize Jesus.*

No, it's not really the body or blood of Jesus. No, it's not "transubstantiated" into the body and blood of Jesus. But spiritually, we partake of both His life and His sacrifice. We live them with Him through this act of Communion. The act of Communion deserves our real respect, inasmuch as the Son of Man instituted the action to begin with.

The Lord's Supper or, if you prefer, the Communion should be practiced regularly. The apostles established that the "breaking of bread" be practiced on the first day of the week. According to Jesus, it is a part of our true worship of God. That, in and of itself, tells us that we should do it often.

In that light, though we know it's proper, once a week doesn't sound like nearly often enough, does it? In fact, churches that assemble the congregation at other times and on other days of the week might do well to observe the Lord's Supper at those assemblies as well.

Further, there is absolutely nothing wrong and everything right in family and friends respectfully and prayerfully commemorating the Lord's Supper at times and places other than the regular assembly of the saints.

Is there such a thing as too much worship?

19

BENEVOLENCE = LOVE

This section is written expressly to discuss benevolence. In case you missed it, we went into this in quite some detail in chapter 17, "Judgment: Doesn't Everybody Go to Heaven?"

Benevolence = Christianity

Benevolence equals Christianity. I cannot express this equation with any more emphasis than to say that benevolence is everything in the Christian life.

"Love one another" has become merely a trite saying in modern times. We even sing the chorus of the hymn "Angry Words" (written by H. R. Palmer and published in 1869), which says, "Love one another. Thus saith the Savior," without any more thought than mouthing the words.

The first time we see this exact phrase is in John 13:34, where Jesus said, "A new commandment I give unto you, That ye *love one another*; as I have loved you, that ye also *love one another*" (emphasis added).

In the very next verse (v. 35), Jesus pointed to the fact that it would be a "badge of identification" for Christians, and He literally repeated the words: "By this shall all men know that ye are my disciples, *if ye have love one to another*" (emphasis added).

Too many believers (and one is too many) take "one another" to mean members of the church. Jesus was by no means limiting our love to our fellow brethren. See His more complete meaning in a passage from the Sermon on the Mount in Matthew 5:43–48.

> Ye have heard that it hath been said, Thou shalt love thy neighbour, and hate thine enemy. But I say unto you, Love your enemies, bless them that curse you, do good to them that hate you, and pray for them which despitefully use you, and persecute you; That ye may be the children of your Father which is in heaven: for he maketh his sun to rise on the evil and on the good, and sendeth rain on the just and on the unjust. For if ye love them which love you, what reward have ye? do not even the publicans the same? And if ye salute your brethren only, what do ye more than others? do not even the publicans so? Be ye therefore perfect [in love], even as your Father which is in heaven is perfect.

Many people throughout history have totally miscued on this passage. They take the summary statement out of context and say that Jesus wants us to strive for perfection. Certainly the Godhead wants us to follow the examples of Jesus, but in this passage, Jesus gave us the definition of perfect love.

Perfect love withholds nothing from a stranger simply because that person is unknown. In an even stronger point, Jesus told us to do only good in return for pain and suffering dealt to us by anyone, friend or foe. God's love bestows the blessing of life—the greatest physical gift of all—to every person on the planet. The fact that too many people misuse their lives in the pursuit of evil does not keep God from giving them the basic sustenance of life. Peter says we should realize that God thinks that everyone deserves a chance at "getting it right" in 2 Peter 3:9.

The above passage from Matthew 5 speaks directly to our requirement to apply God's perfect love to everyone. If anyone is to "see Christ in us," we must show and share gracious mercy and forgiveness along with blessings wherever and whenever we can, upon whomever we can.

The Gap

The gap that must be bridged between our nature and our Christian service is in our own selfish (dare I say *capitalist*?) tendencies. We've mentioned this before, but herein is true application. In Matthew 19:16–22, we're told of a young man who came to Jesus with an earnest question. The young man had heard the message of Jesus and truly wanted to know its meaning.

> And, behold, one came and said unto him [Jesus], Good Master, what good thing shall I do, that I may have eternal life? And he said unto him, Why callest thou me good? there is none good but one, that is, God: but if thou wilt enter into life, keep the commandments. He saith unto him, Which? Jesus said, Thou shalt do no murder, Thou shalt not commit adultery, Thou shalt not steal, Thou shalt not bear false witness, Honour thy father and thy mother: and, Thou shalt love thy neighbour as thyself. The young man saith unto him, All these things have I kept from my youth up: what lack I yet? Jesus said unto him, If thou wilt be perfect [have perfect love], go and sell that thou hast, and give to the poor, and thou shalt have treasure in heaven: and come and follow me. But when the young man heard that saying, he went away sorrowful: for he had great possessions.

Note that Jesus didn't tell the young man that he couldn't be saved without selling all he had. Jesus obviously saw the man's heart and knew that he truly had kept the commandments. We have a great many more examples in the Bible of those saved by faith before Jesus died. Jesus told the young man, "But if thou wilt enter into life, keep the commandments." The young man was in good spiritual shape, because both he and Jesus knew that he had done exactly that for most of his life.

Jesus did, however, tell him the same basic message that was part of the Sermon on the Mount (Matthew 5:43–48 above): perfect love is spread evenly and well. Matthew 19:21 says, "Jesus said unto him, If thou wilt be perfect, go and sell that thou hast, and give to the poor, and thou shalt have treasure in heaven: and come and follow me."

Jesus was saying that since the young man's heart was good enough, the only way he could improve was to get rid of his "baggage" and dedicate his life wholly to apostleship. This is what God wants of *all* of us.

We do have to make a living, and God knows this. It has been so since the fall of Adam. The point of the passage is that if we have anything that so ties us to this world that we can't truly worship God and devote our lives to a Christian life, we're in trouble. On the other hand, if we have things and are willing to use them for the good of God's will, God will give us more so we can give more, and God will give us even more so we can give even more, and so it goes.

The young man might later have done exactly as Jesus told him; we don't know. If he did, I can assure you that the young man became even richer so that he could give more. There is story after story of such occasions and individuals throughout Bible history—Job, Solomon, and so on.

Some four hundred years earlier in the book of Malachi, God told of unsatisfactory sacrifices, improper actions of the priests, and marrying outside of the faith. These produced the love of other gods, ungodly children, injustice (both socially and in business), withholding tithes, and even questions of why people should worship God at all.

In the midst of pointing out the many, many ways that Israel had gone away from Him, God offered a challenge. When speaking of "robbing" Him by withholding tithes, God said in Malachi 3:10, "Bring ye all the tithes into the storehouse, that there may be meat in mine house, and *prove me now herewith*, saith the LORD of hosts, if I will not open you the windows of heaven, and pour you out a blessing, that there shall not be room enough to receive it."

God promised that if the faithful would bring even the sacrifice of tithes alone, He would "open you the windows of heaven, and pour out a blessing, that there shall not be room enough to receive it."

Notice that God didn't say, "I promise." God said, "Prove me now herewith." That phrase has been translated "test me on this." God was saying that if we give as we should, we will be blessed with more. We will not run out but will be given more to give.

Allow me a human example. Have you ever seen a child that makes people laugh—especially its parents? The child repeats the action to make everyone laugh again. The child repeats the action, and everyone laughs again … and so it goes. This is exactly what God does when we please Him. If we please God by giving, He will give us more so we can do it again. If we repeat the action, God will give us more so we can do it again … and so it goes.

The Reason

We would be remiss to not mention another passage of the Sermon on the Mount in Matthew 6:1–4. Jesus tells us that *how* we give is as important as *what* we give. It was important enough to Jesus for Him to use the phrase "take heed."

> Take heed that ye do not your alms before men, to be seen of them: otherwise ye have no reward of your Father which is in heaven. Therefore when thou doest thine alms, do not sound a trumpet before thee, as the hypocrites do in the synagogues and in the streets, that they may have glory of men. Verily I say unto you, They have their reward. But when thou doest alms, let not thy left hand know what thy right hand doeth: That thine alms may be in secret: and thy Father which seeth in secret himself shall reward thee openly.

Our gifts of our service, goods, or money will not go unnoticed. But there are two ways to give. Jesus tells us—in no uncertain terms—that if we give to seek the praises of men, we will get what we want, and that will be that. However, if we give quietly and without "fanfare," we are truly giving for the sake of God and will be rewarded by Him. The latter, obviously, is preferable.

We Can't Be Invisible

It is often asked, "How can we do good works and not be seen?" Being seen is not the problem. The problem is in being quiet about it. Jesus spoke of salt and light in Matthew 5:13–16.

> Ye are the salt of the earth: but if the salt have lost his savour, wherewith shall it be salted? it is thenceforth good for nothing, but to be cast out, and to be trodden under foot of men. Ye are the light of the world. A city that is set on an hill cannot be hid. Neither do men light a candle, and put

> it under a bushel, but on a candlestick; and it giveth light unto all that are in the house. Let your light so shine before men, that they may see your good works, and glorify your Father which is in heaven.

Jesus told us that salt changes what it touches. If we do not change those we touch, we are spiritually of no use. Light dispels darkness. *Good works will not go unnoticed*; they are just like a city on a hill. However, we are called to give "the light of the Lord" to everyone so that "*they* may see your good works, and *glorify your Father which is in heaven*." Look at the emphasis: "so that *they glorify your Father*," not glorify you!

Simply put, show them the light, not the candle!

A Deeper Thought

Remember what Jesus told the young man: "If thou wilt be perfect ..." To those seeking a greater understanding, the deepest point of this thought is that if we are "making a living" for ourselves, we are not working for the right reasons. Right at the end of Paul's letter to the Galatians, he wrote, "Be not deceived; God is not mocked: for whatsoever a man soweth, that shall he also reap. For he that soweth to his flesh shall of the flesh reap corruption; but he that soweth to the Spirit shall of the Spirit reap life everlasting. And let us not be weary in well doing: for in due season we shall reap, if we faint not. As we have therefore opportunity, let us do good unto all men, especially unto them who are of the household of faith" (Galatians 6:7–10).

This totally explains why there are people who are both sinful and, as the world calls it, successful. Sowing to the flesh is sowing in the corruptible and temporary world. Sowing in the Spirit will also give us physical gain, but only if we keep using it for the further glorification of God.

If our hearts and lives truly belong to God, our physical pursuits will be rewarded because God knows that the fruits of our labor will be, first and foremost, returned to Him in the form of service and aid for those less fortunate. This is the true work of the church. You'll see this in the parable of the talents, below.

It should also be noted, even emphatically, that God is not an investment banker. We should not give in hope of a "return on our investment." However, God sees the heart and will know whether or not you will give *Him* a return on *His* investment in you.

Righteousness = Perfection

We began this segment speaking of perfect love. We continue with a brief repeat discussion of righteousness.

Obviously, anytime we think of the Godhead, we think of their pure righteousness. We are told, over and over, that we are to reflect that righteousness. Just before speaking in the Sermon on the Mount shown above (Matthew 5:43–48), Jesus said in Matthew 5:20, "For I say unto you, That except your righteousness shall exceed the righteousness of the scribes and Pharisees, ye shall in no case enter into the kingdom of heaven."

Those who try to separate our spiritual life from our earthly life need to take a long hard look at the fifth chapter of the book of Matthew. Jesus was telling us that our righteousness is tied directly to our love for our fellow man. And we just read in verse 20 that we must be better at it than the scribes and the Pharisees were, or we're in trouble for sure.

I spout wise thoughts from time to time that I can only attribute to "somebody." This is one: "You can be so spiritually minded that you are of no earthly good."

We cannot—no, we dare not—attempt to live our spiritual life separate from our physical one. To do so is to be at the peril of one's eternal soul.

It's That Important?

Doesn't it sound like it? Let me repeat: We cannot—no, we dare not—attempt to live our spiritual life separate from our physical one. To do so is to be at the peril of one's eternal soul.

Now would probably be a good time to look at Matthew 25. Jesus told three parables in this chapter, all of which apply directly to the day of judgment. Notice that the "characters" of each of the three parables are, at the beginning of each story, equal.

The first parable is told in Matthew 25:1–13. Hear the words of Jesus.

> Then shall the kingdom of heaven be likened unto ten virgins, which took their lamps, and went forth to meet the bridegroom. And five of them were wise, and five were foolish. They that were foolish took their lamps, and took no oil with them: But the wise took oil in their vessels with their lamps. While the bridegroom tarried, they all slumbered and slept.
>
> And at midnight there was a cry made, Behold, the bridegroom cometh; go ye out to meet him. Then all those virgins arose, and trimmed their lamps. And the foolish said unto the wise, Give us of your oil; for our lamps are gone out. But the wise answered, saying, Not so; lest there be not enough for us and you: but go ye rather to them that sell, and buy for yourselves.
>
> And while they went to buy, the bridegroom came; and they that were ready went in with him to the marriage: and the door was shut. Afterward came also the other virgins, saying, Lord, Lord, open to us.
>
> But he answered and said, Verily I say unto you, I know you not. Watch therefore, for ye know neither the day nor the hour wherein the Son of man cometh.

The parable of the ten virgins tells us to have done what we need to have done before the time of judgment (before our death). At that point, it is too late. Notice that all of the ten virgins appeared to prepared and felt like they were prepared for the coming of the bridegroom. However, when the bridegroom came later than expected, half of the virgins realized they actually had not done all they should have done.

This parable could be seen as the five wise virgins representing saved souls and the unwise virgins being the unsaved who had to go and rightly prepare. Take it as you wish. We continue with the original thought.

The five "foolish" virgins scurried to do what they should have done in the first place, and they returned to find themselves locked out of the celebration. This could be a person who is on his deathbed, has missed opportunities, is simply a hypocrite, or is part of many other scenarios.

The point is that while an "eleventh hour" (while there is yet time) attempt at righteousness may be acceptable to get into heaven—like the men who worked in the vineyard—but a Christian attempting to do what needs to be done will not be fruitful at 11:59! At that point, there simply is not enough time to do what needs to be done. We must do what we can, while we can.

The second parable is told in Matthew 25:14–30. Hear the words of Jesus.

> For the kingdom of heaven is as a man travelling into a far country, who called his own servants, and delivered unto them his goods. And unto one he gave five talents, to another two, and to another one; to every man according to his several ability; and straightway took his journey.
>
> Then he that had received the five talents went and traded with the same, and made them other five talents. And likewise he that had received two, he also gained other two. But he that had received one went and digged in the earth, and hid his lord's money.
>
> After a long time the lord of those servants cometh, and reckoneth with them. And so he that had received five talents came and brought other five talents, saying, Lord, thou deliveredst unto me five talents: behold, I have gained beside them five talents more. His lord said unto him, Well done, thou good and faithful servant: thou hast been faithful over a few things, I will make thee ruler over many things: enter thou into the joy of thy lord.
>
> He also that had received two talents came and said, Lord, thou deliveredst unto me two talents: behold, I have gained two other talents beside them. His lord said unto him, Well done, good and faithful servant; thou hast been faithful over a few things, I will make thee ruler over many things: enter thou into the joy of thy lord.
>
> Then he which had received the one talent came and said, Lord, I knew thee that thou art an hard man, reaping where thou hast not sown, and gathering where thou hast not strawed: And I was afraid, and went and hid thy talent in the earth: lo, there thou hast that is thine. His lord answered and said unto him, Thou wicked and slothful servant, thou knewest that I reap where I sowed not, and gather where I have not strawed: Thou oughtest therefore to have put my money to the exchangers, and then at my coming I should have received mine own with usury.

> Take therefore the talent from him, and give it unto him which hath ten talents. For unto every one that hath shall be given, and he shall have abundance: but from him that hath not shall be taken away even that which he hath. And cast ye the unprofitable servant into outer darkness: there shall be weeping and gnashing of teeth.

The parable of the talents tells us that we need to use what we have been given to the profit of the Master. The Master in this parable is, of course, God. The profit will be souls saved, both directly and indirectly, by the use of the blessings given us. The servants did nothing to receive the talents, yet two of the three used what they had been given to "bless back" the Master.

The third servant had no lesser or greater status than the other two, therefore he was not disadvantaged by receiving only one talent. This parable appears to apply even more directly to members of the church. This third servant simply chose to do nothing with what he was given. This servant was sent away from the "joy of the Lord." This servant is like a person in our time who won't even extend the effort to invite someone to church.

One point that needs to be made here is that most people see the parable of the talents as evangelistic. To that end, that is what it illustrates. As members of God's church, we should invest our talents into garnering more souls for the Lord. We note here, again, that sometimes we cannot preach with anything but our lives. We can, however, "tend the garden" of the church by raising godly children, teaching and edifying those of the faith, and doing maintenance work required by fellow members—counseling, visitation, service work, etc.

The third parable is not a parable at all. We told this story in chapter 17, "Judgment: Doesn't Everybody Go to Heaven?," so we'll not repeat it here.

Notice that the first two parables were indeed parables. Jesus did not begin his account in verse 31 with any phrasing that indicates a parable. Verses 31–46 are Jesus' own words telling us, plainly and without any possibility of mistaken meaning, exactly how He is going to judge on that day. This story of the judgment serves to clarify the two preceding parables by telling us, specifically, what Jesus will require of us on that day.

I ask you: can it be any clearer? Jesus, the judge of all the earth, has given us the answers to the biggest "final exam" known to man!

Homework

God is love. He desires no more—and assuredly, no less—from us. Please read the book of 1 John (it's short) and especially the fourth chapter.

Look up *love* in your concordance. You'll see for yourself that it is no small thing.

20

EVANGELISM = THE CHRISTIAN LIFE

You Are a City on a Hill

A Christian life is visible to all who view it. "There's just something different about that guy," they'll say. "No matter what, she always seems to see the bright side," they'll say. "He's always ready with a smile and a handshake," they'll say. "When she asks how I am, I can tell she really wants to know," they'll say.

The point is that people will either see your life as a neon sign that blinks continuously, saying, "Jesus lives here," or they'll see you as just another church-going hypocrite.

Sharing Should Come Naturally

Steven Curtis Chapman sang a song in 2001 entitled "Live Out Loud." I offer the lyrics, not in the song form, but as a reading to prove a point.

> Imagine this: I get a phone call from Regis. He says, "Do you want to be a millionaire?" They put me on the show, and I win with two lifelines to spare. Now picture this: I act like nothin' ever happened and bury all the money in a coffee can.

> Well, I've been given more than Regis ever gave away. I was a dead man who was called to come out of my grave, and I think it's time for makin' some noise.
>
> Think about this: Try to keep a bird from singing after it's soared up in the sky. Give the sun a cloudless day, and tell it not to shine.
>
> Now think about this: If we really have been given the gift of a life that will never end, and if we have been filled with living hope, we're gonna overflow. And if God's love is burning in our hearts, we're gonna glow. There's just no way to keep it in.
>
> Wake the neighbors; get the word out. Come on, crank up the music, climb a mountain and shout. This is life we've been given, meant to be lived out.
>
> So la la la la live out loud, yeah, live out loud.
>
> Every corner of creation is a living declaration. Come join the song we were made to sing.

When you are saved, no one expects you to get a soapbox and stand on the street corner. However, none but those of the world would fault you for doing so.

The point is that being saved may not change the way you *make your living*, but it most certainly must change the way you *go about living.*

It's been (rightly) said that your Christian life may be the only Bible that some people read. If that is true for you, what will people think of the Bible after "reading" you and your life?

Spreading the Gospel Message

I continue to envision myself stepping up to the white throne of Jesus at the judgment and feeling quite confident in my faith and knowing that my salvation is secure. It's a good feeling.

However, in my imagined judgment, I become concerned with watching Jesus stand up, shade his eyes symbolically, look over the crowd of millions of souls and ask of me (as he continues to look to and fro), "Who'd you bring with you?" This brings to mind that parable of the talents, doesn't it?*

We should all be evangelists. Previously, we discussed the fact that we all are different from each other. We cannot all become preachers or dedicate ourselves wholly to apostleship.

We also spoke of "being salt." Jesus didn't say that the salt that didn't change the things it touched wasn't salt anymore. Jesus said that the salt that didn't change anything, though it was still salt, was of no use other than for pavement.

By the way, the Dead Sea, before it became known as such, was called Lake Asphaltus or Lake Asphaltine. Because of the mineral drainage of the lands around the lake, its salt was no good for eating. It was only good for traction on wet walks and roads and for weed prevention. This was the salt that Jesus spoke of. Hence came our word *asphalt*.

Again, the point is that our lives should be noticeably different from those of the world. Our language is cleaner, as are our jokes. Our demeanor is noticeably happier and optimistic. People will notice. This is our "lifestyle" evangelism. The apostle Peter put it this way: "But sanctify the Lord God in your hearts: and be ready always to give an answer to every man that asketh you a reason of the hope that is in you *but* with meekness [gentleness] and fear [respect]: Having a good conscience; that, whereas they speak evil of you, as of evildoers, they may be ashamed that falsely accuse your good conversation in Christ" (1 Peter 3:15–16).

Peter is saying that *the right life* is obviously going to be a reason for any confrontation–good or bad—but that we should always give an answer with gentleness and respect so that we will not put God in a bad light with our answers. Don't be cute. Don't be flippant. Know that God is proud of you for speaking for Him by your good conscience.

Anyone who asks you for "a reason of the hope that is in you" in an attempt demean you or your God will go away ashamed of themselves. They will either be ashamed because they attempted in the first place or ashamed because they failed. Either way, both you and God gain ground in the hearts that hear.

Show Me God

There are those who say, "I don't believe in God because He cannot be seen." Let me reinforce the point of living a right life as an example to the world.

Thomas and Philip, faced with a new covenant, were obviously human in their response. Like Moses, they desired to see "just a little more proof." Thomas was concerned that Jesus had said He would be leaving, and Thomas wanted to know the way to follow Him. "Jesus saith unto him, I am the way, the truth, and the life: no man cometh unto the Father, but by me. If ye had known me, ye should have known my Father also: and from henceforth ye know him, and have seen him" (John 14:6–7).

Philip, doubting even more than Thomas did, just wanted to make sure that Jesus really had God's backing. In the next verse (v. 8), he exhibited the human need for a little more proof. Philip, like Gideon, wanted to see "dew on the fleece." "Philip saith unto him, Lord, shew us the Father, and it sufficeth us."

The next verses (vv. 9–11) say, "Jesus saith unto him, Have I been so long time with you, and yet hast thou not known me, Philip? he that hath seen me hath seen the Father; and how sayest thou then, Shew us the Father? Believest thou not that I am in the Father, and the Father in me? the words that I speak unto you I speak not of myself: but the Father that dwelleth in me, he doeth the works. Believe me that I am in the Father, and the Father in me: *or else believe me for the very works' sake*."

Notice two things. First, Jesus said that both Thomas and Philip did not really know Jesus, even after having lived with Him for years. This can also be seen as a "worldly view." Jesus later told them that He had foretold His death and resurrection to them so that when it happened, they would believe. We have the witness of secular history, the Holy Scripture, and the Holy Spirit that these things came to pass—so that we will also believe.

Second, Jesus said, "If you don't believe that I am of the Father, believe me for the very works' sake." This is our mission in this life: to show God to the world by our good works. I often say to let the Holy Spirit do the "heavy lifting." If we show the world God's mercy by benevolence and forgiveness, the Holy Spirit will certainly deal with the hearts that want to know more.

What If I Don't?

God understands that there are different levels of spirituality. In chapter 2, step number two in the steps to salvation, "Belief Leads to Faith," we saw that Jesus Himself recognized that belief and unbelief can and do coexist in the hearts of those who come to Him.

However, while there are different levels of belief, Jesus also pointed plainly to the fact that there are *not* different levels of Christianity. In both Matthew 12:30 and Luke 11:23, Jesus put it plainly when He said. "He that is not with me is against me: and he that gathereth not with me scattereth." Can there be any doubt that Jesus was talking about "gathering" souls?

You can be "young" in Christ. The young, no matter the application, have much to learn. However, Christians—both young and old—are *all* Christians and are fully expected, by God, to act accordingly.

If you are not living as a Christian with an evangelistic, ready-to-share lifestyle, God *cannot* see you as a Christian. In other words, if the world doesn't see you as Christian, God most certainly will not. Plainly put, if people around you don't see Jesus when they look at you, neither will God!

Does this make a difference at judgment?

In the parable of the talents,* Jesus said yes. In that parable, we are shown that we must use whatever level of "talents" we are given to "show a profit" for the Master.

Ezekiel also said yes. We'll not go through it here, but the book of Ezekiel is a good read for the history and character of both Israel and God. Ezekiel 33 gives a warning to the watchman. If the watchman does not warn of the sword and a man dies by the sword, the blood is on the watchman's hands. However, if the watchman gives a warning and the warning is not heeded, the blood is counted against the warned person rather than the watchman.

God went even further with Ezekiel. God told Ezekiel that an evil person who repents is not condemned by previous acts but is "now" considered righteous. Our discussion of a "minimum for a day's wage" is spot on.

---

* Chapter 19, "Benevolence = Love"

God pointed out the other side of the coin as well. A righteous person who does wrong is not saved by previous acts. The idea of "once saved, always saved" is absolutely wrong.

We must "work 'til the day is done." That is, we must *continue* to grow in the Spirit to an even stronger faith, greater works, and righteous life.

PART V

Theology: Study

This is the "good to know" section of this work. Herein will be noteworthy scriptural lessons that will range from observations to full-blown discourses. They also (depending on one's point of view) will range from points of small consequence to major points.

Part V will focus on the following:

- the crucifixion: a more "reasoned" study of God's manifest wisdom
- testing: a study of life's circumstances, good and bad
- Did Jesus go to hell?
- marriage to God: our spiritual relationship with the Godhead
- a more "reasoned" view of the book of Revelation
- Lazarus and the rich man: when is the judgment?
- the difference between providence and miracles
- our purpose and the purpose of God's armor

- what God's glory really is
- continual cleansing and the errors of that belief
- the parable of the prodigal son: more than just another casual story
- the unfaithful (shrewd) steward: a difficult passage explained

21

The Crucifixion

When I think of the crucifixion of Jesus, I remember the words of the title song of *Jesus Christ Superstar* (1970). The first couple of lines go like this:

> Every time I look at you I don't understand
> Why you let the things you did get so out of hand.
> You'd have managed better if you'd had it planned.
> Why'd you choose such a backward time in such a strange land?

Judas (originally played by Murray Head on the album) brought up a question rarely asked: "Why at this particular time?" His song continued with, "If you'd come today [modern times] you would have reached a whole nation. Israel in 4 BC had no mass communication."

This study looks at the time of the crucifixion from a more "reasoned" point of view than most biblical scholars hold. We will not detail the many physical aspects of the crucifixion; that's been done and done again. We will, however, be looking at the *what*, *when*, and *why* of this most wonderful gift of God to humanity.

If, for whatever reason, you disagree with my statement that the crucifixion of Jesus is a gift from God, please refer to chapters 1 and 2 of this book. We'll hold your place here.

The Hebrew/Jewish Aspect

From the Hebrew/Aramaic/Jewish standpoint, the Jews were more than ready for a Messiah. God had "pulled their fat out of the fire" on many occasions—too many to count. The devout Jews knew that there was a Messiah coming, and the persecution by the Roman occupying armies helped to keep the thought of a redeemer in their studies and discussions.

This is not to say that the devout Jews were the Pharisees, Sadducees, scribes, and other temple leaders. This is probably the main theological reason for Jesus coming at that time. The leadership had made the religious practice of Judaism so legalistic that praising God and worshipping Him had actually become burdensome to those who wished to "do well in the eyes of the LORD."

The Jewish religion had become more ritual than worship or lifestyle. "Keeping the law" had become tedious, because the temple leaders kept qualifying the law in smaller and more tedious increments. The Pharisees were more flexible and willing to change with the times, while the Sadducees kept to a strict interpretation of the law. If you needed a "loophole," you went to the Pharisees, who were not unlike the Christian moderates and religious liberals of today.

However, the Pharisees were also responsible for extensions of the law, such as "On the Sabbath, do not spit on the ground, because one might be perceived as plowing by stirring the dust," or "By examination, we have added gnats to the list of unclean animals. Therefore, pour your wine through a cloth to assure you do not consume one accidentally."

As God saw it, the biggest problem of the time was that the law was never meant to be "practiced." The law had been given to provide guideposts and guardrails by which a person could live his life as God intended. It had gotten to the point where God was remembered less and less, and rituals were remembered more and more. There are religions yet today that practice law and ritual with little thought of whom or what or why they worship.

The Geopolitical Setting

We all know the story of Jesus: He was born in Bethlehem, was lost in the temple at age twelve, turned water into wine, was tempted in the desert, gave the Sermon on the Mount, stilled storms, raised the dead, healed the sick … and the list goes on.

Most of Christianity has given no thought to world history at the time of Jesus. Without drowning us in civics, let's look at what the world was like in the time of Jesus.

Politics of the Jews

The Jews were in a state of religious turmoil. The "accepted" Jews were either *Pharisees* or *Sadducees*. The Pharisees were a bit more popular because of their "loophole" theology and the fact that they believed in life after death. The Sadducees were the conservatives of the time and had a strict interpretation of the law. They also held a sad-Sadducee belief that all forms of life on earth ended with death—and no afterlife.

There were other political groups as well. The *Essenes* were not as large a group, and they are sometimes called a sect because of that smaller size. They practiced a more communal "Jesus style" of life outside of Jerusalem. In fact, since Jesus *was* a Jew, He is usually considered to be Essene. The Essenes didn't recognize the authority of the temple leaders and practiced their faith where they lived in the hills around Qumran. By way of note, the Dead Sea scrolls were found in this area.

Another group was called *Herodians*. By the name, one can see that these adherents had their ears tilted toward Herod, the king. We will look more into that political state in a moment.

Another group, after being labeled as zealots, assumed that label as a title. The *Zealots*, as the name implies, were both radical and impulsive. A bit later, the name came to be applied to the revolutionary religious/ political party.

There were also the *Levites*, who were in charge of the temple. This group would include the high priest, chief priests, priests, and Levite "orderlies."

The Jews' "supreme court" of the time was the *Sanhedrin*. This was a rather dynamic group of elders—and those who were rich enough to buy a seat or politically strong enough to get a seat. The Sanhedrin heard the more controversial and difficult cases of Jewish legal and religious issues. The group was originally formed by Moses with seventy members.

The *Kings*, Herod the Great and Herod Antipas, were rulers during the life of Jesus. They were true kings, but the Herods ruled at the pleasure of the Roman emperor, and they understood that fact very well.

Given the religious and political atmosphere of the time, one can readily imagine both the petty and grand controversies and contentions concerning religious practice that could occur on a daily basis. Suffice it to say that unity was not the order of the day for the Jews at the time of Jesus.

Come to think of it, when Paul later continually preached about unity, he could well have been saying, "Don't be like *them*."

Politics of the Romans

As if the Jews' problems were not enough, their nation was occupied by a Roman army that cared nothing about a Jewish God. The Romans had established a rule that was followed at the point of a sword. The closest comparison in the time line of human memory would be the German occupation of Europe.

At the order of Mark Antony, Herod (not yet "the great") returned—with aid from Sossius (Roman Governor of Syria), after having been previously ejected by the Maccabees—and took Jerusalem about 37 BCE. This eliminated Hasmonean (the priestly Maccabean family) rule forever. Israel would not again be an independent nation for nearly two thousand years.

Perhaps the largest problem for the Roman occupation was that the Jews annually celebrated their historic freedom from the oppression in Egypt at the celebration of Passover. Many Israelites (rightly) believed that the Messiah would come during Passover. The Roman governor actually moved from Caesarea to Jerusalem at the time of the Passover to more quickly quell the unrest that inevitably arose during the Passover season. The governor's annual move only served to add to Jewish indignation.

To the Romans, "keeping the peace" sometimes meant almost daily concessions, which we see in the Scripture when Pilate "washed his hands" and freed Barabbas. The politics of that particular moment in time are best shown in John 18:28–19:22.

The Compromise of Rulers

As long as the Jews were "quiet," the Romans basically let the Jews be Jews. They conceded in not requiring the Jews to worship the emperor or to perform in military service. These and other Roman requirements would have indicated that the emperor was a God.

For the most part, the Sanhedrin handled whatever was considered a problem of Jewish (Mosaic) law, while any violation of civil or Roman law was handled in the Roman court. Examined in that light, one can readily see what a political "hot potato" the conviction and death of Jesus quickly became.

For clarity, we'll note that Jesus went from the garden of Gethsemane to Annas (father of Caiaphas) first and then stayed through what we would call the early hours of the morning. From Annas, Jesus was taken to Caiaphas and the Sanhedrin, to Pilate, to Herod, and back to Pilate—all in the course of about three hours. We're not told how long the "proceedings" took with the Sanhedrin, but Jesus left there at "first light" (approximately 6:00 a.m.), and the Christ began carrying His cross to "the place of the skull" at approximately 9:00 a.m.

Think on this. Jesus appeared in four different courts. Jesus, of course, had to travel—bound as a prisoner to each court within a growing parade of people who beat Him along the way. Adding to that the time taken for at least one formal flogging and the occasion of shame with a cohort of Roman soldiers, one has to think something like, "Hot Potato, indeed." The time in each court was fleeting at best.

The Timing: Why This Particular Time?

I'm told by some that we should never ask why in response to a decision by God. To the contrary, God takes pleasure in seeing His children in *fruitful and honest* study of Him and His history. God can certainly see us involved in various activities and exploits that are less savory. So, how much more must it please Him to see us seeking Him as we are told to do in Hebrews 11:6: "Without faith it is impossible to please him: for he that cometh to God must believe that he is, and that he is a rewarder of them that diligently seek him."

Seeking God does not mean to get a glimpse and say, "Tag! You're it!" The word *diligently* cannot go unnoticed. We'll not go into semantics, but one must believe that *diligently seeking* includes asking why.

Because of the Jews

God does not like confusion, especially when it comes to His instructions for living. The time leading up to the time of Jesus was filled with confusion, error, and intentional misguidance. We've discussed all of that previously. The point is that God knows when humanity has gone "almost too far to get back." As we've discussed elsewhere, God completely started over with humanity when humans became too decrepit to redeem.

Spiritual life in the New Testament times of Jesus had gotten to that point. The spiritual freedom that God wishes for all of us had turned into spiritual burden. God saw that this "trend" was only going to get worse.

Given that God wasn't pleased with the way things were going, conflict between Jesus and the temple leaders was inevitable. What *was* rectifiable, though, was the attitude of the temple leaders. It's been said that "selfishness gets you into trouble, but pride keeps you there." This was the attitude problem that put our Savior and the temple leaders at odds.

Given human nature, any person of that time who might have come to reform the ways of worship would have met with strong, if not absolute, resistance. History bears this out. Simply put, Jesus was teaching about a relationship with God that no longer required the leaders' services. Jesus spoke of a kingdom in which one's body was the temple and scorekeeping was no longer necessary. Jesus said in John14:6, "I am the way, the truth, and the life: no man cometh unto the Father, but by me."

The temple leaders felt their job security being threatened. They began to think that all they had to do was silence this Jesus fellow, and then things could get back to "normal."

At the beginning of what we call Passion Week, the temple leaders actually recognized what Jesus was talking about, but in their pride, they would neither relent nor repent. The story is recorded in Matthew 21.*

The Jewish part of the scene was set for the death of Jesus. God was showing us Isaiah 46:10 again, saying, "My counsel shall stand, and I will do all my pleasure." God's plan, once begun, would, without fail, be completed.

Because of the Romans

The Roman Empire of the New Testament period had been established eight hundred years earlier with the founding of Rome. Their empire completely encircled the Mediterranean Sea and beyond.

The Romans at the time of the Christ were both excellent and practiced at killing. There was no better time, before or since, to physically put Jesus to death. There are a great many historians who believe that the Romans had professional "crucifixionist" soldiers because the practice was so common.

To the Romans, the "beauty" of crucifixion was that the victim's shame could be displayed and that death on the *crux* (Latin) was excruciatingly painful and long in coming. Death might take two or even three days for a strong man.

The other side of the coin—the physical side of crucifixion—is not *completely* examined by most. While we won't look at the science of crucifixion, we *will* look at the pain that Jesus had to endure.

The True Suffering of Jesus

Most of us only lament the suffering of Jesus. It is only right that we are full of both sorrow *and praise* for the unselfish act of Jesus: giving His life for our sins.

---

* For more detail, see chapter 7, the section titled "Jesus Changed Everything While Changing Little."

Along with the human dread that Jesus felt, there were actually four genuinely different levels and areas of pain that Jesus was required to endure:

1. The pain of being made sin
2. The pain of crucifixion
3. The pain of abuse, flogging, the crown of thorns, etc.
4. The mental anguish of betrayal and abandonment

We will look at these four areas in detail.

The Pain of Being Made Sin

This is most likely the real reason God chose the Roman period. Let us look once more at the one we are talking about. Jesus is God the Son, Creator of the universe, Creator of humanity, the Word, the archangel, and the Christ (the Anointed). By His very nature, He is the enemy to sin. God the Son came to this earth to be Jesus, a human, and to live among sinners.

Think on that. Jesus came and lived His life in this sinful world. Sin is against His very nature. Jesus came and lived in "the camp of the enemy," yet Jesus lived a right life as an example for all.

Jesus came, first, to show us how to live. However, His plan was to ultimately die as the perfect sacrifice that would perfect our worship and our salvation. "For he [God] hath made him [Jesus] to be sin for us, who knew no sin; that we might be made the righteousness of God in him" (2 Corinthians 5:21).

Imagine, if you can, what this meant to Jesus, the Christ, God the Son, who had never known sin throughout eternity, except as a crippling, life-ending thing to hate with all His being. Sin was the one thing that would make God the Father turn His face away and not hear any of His children. Jesus was about to become sin—not simply the sins of one person, but the unatoned sins of all people from the beginning of sin itself.

The beauty of the sacrifice is that, being perfect, it stood to atone for any sins of anyone who would claim the name of Jesus as High Priest and the Son of God, according to God's plan of salvation.

The point is that God, being perfect, only experiences pain in the form of rejection from His children. Those pains are the pains of rejected love. God, being perfect, cannot even look upon sin. When God made Jesus to be sin, He had to turn His face from His Son because of the sin Jesus then carried. The Light of the World was turned away from Him, and the sky turned black (Matthew 27:45).

Most people think only of the physical pain that Jesus had to endure. Think of the pain of a perfectly sinless person who knew He was the Son of God but who literally became sin. In modern terms, it was like matter meeting antimatter in the soul of Jesus.

This pain—in (1) becoming the very thing (sin) that Jesus had hated from the time it entered the garden and (2) consequently being separated from God the Father and the Holy Spirit is a most exquisite pain, which we can never even imagine (until judgment day, but that's another study). To try to imagine such pain can only cause pain at the thought.

Crucifixion is the most vile, repugnant, vicious, hideous, insidious, and excruciatingly painful means of death ever created by humanity. The time when crucifixion was in vogue was the right time for the death of Jesus, in that the torture of crucifixion would actually serve to help Jesus take His mind off the real pain of becoming sin and being totally separated from God.

Yes, it was that much pain, and more.

The Pain of Crucifixion

Crucifixion is the worst pain that humanity has ever been able to manufacture. We mentioned that crucifixion was perhaps the only form of execution that would have helped Jesus to bear the pain of being made sin.

But what of the pain of the crucifixion itself? What of the hideous, hateful, ugly pain of both imagined shame and the innumerable real human pains of crucifixion? What, if anything, helped Jesus take His mind off the pain of the crucifixion itself?

Notice the stair steps of Christ's pain. The pain of crucifixion helped Jesus not to think about the pain of being made sin. Next, we examine the idea that the abuse and incessant beating of Jesus' body actually served to take His mind off the actual pain of the crucifixion—the nails driven into

His hands and feet, the near suffocation, the muscle cramps, the spasms, and so on.

The Pain of Abuse

Jesus was "found" in the garden and identified by Judas. He was arrested and taken to Annas and Caiaphas—in a raucous fashion, to be sure. After finding Jesus "guilty" of blasphemy, the Sanhedrin started spitting, slapping, pulling hair, and trying to hurt Jesus in order to manifest their superiority. Then Jesus was off to see Pilate, all the while being hit, spat upon, slapped, and hit some more. Pilate heard that Jesus was Galilean, so off Jesus went to Herod, all the while being hit, spat upon, slapped, and hit some more. Herod questioned Jesus, but Jesus gave no answer. Herod could find no entertainment in Jesus, except in mocking Him and putting Him into a "gorgeous robe," so back Jesus went to Pilate, all the while being hit, spat upon, slapped, and hit some more.

After not much discussion between Pilate and the Jews, Barabbas was freed, and Jesus was flogged and condemned to be crucified. A band of soldiers (a cohort numbers 480 men), apparently because of the scarlet robe Jesus was then wearing, gave Him a crown of thorns and beat him about His bleeding head and all over His body. It's unthinkable what 480 Roman soldiers might have done to inflict pain on a man they knew was about to die. They then put Jesus' own bloody clothes back on Him and released Him to the crucifixioners.

Jesus, as with all condemned, was made to carry His own cross to the place of crucifixion. Because of His weakened state, Jesus faltered, and Simon, the Cyrene, was compelled to carry it for Jesus. The party went down the Via Dolorosa (traditional) to Golgotha, and Jesus was crucified.

Jesus had been beaten in no organized fashion from midnight until approximately 9:00 a.m. There was the exception in the court of Pilate, where Jesus was officially flogged. During this period of Roman history, a flogging was "forty stripes, save one," or thirty-nine stripes. This was another method of inflicting pain, perfected by the Romans. The Romans had found that after thirty-nine stripes, the person was unable to feel the pain as it was inflicted. In other words, the "criminal" was hurting all he was going to hurt after thirty-nine lashes. They found that any stripes beyond this number was equal to beating a dead horse.

The flogging and almost continual beating Jesus endured on the way to the crucifixion was twofold in the preparation of Jesus for crucifixion. First, His nerves were not registering new pain. That is to say that Jesus was in pain, yes, but it was more of an "everywhere" pain rather than that of any particular injury. This would be accompanied by a numbing of the senses. Second, a direct result of mind-numbing pain is physical shock. The body actually begins to shut down all but the most vital functions in an effort to rescue failing life. This is why we are told in modern times to do all we can to keep a person from going into shock. In that state, it is often easier to die than to live.

Do you remember the earlier fact that a crucifixion sometimes took two or three days to kill a strong man? The benefit—if you can call it that—of Jesus' beatings and abuse was that death came quickly to Him.

However, this abuse was hardly the first pain that Jesus experienced that woeful night. We must realize that Jesus was in pain—even mortal pain—before He was arrested.

The Pain of Betrayal and Abandonment

The one thing that most people do not even pause to realize is that Jesus was in a genuine, physical state of depression and anguish before His arrest. Jesus was near death before any of the physical abuse even began.

Jesus was betrayed by Judas. Judas was perhaps one of the more trustworthy of the apostles in that he was entrusted with "the purse." Judas was entrusted with funding the ministry, and apparently, he was good at it. Yet Judas betrayed the Savior of the world.

Jesus knew that Peter, one of the "inner circle," was going to deny Him. Later, Peter—the one who had proclaimed that he would die with Jesus if necessary—followed "from afar" and denied that he ever knew Jesus.

Besides knowing that all the men He had loved and trusted with His teachings were going to desert Him, Jesus knew the fate that was to befall Him. Jesus took Peter, James, and John into the garden and told them that He was exceedingly sorrowful. The word *perilypos* means "grieved all around" or "surrounded by grief," and it was, as Jesus said, "to the point of death."

It is quite possible for someone to die of anguish. The physical symptoms of that failure—bursting capillaries—made Jesus start to "sweat drops of blood." Luke tells us that as Jesus was praying that "this cup be taken from me," an angel came to strengthen Him. Jesus was in agony, we're told. *Agony* is defined as the internal struggle that precedes death.

Even so, Jesus knew that God's plan needed to be carried out. He prayed earnestly and "more earnestly" that if there were any way around this crucifixion, He wanted to go that route. But ultimately He said, "Not my will but thine be done."

The rest of the apostles scattered like a flock of birds as soon as Jesus was arrested. Mark said that even a bystander boy wrapped in a bed sheet, apparently awakened by the noise, ran away when confronted by the arresting mob.

Imagine the deep, deep sorrow and physical depression that Jesus experienced. Were it not for the angel sent to strengthen Him, He might well have died in the garden.

The apostles slept while Jesus prayed. In this, Jesus had actually been abandoned before His arrest. No matter what, Jesus was totally alone after His arrest—except for the presence of God. Abandonment by God would come later. Jesus knew that also.

Jesus was on "the tree" for over three hours—and possibly between four and five hours—depending on how quickly the crucifixionists did their job. The sky became dark at what we call noon, and the Christ's body was found lifeless at what we would call three o'clock in the afternoon. This gave the faithful time enough to get Him off the cross and into Joseph's tomb before the Sabbath that would begin in only three hours from that point.

In Conclusion

God had left no detail to chance.[†] The only things that God could not control were the free will of Jesus (Matthew 26:53) and the pain that Jesus

† For background and study, see chapter 8, the section titled "Focusing on Omniscience," and chapter 13, "God's Plan ≠ God's Will."

had to endure. However, God, in His wisdom and forethought, did all He could do to make it all more bearable, if you will.

As with all of God's plans, the time of the crucifixion was right from both the *religious* standpoint—in making things right again—and from the *physical* standpoint—in providing for the Son as He endured the most painful execution possible.

22

Testing, Testing: Is That You, God?

This is a Test

The man said, "Surely God must be testing me." Who's to say? The man may be right.

Wouldn't life be grand if a voice came through the speakers of your mind when something unexpected happened, saying something like, "This is a test. This is only a test. Had this been a life-changer you would have also been informed on how to proceed for further instruction."

There are many different problems, trials, tribulations, adversities—whatever you want to call them—and we have them for many different reasons. But let's not be totally on the down side here. We also see many good times, with expected and surprise happenings that leave us feeling better than before. Yes, good times can be considered tests as well.

Not only are there many different problems, but there are also a great many reasons for receiving them. Understanding this is the purpose of this chapter.

Tried and True

The phrase *tried and true* indicates both a test and a result. God will test you only for good reason.

At what was perhaps the most important turning point in the history of humankind, Abraham was tested (Genesis 22). God's plan to give the life of what would be His only begotten Son was in the balance. God saw that Abraham was willing to sacrifice Isaac. Thereby, God was able to see that humanity was capable of a level of faith equal to God's own plan of salvation.

We all will be tested, at least to a minimum. To every person who has heard the gospel, that minimum will be the act of following Jesus to the grave,* dying to sin, being buried with Him in the watery grave of baptism, and coming up from that grave as "a new creature" (2 Corinthians 5:17) to walk in the will of God.†

God tests us for many reasons. Sometimes a person has to be reminded that God is indeed in control. A doctor with a "God complex" or the person who thinks something like, "I have built an empire, and it is all mine," is seen as shaking his fist at God—and believe me, God sees. In Luke 12:16–21, the parable of the rich man shows us an example of a "good times" test. The rich man failed miserably.

The Test of the Blessed

The other side of that particular coin reminds me of a woman I knew at church who was "never hurting for money." Whenever someone needed something like a wheelchair or such, the item would simply appear in the foyer by the backdoor of the building, but no one ever knew who was responsible for providing it. I have no doubt that she was blessed because she was a blessing. She showed us all what God's love looks like, neither desiring nor expecting recognition.

In fact, I can show you this point in Scripture. In James 4:13–17, James gave firm guidance against the pride of success. Belittling others and boasting are undesirable side effects of being blessed that must be avoided. This is not just a story for merchants and business owners; it more than applies to all of us who have been or will be blessed in one way or another.

James said that if we tell of any plans for the future, even for tomorrow, it is sinful boasting—unless God is given credit for granting us the life with

---

* Part I, "Salvation"

† Chapter 13, "God's Plan ≠ God's Will"

which to pursue those plans. James's point—and ours, here—is that we are only stewards of God's property. Even we ourselves belong to God, much less the things men deed to us. In verse 15, James said, "For that ye ought to say, If the Lord will, we shall live, and do this, or that."

Simply put, we're told to think this way: if the Lord will bless us with life for tomorrow, we plan on doing this or that.

The point I wish to make about verse 17 is often totally overlooked in this passage. Preachers and teachers make such a point of the "Lord willing" part of the passage that verse 17 is rarely examined. Verse 17 sounds like an "oh, by the way" type of entry, but it is so vital to a right life that it must be examined closely. James 4:17 reads, "Therefore to him that knoweth to do good, and doeth it not, to him it is sin."

James issued a pretty straightforward statement, but it seems, perhaps, to be a little disjointed from the "Lord willing" message. Remember that one of the basics of Bible study is the context surrounding any verse. Remember that James was speaking to merchants and was concerned about those merchants bragging on themselves without remembering God.

Given the context of verses 13–16, we see that James was saying, "*And* along with your not giving God the credit, you know that you should be giving proportionately to the church's work for the poor, the widowed, and the orphans. In that you know God's blessings are for you to share, if you do it not, you are a sinner."

This verse can also be laid at each of our doorsteps. Let's read it again, from NIV this time: "Anyone, then, who knows the good he ought to do and doesn't do it, sins."

That's truly a statement that fits every person at every time in every place. If you know what is right and do not do it, it is sin. What if the person doesn't know what's right or wrong? Then *you* need to show that person the gospel of the Christ.

Is That You, God?

One may ask, "How do I know if God is testing me?" That is actually a very easy question to answer. However, it is answered with another question: "How close are you to God?" I know of no one who has been tested to the fullest measure of their faith by God, who was not conversant with Him.

This is not to say that some—even some who have denied Jesus—have not been challenged and changed. I reference Saul/Paul on the road to Damascus (beginning in Acts 9). This, though, was not a test. It was miraculous, but it was on a different level for a different purpose.

The most common argument against the "conversant with God" statement is Moses' being raised in the heathen, polytheistic empire of Egypt. The truth is that Moses was Hebrew, a Levite, and he knew it. The story is told in Exodus 2. Moses' mother, Jochebed (yo-keh'-bid), literally nursed him until his weaning. Weaning in those days occurred from age two to age five. We know that the faithful Jochebed taught Moses about little else besides God and Hebrew history.

The point is that Moses fled Egypt to Midian, took a wife, joined and made a family, and no doubt worshipped the God of Abraham at every opportunity during this part of his life with Reuel (Jethro), the priest of Midian and Moses' father-in-law. Moses was tested at every turn of his life, *and* Moses was conversant with God, at least from the time he renounced his Egyptian citizenship until his death.

In actuality, God doesn't test someone unless He thinks (or perhaps hopes) that the person has a pretty good shot at success. If you are being tested by God, be cheered by the fact that God thinks you worthy of the test to begin with.

If Not a Test, Then What Is It?

How can a good God do such bad things to His creation? This question, worded many different ways, is asked over and over again. We partially addressed the answer in chapter 8. Suffice it to say that *nothing evil comes from God.*

I slip a special note in here. The world fears death. The believer will hardly fear it, except for the desire to remain with loved ones. The older-in-Christ believers will more often come to embrace death as a reward rather than a thing to be feared. In this section, we include death as a "bad thing" along with other adversities. I make this note to acknowledge that death holds far different meanings to believers and unbelievers.

We started this segment with a man saying that God must be testing him. Comments like that are common during hard times of any sort.

Earlier in this chapter, I wrote, "There are many different problems, trials, tribulations, adversities—whatever you want to call them—and we have them for many different reasons." Let's look at why adversity besets us.

There are six scenarios in which we will see sickness, hardship, and sometimes even death. The first four are actually from God; that is, God "unleashes" Satan. The last two are everyday cause-and-effect situations.

Scenario #1: God Is Glorified

This is the highest compliment a human can ever receive. Look at the story of Job. Satan said to God, "Let me at him. I can make him curse you." God believed that Job would remain faithful to their relationship, and He was willing to put His belief on the line to show Satan—and us—that true faith can overcome Satan himself (James 4:7).

If you are feeling tested, give thanks to God and give Him the praise He deserves. People may write stories about you too. But even better for you, God rewards the faithful with more than the faithful one's greatest dreams. Read the book of Job.

Scenario #2: God Judges and Seeks Retribution

There were times in biblical history when God decided that a person or a people should simply be punished for some reason, most often for a covenant violation. God will not allow people to renege on a covenant without bearing the consequences. God considers the covenant of His care to be the same as a marriage. The Bible speaks often of God seeing His people as adulterous or as entering whoredom with other gods of other people.

In chapter 4, we said that God is *the* most fair. God's justice is simply a balance scale. Both sides of any relationship with God will be weighed. If you do not have a firm grasp of this most important part of God's simple logic, stop here and go back to absorb it.

It is a given that God expects us to keep our end of the bargain in any covenant relationship. It's also a given that God keeps a far better accounting than we humans ever could. With that, we see that God can see—before we even think of it—when we are nearing the point of no return. Spiritually speaking, *the point of no return* is the point at which God can see that a people (nation) or a single person will not return to the covenant, ever. Our life is the most that any of us can give to repay the debt for breaking a covenant.

God ended the world one time, except for the family of Noah, and had it not been for the intercession of Moses, He would have done it twice again. Through the new covenant, we have been given a means for avoiding spiritual death as well.

God, who knows even the intentions of the heart, can tell when we have passed the point of no return, as the people of Noah's time had done (Genesis 6:5–7). God seeks retribution when the debt needs to be paid.

Take note that *retribution is not punishment*. It is simply a balancing of the scales.

Scenario #3: God Disciplines

Paul spoke to the church in Corinth about their being judged by God for improper practice of the Lord's Supper in 1 Corinthians 11.[‡] Paul pointed out, specifically in verse 32, that God's judgment of a Christian is not punitive but for discipline—as a parent disciplines a child.

The one thing that most people don't realize is this: discipline is not punishment. As parents, we must see that if we dispense punishment under the guise of discipline, we are neither teaching nor training our children. By wrongly applying punishment, we foster either resentment or fear, neither of which produces the desired result.

As He instructs His children, God very often has to remind them of the source of their blessings and protection. This also can (and should) be considered complimentary, in that God thinks enough about you and me to apply discipline in the first place. Please remember that God, with a simple wave of His hand, can remove the universe from existence. Yet God, in His love, is concerned that you and I, individually, remember Him and seek His forgiveness, love, and fellowship by acknowledging His discipline.

Think about our human world. The army wants all its troops to look and think alike. The army begins at boot camp, making all the recruits look alike and then "breaking" them down. The troops are then on the same

---

‡ Chapter 18, "The Lord's Supper: Communion"

level and can be trained for whatever duty is intended. The army leadership becomes "lord and master." A trained soldier comes to think that all things come from the army and that orders are to be obeyed without question.

This is the reason that God must see a contrite, repentant, and sometimes even broken heart. God can see whether or not you are going to ask Him for help or blame Him for your "predicament." When you become "trainable," God will take you and shape you to fit His plans. When God looks at the true believers, He sees that we have become like Jesus, washed by His blood. We all look alike in that regard. We are "troops" ready to be trained.

Scenario #4: Retribution Combined with Discipline

We have all heard that we should learn from the mistakes of others. On many occasions, God has pointed to the failings and resultant punishment of a person or a people and has admonished, "Do the same, and receive the same punishment" (Deuteronomy 24:9).

God has even backed off of punishment, but only if an established statute has not been violated, and only at the request of "a righteous man" (James 5:16). We have discussed many examples of intercessory prayer in chapter 12, but that is in no way exhaustive of the many examples of these types of prayer in the Bible.[§]

The point here is this: *what might be punishment for one should be considered discipline by all.* We do not have time to make all the mistakes on our own. We must consider history to be necessary not only for heritage but for education. We should be careful to not make the same mistakes that others made before us.

This brings to mind the second of three times that we hear of Miriam, the sister of Moses, in the Scripture narrative. This particular event occurred immediately before Moses sent the spies into Canaan. The twelfth chapter of the book of Numbers tells us of an adult version of sibling rivalry. God squashed it like a bug when He struck Miriam with leprosy, because Moses was so meek as to not contest her seditious talk. She was directly punished. Aaron, the newly named high priest, judged her to have been struck with leprosy. (The high priest's judgment made it official.) He immediately begged Moses not to lay the sin where it belonged: on him and their sister.

§ Chapter 12, "Prayer: Is This Thing On?"

Notice that Aaron correlated the sin with the punishment. He considered sin and punishment not only equal but inseparable. He saw, as we all should, that we cannot have one without the other. They come hand in hand.

Moses then asked God to heal Miriam. God did heal her—instantly—because of the intercession of Moses. However, God would not let her insubordination go unpunished. In Numbers 12:14, God said, "If her father had but spit in her face, should she not be ashamed seven days? Let her be shut out from the camp seven days."

The minimum statute of "isolation" time for touching a dead body, for shaming one's family, or for breaking any such statute was seven days. God was saying that the minimum statute for any shameful thing was seven days and that Miriam, even though she was healed, was going to have to endure, at the very least, a minimum form of punishment.

A major point to realize here is that Miriam was, in actuality, not nearly as severely punished as God had originally intended because of the intervention and intercession of Moses. However, God had to be fair and certainly could not declare that Miriam had not sinned and would not be punished. God, again and again, proves the meaning of "firm but fair."

Throughout our history, we have seen the consequences of sin as applied to God's children, from the most righteous to the least. Miriam received the gift of forgiveness for her sin, but she was not relieved of the responsibility of the consequence of that sin.

All of us, whether believers or not, should never believe that forgiveness of sin is equal to forgiveness of the consequences of that sin. The saved are forgiven of their sins and often receive special blessings from God after entering the covenant relationship. Even so, the forgiven must still live with the consequences of previous sin.

Sin does not care about saved or sinner. Sin treats every human being exactly the same, with equal consequence for all. No one is immune, because sin always gets the first punch. That is to say that sin comes with baggage, and it immediately straps that baggage (consequences) squarely onto the back of the sinner to be carried—whether we like it or not, and whether we are forgiven or not.

Punishment for one person should be considered discipline for those around him. Using the punishment of a person or a people as an example is not uncommon in the biblical history of our God. No doubt, Miriam also learned a lesson from what began as punishment but ended with forgiveness.

Scenario #5: Satan Is Ruler of the World after "the Fall"

The idea that Satan is ruler of the earth is difficult for some to accept. There are those who quote that old phrase, "God is in control," and apply it to this sinful world, and then they wonder, "Why did God do that?"

No one can, with a true understanding of the purity of God, believe that sin, evil, badness, or any other "not good" thing could ever come from God.

As soon as sin entered the world, God saw His creation as tainted. From that point forward, God set the earth on autopilot and began caring only about our eternal souls. God has always cared for us as His children. However, Satan continues to roam the earth and tries at every turn to get people to curse God for any reason and by any means possible. Temptation and evil are both very real.

Satan considers it open season on the souls of humankind. The unsaved do not have the protection of the covenant and are "low-hanging fruit" as far as Satan is concerned. I've often said that Satan doesn't go to the dens of iniquity. Those souls are already in the bag. Satan goes to church! When you want to catch fish, you go where the fish are.

Scenario #6: Our Own Failings

I will not disagree with the old saw that says *all things happen for a reason.*

Most people take that to mean that God has made this or that happen in order to get whomever to a better place or understanding. They will say that God placed a burden on you for your own benefit. God *may* actually discipline someone, but more often than not, we repeat that worn-out phrase because we can think of nothing else to say. It is a favorite at funeral homes.

Others repeat that same line to mean that we are only pawns in a great game of spiritual chess and that we shouldn't even question whatever has happened because we will never understand it anyway.

I will not disagree with this old saying because it is true. Everything *does* happen for a reason. However, it is *not* true for the reasons just shown.

The statement is true by means of simple cause and effect. To state it even more simply, every sin carries with it a bag full of consequences—none of them good.

Biblical and secular history is chock-full of stories of men and women, great and small, who sinned against God and met the consequences of their actions. The consequences did not happen by God's plan; they were the result of each person's individual decisions and actions. God allowed these things to happen, yes, but He did so out of His ultimate fairness and justice. God neither desired nor planned any bad thing (consequences of sin) that happened to Abraham, Moses, or David—or you or me.

Satan is not sitting on the sidelines. He will always attempt to get us to curse God and turn our backs on Him through sin itself or through guilt and our feeling "too sinful" to come to our Father or to return to Him. After participation in sin, we may receive consequences in the nature of physical, mental, and/or spiritual afflictions. They are the consequences of sin and its simple existence in the world.

The Greatest Test

We've been talking about committing sin and realizing the consequences of sin. We've also seen that sin is simply in the world, and we are going to see it, smell it, and even touch it more times that we'll care to remember. One of the foremost things to realize and remember is that we are tested by the world and by Satan himself on a daily basis.

To be sure, there is no *modern* "list" that can itemize what is sin. There does exist a list, however. We can refer to the Old Testament for a list of rules. God never changes His statutes (laws). Many are confused by the old and new covenants. Refer to part II, "God's Logic," for review and clarification in this regard.

At this point in the study, we need to address what some call the *sin of omission*. This is, perhaps, the greatest test of all. Given that we all have different points of view, if this is not the greatest sin, it is certainly the most pervasive. The sin of omission is that of *not doing* what is right for the true Christian life. Just as there are different levels of faith, there are varying degrees of omission as well.

For the saved Christian, "busy-ness" comes into play. In chapter 19, we spoke of the ten virgins who thought they were ready for the feast. The foolish virgins were the ones who were so busy getting ready for the feast that they failed to prepare for any delay in the coming of the bridegroom.

Every time you think, "I'm too busy," in terms of God's work, you are committing a sin of omission. This is especially true of prayer. We must make time for communion with God. Remember that our lives are containers and that we must continue to "eat" spiritual things in order to become more spiritual. We must "give our bodies as a living sacrifice" to God.

We're all guilty of doing "something else" rather than asking God what He needs done. God might have pointed to something, and we might have recognized that God was pointing it out to us. Still, we decide to put that "on the shelf" to be done later, while we go about plans of our own making.

If Satan can't make you bad, he'll make you busy. Realize that Satan *wants* you to worship. He wants you to worship anything except God Almighty.

Now, pack your bags; we're going on a guilt trip. *You always make time for the things that you think are important.*

To the saved Christian, the definition of sin in James 4:17 is the truest definition of the sin of omission: "Therefore to him that knoweth to do good, and doeth it not, to him it is sin."

The Holy Spirit lives in the heart of the saved believer. An old joke truly fits this scenario: "There's a mechanical failing in many cars: the nut behind the wheel." Yes, the Holy Spirit may live in us, but for Him to be effective, we have to *let Him drive*!

We should never turn away from God's work. We should always ask for a greater indwelling of the Holy Spirit so that we can better do God's bidding. Please refer to chapter 12 on prayer for a guide to a closer communion with our God.

Rationalization is a great tool for clearing one's conscience, but to the person with a good heart, it simply won't work—for a while. If the conscience is abused enough, it will callous over, just like your heel in a bad pair of shoes.

The most pitiful sin of omission is actually intentional. This is the sin of knowingly omitting God from your life. Jesus called this the *blasphemy of the Holy Spirit*.

People have written so much about this "unforgivable sin" that they have tried, it seems, to make it one of the most ambiguous and misunderstood thoughts of the Bible. Here, I want to make it as simple as Jesus did when He spoke of it in both Matthew 12:31 (a deeper description) and Mark 3:29.

Blasphemy of the Holy Spirit is the act of defiantly speaking against God, or even more literally, of sinning intentionally. In other words, *blasphemy of the Holy Spirit* is knowingly speaking ill of God or knowingly doing other than the will of God.

Take note of the biggest sin of omission: if one does not answer the gospel invitation, this too becomes an act of sinning against God. *This* is the unforgivable sin.

I'm reminded of the song "Free Will" by the group Rush. It's an insightful song that says, "If you choose not to decide, you still have made a choice." That's exactly what Jesus said. There is no "neutral" in your spiritual transmission! Concerning God, to remain neutral is to remain lost. The unsaved who have heard the gospel message are doing just that. Saying "maybe later" puts one's soul in peril. Doing other than what God wants is to blaspheme the very Spirit of God.

At the time of these biblical passages, Jesus had just been accused of healing by the power of "Beelzebub, the prince of the devils." Jesus noted that this was speaking directly against God and that those who did so were *blaspheming the Holy Spirit* of the Godhead. Jesus made His point clear when he said in Matthew 12:30, "He that is not with me is against me; and he that gathereth not with me scattereth abroad."

It can be no clearer.

I will also state here that even the "unpardonable sin" *can* be forgiven if even the most flagrant violator repents and becomes saved, as Saul/Paul and others did. The point is that if a person dies in the unsaved condition after knowing the truth of the Word, there is only one judgment. That person's soul must go to "the place reserved for the Devil and his angels."

We sometimes have another word for some of these tests designed by Satan. We call them temptations. These tests are often vague and appear to be innocent, such as "time conflicts," and so on. Any "temptation" that makes your conscience uneasy is a sin. "If the shoe fits, wear it," so to speak.

We must fear spiritual atrophy. Spiritual atrophy is gradual. Satan is willing to take his time with you. Your spiritual life needs regular exercise.

Remember that if you do not purposely fill your life with light, darkness grows within you.

It's Up to Each of Us

Yes, *all things happen for a reason.* Sometimes things happen for some pretty silly or even stupid man-made reasons, but the things that "happen" to us personally are usually consequences of our own actions. We're told in Matthew 7:17–18 (NIV), "Likewise every good tree bears good fruit, but a bad tree bears bad fruit. A good tree cannot bear bad fruit, and a bad tree cannot bear good fruit."

Good things happen for a reason too. It's just that we tend to forget God when things are going good. Satan wants us to blame God for our troubles when, in fact, God has merely "let the chips fall where they may."

Sin is rampant in the world. Bad things sometimes happen to good people. God is not mocked. The believer who understands both the consequences and, sometimes, randomness of sin will also be visited with a stronger faith and an increased presence of the Spirit of God.

23

Did Jesus Go to Hell?

Where did Jesus go after He died?

This is another issue that is not a "salvation issue." However, it is a question that often sparks lively debate, and we address it for that reason.

The thing that *is* a salvation issue is this: it's our soul that has a body, not our body that has a soul. Our body is our temple, the place where we find the Godhead, the place where we go to worship God in spirit and in truth. Paul said it in no uncertain terms 1 Corinthians 6:19–20: "What? know ye not that your body is the temple of the Holy Ghost which is in you, which ye have of God, and ye are not your own? For ye are bought with a price: therefore glorify God in your body, and in your spirit, which are God's."

But let's get back to the subject: the soul of Jesus. As it is with every soul that walks the planet (except those whose bodies are alive on the ultimate day of judgment), Jesus' soul went somewhere after His body died.

Some people believe that Jesus went to hell (*the* prison) to judge the antediluvian (before the flood) dead that God and Noah left behind. This is not a "stretch," so to speak. At the time of Jesus, the fate of those lost in the flood had long been sealed. Spiritually speaking, it certainly would have been a convenient time to dispense with some "unfinished business." This is what many believe to be the meaning of 1 Peter 3:18–19, which says, "For Christ also hath once suffered for sins, the just for the unjust, that he might bring us to God, being put to death in the flesh, but quickened by the Spirit: *By which also he went and preached unto the spirits in prison*."

However, to say that Jesus went anywhere to judge anyone is contrary to God's own decree about the day of judgment, of which Jesus spoke and bore witness—not to mention the account in Revelation of Jesus sitting on the white throne of judgment. A second point is this: if Jesus had "preached" to the lost souls in hell, it is certain that none of them would have failed to repent. If any of us were to be given a get-out-of-jail-free card after being sentenced to an eternity in hell, we'd jump on it like a bird on a June bug.

Look at the language Peter used, remembering that the translation was to Old English. Peter was saying that Jesus was certainly put to death but that He was "quickened" by the Spirit—*that same spirit* that went with Jesus (in the time of Noah before He was "Jesus") when He attempted to get the people of Noah's time to repent. Those people were "now in the *prison* of hell."

Peter was identifying the Holy Spirit, not Jesus.

As an aside, notice that Peter told us something we hadn't been told before. God obviously gave every opportunity to the people of Noah's time for repentance. Peter, inspired by the Holy Spirit, told us that Mi-Ki-El even went to preach to the people before God decided to destroy humankind. God went directly to the people, and they *still* did not repent. No wonder He decided they weren't worth saving.

Given that experience, it is also evident why God told the rich man (in the story of the rich man and Lazarus) that sending "one risen from the dead" would do no good. God had tried it already!

So, did Jesus go to hell? No, Jesus did not go to hell. Think on this. Why would the God of heaven sully His shoes by taking one step into the perdition reserved for those opposed to Him? Jesus was in heaven before He came, and His soul returned to heaven upon His death.

The sovereign, almighty God who, with a word, created all that we know and do not yet know, He who breathed life into us and grants life to us daily, needs only to speak judgment, and it shall be done.

Apply this bit of logic: God the Son had just been made sin for the sake of the entirety of humankind. Why would He wish an audience with sin for any reason?

The story of Lazarus and the rich man supports the notion that judgment is immediate at one's death. No one will be damned or saved by believing one way or the other about personal judgment versus one very large judgment day. However, if singular judgment applies, the people who died in "the deluge" had long since been judged and permanently placed in hell.

Jesus, Without God

There is one thought that comes to mind when thinking of possible definitions of hell. One popular way to think of hell is to say that it is "anyplace that God isn't." In that sense, from the sixth hour to the ninth hour of the Jewish day while Jesus was on the cross, Jesus was in hell, because God was not present.

God turned His face from the scene for those three hours because Jesus had been made sin. This was why the sky turned dark. God cannot even look directly on sin; His purity won't allow it. Jesus acknowledged that fact, and it was recorded for us in Matthew 27:46: "And about the ninth hour Jesus cried with a loud voice, saying, Eli, Eli, lama sabachthani? that is to say, My God, my God, why hast thou forsaken me?"

Note what Jesus said in the parable of the lost sheep in Luke 15:4–7. Jesus ended the parable this way: "I say unto you, that likewise joy shall be in heaven over one sinner that repenteth, more than over ninety and nine just persons, which need no repentance."

Jesus said that He came to seek and to save the lost (Luke 19:10)—not the lost who have no means of repentance but the ones that He, and we, can bring to repentance. People who were in a "lost" or unsaved condition when they died cannot repent; and we certainly cannot repent for them.

The point is that, in either case of judgment, there was no reason for Jesus to even give a thought about the people who had died in the deluge.

24

Married to God?

Many people who become Christians* think that they have accomplished a simple act of salvation. In and of itself, that is true. However, consider again the student who says, "The more I learn, the more I see there is to learn."

God Is Our Bridegroom

In Exodus 4, we find God's plan for getting the people of Israel to leave to do sacrifice at Goshen. God told Moses to return to Egypt with Aaron. God also told Moses, in verse 23, "Let my son go, that he may serve me: and if thou refuse to let him go, behold, I will slay thy son, even thy firstborn."

God was telling Moses to circumcise his firstborn son, Gershom. Moses was hesitant, almost to the point of reluctance. God had already gotten mad over the reluctance of Moses in the first part of this chapter. On Moses' way to Egypt with his family, the Lord came to claim his son by death. "The Lord," in this instance, has also been translated to "the Angel of the Lord."†

In verse 25 we read, "Then Zipporah took a sharp stone, and cut off the foreskin of her son, and cast it at his feet, and said, Surely a bloody husband art thou to me." This translates out of the Old English to mean,

---

* See part I for details.

† See the names for Jesus in chapter 9: "The Angel of the Lord or Angel of God" for deeper discourse.

"Surely you are a *bridegroom* of blood to me." This refers to the covenant of circumcision.

This is the first instance of God (Mi-Ki-El, or Jesus) being called a bridegroom. The Lord obviously approved of this "last-minute" compliance, because He let the boy go and sent Moses on to meet Aaron.

Isaiah declared God to be a bridegroom in Isaiah 61:10 when he spoke praise for salvation and more. He said, "I will greatly rejoice in the LORD, my soul shall be joyful in my God; for he hath clothed me with the garments of salvation, he hath covered me with the robe of righteousness, as a *bridegroom* decketh himself with ornaments, and as a bride adorneth herself with her jewels" (emphasis added).

John the Baptist spoke of Jesus and himself directly when he said, "He that hath the bride [the church] is the *bridegroom*: but the friend of the bridegroom [we would say, the "best man"], which standeth and heareth him, rejoiceth greatly because of the *bridegroom's* voice: this my joy therefore is fulfilled" (John 3:29, emphasis added). Jesus alluded to Himself as a bridegroom a number of times in the Gospels.

In Exodus 34:14, we are told—in no uncertain terms—of God's feeling for His people as His bride. "For thou shalt worship no other god: for the LORD, whose name is Jealous, is a jealous God."

Over and over again, God spoke of times when the people strayed from Him as "whoredom." In Ezekiel 16:28, He pronounced judgment and said, "Thou hast played the *whore* also with the Assyrians, because thou wast unsatiable; yea, thou hast played the harlot with them, and yet couldest not be satisfied" (emphasis added).

The book of Chronicles tells of the various tribes of Israel. Of the half-breed tribe of Manasseh, who were later called Samaritans, 1 Chronicles 5:25 says, "And they transgressed against the God of their fathers, and went a *whoring* after the gods of the people of the land, whom God destroyed before them" (emphasis added).

Since the History of Humanity Began

Jeremiah 2 is as modern as it is ancient. We can see God speaking to us just as easily as we know that He was talking to Israel. God actually recounted the freshness of a young nation and its love for Him, the Lord

God. In verses 2–3, God spoke of Israel as having the love of newlyweds, and of the protection He afforded to the people who were married to Him. He told Jeremiah, "Go and cry in the ears of Jerusalem, saying, Thus saith the LORD; I remember thee, the kindness of thy youth, the love of thine espousals, when thou wentest after me in the wilderness, in a land that was not sown. Israel was holiness unto the LORD, and the firstfruits of his increase: all that devour him shall offend; evil shall come upon them, saith the LORD."

God's love is evident in the Scripture. God remembers that because the people were married to Him by the covenant of blood in Exodus 24:6–8. He protected them from anyone who tried to take them or hurt them, dispensing punishment on those people as would a husband would protect his bride.

What's Modern About That?

Let's bring this into a modern context. This sounds like the early times of the United States. There were plenty of people who didn't worship God, but the country was established with "In God We Trust" as our working, viable motto. God protected us. Our enemies fell away and often met punishment, either before or after attacking us.

Then we became secure within ourselves. Our country was led by people who "knew not the Lord," and our law and way of thinking traveled further and further away from God. Verses 8–9 (NIV), say, "'The priests did not ask, 'Where is the LORD?' Those who deal with the law did not know me; the leaders rebelled against me. The prophets prophesied by Baal, following worthless idols. Therefore I bring charges against you again,' declares the LORD. 'And I will bring charges against your children's children.'"

In verses 11–13 (NIV), God continued, saying, "Has a nation ever changed its gods? (Yet they are not gods at all.) But my people have exchanged their Glory for worthless idols. Be appalled at this, O heavens, and shudder with great horror," declares the LORD. My people have committed two sins: They have forsaken me, the spring of living water, and have dug their own cisterns, broken cisterns that cannot hold water."

God was saying that if we forget we are married to Him, He can do no less than to "put away the adulterous bride" as written in His own statutes. Our country has "whored" out to other nations, just as God said Israel did. We have adulterated our morality with ideas about "relative truth." To be "tolerant" we have removed God from our lives and the lives of our children. We would do well to "eat" the words of Jeremiah that were given to him by God in verses 23–28 (NIV).

> How can you say, "I am not defiled; I have not run after the Baals"? See how you behaved in the valley; consider what you have done. You are a swift she-camel running here and there, a wild donkey accustomed to the desert, sniffing the wind in her craving—in her heat who can restrain her? Any males that pursue her need not tire themselves; at mating time they will find her. Do not run until your feet are bare and your throat is dry. But you said, "It's no use! I love foreign gods, and I must go after them."
>
> As a thief is disgraced when he is caught, so the house of Israel is disgraced—they, their kings and their officials, their priests and their prophets. They say to wood, "You are my father," and to stone, "You gave me birth." They have turned their backs to me and not their faces; yet when they are in trouble, they say, "Come and save us!"
>
> Where then are the gods you made for yourselves? Let them come if they can save you when you are in trouble! For you have as many gods as you have towns, O Judah.

There's more. You should go there and read and digest it.

Yes, We Are Married to God

We have an illness in our society's relationship with God. Divorce in a relationship is quite the same as using abortion for birth control. Our society has seen both for so long now that neither seems wrong to a great many people. We have conditioned ourselves to simply turn a blind eye and call it a matter of choice.

The modern version of the traditional wedding vows reads all but identical to the way the vows read a century ago (without the word *obey*) except for the part where one promises, "As long as we both shall live." That phrase, in the modern version, is now, "As long as our love shall last." How can this be seen as anything less than the wedding vow itself giving permission for divorce?

A point to consider is that a quasi-psychologist on television once stated, "Relationship commitment is *not* 50:50. Relationship commitment is 100:100."

We are living under God's new covenant. God agreed to be our God and thereby afforded us all the privileges and protections He has promised—if, and only if, we first enter that covenant agreement with Him‡ and then remain faithful as if it were (rightly) considered to be a covenant of marriage.

We break our vows when we commit adultery with other gods, goods, and man-made moralities. God is longsuffering, but if a society's moral decay proceeds to a point where the wrongs have a greater influence than the good, God has historically proven that He will either personally stop it or simply turn the other way and allow it to fail miserably.

Realize that God is faithful. However, if we break our covenant obligation to remain faithful in a right life, God is well within His rights to remove Himself from any covenant obligation. We would do well to view the history of humanity and recall the times when God did exactly that.

‡ For instruction on how to enter the covenant with God, see part I.

25

Revelation: It's Not about Soothsaying

Context is vital to any real understanding of history and historical writings. This truth has no stronger argument than in the book of Revelation. Let's first talk about the *setting* of the book.

The "Where"

The story *about* the book of Revelation is that it was written by John. He identified himself four times in the book. Most agree that this is John, the apostle, who was exiled to what was probably a Roman penal colony on the island of Patmos off the coast of what is now Turkey, southwest of Ephesus and the other six of the seven churches of chapters 2 and 3.

The New Christians

One must remember that the Christians of the day were converted Gentiles, previously pagan idol worshippers. The Jews, to whom Jesus ministered first, were very ready for the Messiah (or so they said), but they had not found Jesus to be a Messiah to their liking and had decided to wait for the next one.*

---

* See chapter 7, "Judaism: New and Improved," "Change of the Chosen," for greater detail.

Most of the pagan worship of the period included drunken parties, orgies, and other acts of immorality. This was radically different on every level from Christianity, which espoused fidelity, chastity, and benevolence, and considered things like gluttony to be a sin.

These new Christians of these seven churches were attempting to live a right life in the middle of one of Satan's greatest strongholds. They were faced with "come on in, the water's fine" at every turn of their daily life.

Roman Emperor Worship

Add to the various hazards of backsliding the Roman enforcement of emperor worship. History shows us that up until the crucifixion of Jesus, the stipulation of emperor worship had been disregarded in the area around Palestine—as long as the "good little Jews" stayed "good little Jews." However, the Romans felt they were beginning to lose control as "this new Christian religion" began making greater and wider waves in the Jewish pond.

The Romans deemed that something had to be done. They must have thought that forcing "those Christians" to worship the emperor would break them, or at least the Romans would have something with which to charge them so they could suppress, jail, and kill them.

The "Why"

John wrote the book of Revelation to edify and encourage his Christian contemporaries. John was showing the faithful believers that the points were already on the scoreboard … and God wins!

The number seven is used fifty-two times in John's writing of Revelation. To the people of the period, the number seven was the designation of completeness and fullness. This, in and of itself, is proof of the finality of the book.

Revelation tells us that believers go to heaven. Satan is defeated. God and His faithful will live, spiritually complete, for eternity.

Let's Set the Stage

Apocalypse, translated literally from the Greek, means nothing like "the end of the world." Rather, it means "a revelation or discovery of what was concealed or hidden." Obviously, the book of Revelation was apocalyptic. Because of this book, the writing style has also been labeled *apocalyptic*.

One very real reason that the book of Revelation has received notoriety of late is a resurgence of fascination with "the mystical." Witchcraft and phantasms are now in vogue. Witness the entertainment industry, which is garnering billions of dollars from people who often find those lies and fantasies easy to believe. You can probably name a few such movies or TV shows yourself.

There are labels attached to the different views of the interpreters of Revelation.

Preterists	believe that Revelation is a first-century book written for first century Christians, with application for all of us. The events told by John are of that era with most events having already occurred.
Historicists	believe that Revelation is a description of a series of events from the time of writing through the end of time.
Futurists	believe that Revelation is an "end-times" prophecy.
Idealists	believe that Revelation is a symbolic story of God's good over Satan's evil.

You'll see these listed views either espoused or denied within this section of this work. There will be no specific argument either pro or con. The truth is the truth. The truth proves or disproves.

Remember also that John did not try to explain the book any better than to report what he saw (which was given to him to tell). If he had, the Romans would have squashed his book. This again shows the wisdom of the Spirit that inspired the writing. This was a time of tremendous persecution.

To the pagan Romans, Revelation was merely a harmless book of fantasy. Come to think of it, we've seen some pretty good fantasy come from its recent interpretation as well.

Like many other passages of Scripture, the book of Revelation has been both construed and misconstrued to fit what any-given person wants it to say. As we always should, we'll look at the Scripture for proof of the Scripture.

Earthly Kingdom

"But the day of the Lord will come as a thief in the night; in the which the heavens shall pass away with a great noise, and the elements shall melt with fervent heat, the earth also and the works that are therein shall be burned up" (2 Peter 3:10).

"The sun shall be turned into darkness, and the moon into blood, before the great and the terrible day of the LORD come" (Joel 2:31). (This is repeated in Acts 2:20 as a New Testament reference.)

"As if a man did flee from a lion, and a bear met him; or went into the house, and leaned his hand on the wall, and a serpent bit him. [the man can't get away] Shall not the day of the LORD be darkness, and not light? even very dark [sun is "turned off"], and no brightness in it?" (Amos 5:19–20).

"Neither their silver nor their gold shall be able to deliver them in the day of the LORD'S wrath; but the whole land shall be *devoured by the fire* of his jealousy: for he shall make even a speedy riddance of all them that dwell in the land" (Zephaniah 1:18, emphasis added).

Other Scriptures bear the same meaning. I used mostly Old Testament references to emphasize that the picture of the "end of days" has not changed since even early biblical history. Notice the repeated statement that all the heavens and the earth will be destroyed. This seems to quiet any talk of an earthly kingdom, doesn't it? John himself wrote in Revelation 20:11, "And I saw a great white throne, and him that sat on it, *from whose face the earth and the heaven fled away*; and there was found no place for them" (emphasis added).

John told us that heaven and earth were gone (fled away). When John said, "And there was found no place for them," he was saying that there was no need of them anymore.

The New Jerusalem

The New Jerusalem is said by John to be "descending out of heaven." This was after he had been taken "in the spirit" to a "great high mountain." This simply means that the New Jerusalem appeared to him from out of the spiritual realm. It would be "descending" in that heaven has always been seen as above man. God brought it "down" and gave it a physical appearance so John would be able to describe it.

John had been transported by our supernatural God to a place where the spiritual and physical could mix long enough for John to get a grasp of the beauty of heaven. Note that this action would probably resemble, to whatever degree, the transfiguration. John's description was simply the best he could humanly offer. Most people think he did a pretty good job.

Given that the New Jerusalem "descending" was not for the purpose of descending to earth for an earthly kingdom—for there will be no earth on which to put it—it must be that John was talking about a spiritual place for spiritual (faithful) souls.

We must also remember that John was, as were all the other authors of the Holy Scripture, writing to a people living thousands of years ago. We who have advanced science in our pockets and purses might give a description more befitting the twenty-first century.[†]

What About the Thousands?

This is where the interpretations get really dicey. That's just the right word by the way, as *dicey* is defined as "unpredictable and potentially dangerous."

There is a cardinal rule in the study of any historic writing. I think we can all agree that the Bible is both historic and historical. The rule is that we must first define the Ws—who, what, when, where, and why in order to apply proper context.

We all continually try to apply the thinking—and even morality—of the twentieth and twenty-first centuries to the words and actions of people who lived thousands of years ago. Even our modern anthropologists would

† See chapter 21, "The Crucifixion" for a better understanding of God's timing, and how much more He sees than we do.

agree that to do so is error. Many people say things like, "Why didn't they just do ..." or "I certainly wouldn't have thought that" or "If they'd only read the letter to the Romans" or such like—all to no avail.

In the case of Revelation, the Ws are:

Who	was John. *To* whom was the churches.
What	is the encouragement to remain in the faith and John's proof that God wins.
When	was somewhere around the end of the first century.
Where	*From* where was the Island of Patmos. *To* where was the Aegean coastal area of Asia.
Why	is the same as the "what."

In this case, the *when* is vital to understanding the error that many believe. The first issue is all the numbers listed in the book. The second issue is the historical time line of the book. We'll consider the first issue—the numbers—here. Without going into a monstrous study of numerical systems, we have to look at the history of numbers themselves.

"A Thousand" Is Not 1,000

The "thousands" of the book of Revelation are not "999+1 = 1,000." World history explains it in one simple sentence. Until about AD 500 in India (at the earliest), the number zero had not been "invented" as a placeholder or given numerical significance in a base-ten numerical system.

There was no such number as "1,000" in a decimal system (in any form of common use) before the end of the sixth century.

The closest thing to an organized numerical system that existed at that time of Jesus and John was the *Mesopotamian numerical system*, which was based on counting the tips and knuckles of the four fingers of the right hand (12) and multiplied by the digits of the left hand (5). This made the Mesopotamian system a *base 60* (sexagesimal) system, not a *base 10* (decimal) system that would use the numbers 10, 100, 1000, etc., as we think of them.

The point is that in the time of Jesus and John, the base 60 system had imbedded itself into the world of mathematics and accounting. The Mesopotamian system had been in use for about 1,500 years or so.

The idea of "zero" as we know it today started in India. However, the idea of zero as a "placeholder" was not even a thought until late in the fifth century, at best. The base 10 system didn't get to Europe until the eleventh or twelfth century.

In fact, the base 60 system has not gone away, even today. We use it in our measurement of time and also in the measurement of degrees, minutes, and seconds of our navigational systems, to name only a couple of examples.

The people of the time of Jesus and John would have interpreted 1,000 to be equal to 60^3 (60 to the third power) which would be 216,000 in the *base 10* system we use for counting today. That would only be, of course, if the Christian readers of the time were involved in higher mathematics rather than just trying to make sure they had enough to feed the family for the day and stay at least one step ahead of the Roman persecution.

John could not have written a number that simply *did not exist* at the time of the writing. There had been considerable "evolutions" in mathematics by the time of the authorized King James translation.

With these "new eyes," we can readily see that considerable liberty was taken by those translators when it came to the numbers contained in the Bible, and especially in the book of Revelation. Note that the King James Version was translated about fifty years after the Italian church's Council of Trent. Arguably, the largest single decision of the Council of Trent was that "traditions of the church are equal to the Scriptures." The Italian church at the time of the King James translation was very likely to take any liberties it felt like taking.

So, What *Are* the Numbers?

Given that interesting bit of numerical history, we can look at what John wrote with "ears that can hear."

The word John used that has been interpreted to be *ten thousand* is the Greek word *myrias*. We use the word *myriad* nowadays to mean exactly what John meant: a large number that cannot be measured. *Myrias*, the word that John used, is a plural of the primary word *murioi*, which means "very many." That would mean that John was saying that it was *innumerably many.*

Also, we must remember that the Greek used by John and the other authors of the New Testament (including the educated physician, Luke) was more a vernacular of the common people than the aristocratic Greek that we now study. Think of it as American English versus British English or Tex-Mex versus Castilian Spanish.

This one word, *myrias*, got translated in the King James version of Revelation and other books thus:

- ten thousand times ten thousand (Revelation 5:11).
- two hundred thousand thousand (with the added word dyo (duo = two) for more emphasis) (Revelation 9:16).
- innumerable multitude (Luke 12:1)
- ten thousand (Matthew 18:24)
- innumerable company (Hebrews 18:22)
- fifty thousand (Acts 19:19)
- thousands (Acts 21:20; Jude v. 4)

Notice that the *authors* used the descriptive word rather than listing a real number. They were not even trying to make an estimate. The King James translators apparently thought they needed to explain what an "innumerable number" was. Whatever the reason, we can see that they were hardly consistent.

Another word John used that has been interpreted as "a thousand" is *chilioi*. It is an adjective traditionally used as "a thousand *of something*." It is defined as "a plural of uncertain affinity." The word John used that has been interpreted as "thousands" is *chilias*. It is a feminine noun. This can actually be interpreted as a large number, but not too large. It is usually considered to be "one thousand."

The reason for using both *chilioi* and *chilias* is that in the Greek and other languages, the adjective must agree with the noun. If the noun is plural, so must be the adjective.

How Do We Know If It's Real or Figurative?

Without going further into etymology (the study of words), we'll look at literal and figurative uses. Note, if you will, that when we're told of a *real accounting*—such as the two occasions recounted by Jesus in Matthew 16:9–10—we're told an exact number: in this case, the number of people.

The "four thousand" and the "five thousand" people that Jesus fed on those two occasions were numbered in the Greek as *tetrakischilioi* and *pentakischilioi*, respectively. This translates exactly to "four times a thousand" and "five times a thousand."

Remember and truly realize two very important things we take as given:

1. All the Holy Scripture is inspired through each author by the Holy Spirit of the Godhead.
2. As such, the Scripture is cohesive over the course of about 1,600 years and was written by about forty authors.

Given these facts, it should be impossible to reason that that this one book would be totally misaligned from the others. The point is that if the detailed numbering of angels, saved souls, and years given to us in Revelation was important, God would have expressed the exact numbers to John. Another point is that even though the numbering in Revelation is not exact, it *is* accurate.

"A long time" is not exact, but we know that it is not "a blink of an eye." "An innumerable multitude" is not exact, but we definitely know it is not "a handful."

One Big Human Misconception (to Add to the List)

In realizing that the numbers of Revelation are inexact at best, we can look at the 144,000 of chapter 7 with new eyes. Remember, also, that we have seen—in this work and elsewhere—that God looks after the faithful. What we see in the "sealing" of chapter 7 is the blanket of protection that God placed over the messianic (Christian) Jews of Jerusalem and their company.

There were a "great number" of Christians converted from all of the twelve tribes of Israel. God "sealed" them with safety and "held back the four winds" before the great attack on Jerusalem. The faithful were afforded time to gather and get away. This is proven historically, in that not a single baptized believer was in Jerusalem in AD 70 when the Romans razed the city. God had abandoned the city, and He took His children with Him.

The Exact "When" Doesn't Matter

If we read the book of Revelation with one eye on the Scripture and the other on the history books, we will see that what we call history is what John was told to write. John was told in Revelation 1:19 to "write the things which thou hast seen, and the things which are, and the things which shall be hereafter."

This applies directly to the argument over when the book of Revelation was written. The answer to that question is: it doesn't matter. Most people say that John wrote the book around AD 95. These folks say that the book can't be speaking of the destruction of Jerusalem, because that occurred in AD 70. They say that this would mean that the book was not foretelling the future. We will discuss prophecy later in this same chapter.

Jesus told John to write "the things which are [that then existed or had occurred already], and the things which shall be hereafter." No matter when the book was written, we're told from the mouth of God that the events had either occurred or had yet to occur. Therefore, there is no argument between content and timeline.

Revelation Simplified

Think on this. We accept that every other book was written to the people it was addressed to, e.g., Ephesians to the church at Ephesus, Philippians to the church at Philippi, Thessalonians to the church at Thessaloniki, etc. Why then do we so readily forget that Revelation was written to the seven churches to which it was addressed?

Revelation was written for the edification of the churches that existed in that day. As with all the other Spirit-inspired books, Revelation holds lessons for us today as well. John warned the churches of persecution and temptation from without and within. He told them what was and what would be soon, just as he was told and shown.

What makes the book of Revelation so special is that the Word of God, through John, gave us a "look behind the curtain." These are very real happenings recorded for us in what we would now call "real time." We are given a very real and rare look at what went on in the spiritual realm while also knowing, historically, what went on here on earth.

A Reminder about Prophecy

Let's remember that a *prophecy* is not truly defined as a foretelling of the future. It is better defined as an interpretation, in our case, of the Word of God. The Word of God did reveal God's future plans on many occasions through prophets (interpreters). This is where we get our misaligned meaning of the word *prophecy.*

We should consider a biblical prophet to be an interpreter of the Word of God, either of the Scripture or of direct contact, as was the case with John, the author of Revelation.

This is why John was given the little scroll to eat in Revelation 10:8–11. Just as Ezekiel did in the third chapter of his book, John had to eat it so it would become a part of him and he would not lose a word of what was written. Not forgetting anything, John could give a right and true interpretation.

The Revelation Scripture on Prophecy

If you will, allow me to replace the word *prophecy* in the passages that follow with the phrase "interpretation of the Word of the Lord (Jesus) by John." By doing that, the word *prophecy* loses its mystical sound, and we can once again take the book of Revelation as what it is: an inspired book to edify and unify the church.

"Blessed is he that readeth, and they that hear the words of this [interpretation of the Word of the Lord (Jesus) by John], and keep those things which are written therein: *for the time is at hand*" (Revelation 1:3, emphasis added).

"And I fell at his feet to worship him. And he said unto me, See thou do it not: I am thy fellowservant, and of thy brethren that have the testimony of Jesus: worship God: for the *testimony of Jesus* is the spirit of [interpretation of the Word of the Lord (Jesus) by John]" (Revelation 19:10, emphasis added).

[Jesus said,] "Behold, I come quickly: blessed is he that keepeth the sayings of the [interpretation of the Word of the Lord (Jesus) by John] of this book" (Revelation 22:7).

"And he saith unto me, Seal not the sayings of the [interpretation of the Word of the Lord (Jesus) by John] of this book: *for the time is at hand*" (Revelation 22:10, emphasis added).

"For I testify unto every man that heareth the words of the [interpretation of the Word of the Lord (Jesus) by John] of this book, If any man shall add unto these things, God shall add unto him the plagues that are written in this book: And if any man shall take away from the words of the book of this [interpretation of the Word of the Lord (Jesus) by John], God shall take away his part out of the book of life, and out of the holy city, and from the things which are written in this book" (Revelation 22:18–19).

26

Lazarus and the Rich Man: When Is the Judgment?

Does it matter when the judgment is? In a word: no.

This is yet another thing that is hardly a "salvation issue," but it does address the judgment and the question of whether or not judgment is, indeed, a meeting of all the souls at one time or an individual meeting with Jesus at the point of death.

This study will not attempt to give a definitive answer. Only those who have gone before us can tell those of us who have not yet gone. The point that we hope to make here is that either scenario will result in the same outcome for eternity.

The question arises with Jesus relating the story of Lazarus and the rich man in Luke 16:19–31. Jesus told of a beggar named Lazarus and what happens to those "rich" of the world who "know not the love of God." Jesus related the story thusly.

> There was a certain rich man, which was clothed in purple and fine linen, and fared sumptuously every day: And there was a certain beggar named Lazarus, which was laid at his gate, full of sores, And desiring to be fed with the crumbs which fell from the rich man's table: moreover the dogs came and licked his sores.
>
> And it came to pass, that the beggar died, and was carried by the angels into Abraham's bosom: the rich man also died, and was buried; And in hell he lift up his eyes, being in torments, and seeth Abraham afar off, and Lazarus in his bosom. And he

> cried and said, "Father Abraham, have mercy on me, and send Lazarus, that he may dip the tip of his finger in water, and cool my tongue; for I am tormented in this flame."
>
> But Abraham said, "Son, remember that thou in thy lifetime receivedst thy good things, and likewise Lazarus evil things: but now he is comforted, and thou art tormented. And beside all this, between us and you there is a great gulf fixed: so that they which would pass from hence to you cannot; neither can they pass to us, that would come from thence."
>
> Then he said, "I pray thee therefore, father, that thou wouldest send him to my father's house: For I have five brethren; that he may testify unto them, lest they also come into this place of torment."
>
> Abraham saith unto him, "They have Moses and the prophets; let them hear them." And he said, "Nay, father Abraham: but if one went unto them from the dead, they will repent." And he said unto him, "If they hear not Moses and the prophets, neither will they be persuaded, though one rose from the dead." (Luke 16:19–31)

Jesus didn't introduce this story as a parable by saying "is like unto," "hear another parable," or "harken and understand." Neither is the story introduced as a parable, as many parables were, by the Scripture itself.*

Many, if not most, commentaries and scholars make that same distinction. Many also make the same point that I do: the story is viable whether it's a parable or an account of Jesus' own memory. I'll not get into the many details intimated in the story, for it would remove us from our discourse. Suffice it to say that many believe Jesus to be telling a true story rather than a parable.

Jesus Gives a Hint

As we mentioned, many point out that Jesus told the story like a person relating a memory. It's certain that if the story of Lazarus is true, Jesus was telling it from memory. This, of course, favors the idea of individual judgment.

---

* See also chapter 32, "The Shrewd Steward."

Those who believe this story to be evidence of individual judgment also point to the "two other malefactors" who were crucified with Jesus. You know the story. "And Jesus said unto him, Verily I say unto thee, To day shalt thou be with me in paradise" (Luke 23:43).

This certainly shows that this particular malefactor was not going to wait on a cumulative judgment day.

In chapter 23 of this book, "Did Jesus Go to Hell?," we discussed Peter's words about "those in prison" referring to the dead after the deluge of Noah's time (and unknown others). The phrase "in prison" could be seen to allude to their sentence having already been pronounced.

Was It Heaven and Hell?

If the story of Lazarus and the rich man is a true story, which it seems to be, it indicates that judgment is a single event for individuals at the point of death.

The point of the story is not *when* the judgment is, but that there *is* a judgment!

If the story is from the memory of Jesus, Lazarus went to "the bosom of Abraham"—as heaven was known to the Jews at the time of Jesus. The rich man went to hell and was tormented from the moment he got there.

What About the Bible?

What about the return of Jesus? The Bible and the words of Jesus speak about the return of Jesus to the earth on the final day of Earth's existence. It doesn't matter whether you believe this to be *the* judgment day for every soul that has ever occupied a body, or simply the largest judgment day out of the many others that have already occurred with the daily deaths of saints and sinners throughout history. The point is this: "It is appointed unto men once to die, but after this the judgment" (Hebrews 9:27).

27

Are There Still Miracles?

The modern definition of *miracle* is "an event that appears inexplicable by the laws of nature and so is held to be supernatural in origin or an act of God."

There are many of the church who will tell you that we no longer live in the "age of miracles." This, in actuality, is true. We will no longer see someone simply call into the sepulchre of a man who has been dead for four days and raise that person from the dead. Jesus did that in the eleventh chapter of John.

These acts were considered to be "signs and wonders" by both those who performed the acts and those who witnessed them. I believe that this is a good distinction and should be used today as well.

We no longer see "signs and wonders" as proof of God's power, because we have the New Testament Scripture, and those people of Jesus' time did not. We have the written testimony of many apostles and the witness of the Holy Spirit for us to believe.

However, we see miracles daily. Why do you think we use the phrase "the miracle of life"? I remember the song "I Believe," which says, "Every time I hear a newborn baby cry, or touch a leaf, or see the sky … then I know why I believe."

Most Christians have had something happen in their lives that simply cannot be explained. People often speak of living through a car wreck that should have killed them, or of being spared calamity by something, somehow moving them by only a matter of inches—or keeping them from it. The believing Christian takes pause and says, "Thank you, Lord," because, to the Christian, *coincidence is when God wishes to remain anonymous.*

Semantics

The problem arises when we don't see God's action as a very real part of our Christian life. When we attempt to "explain away" the daily miracles that occur, we rob God of the praise that He alone deserves. I, personally, have seen this happen—in church. Things like healing and special needs being met are very carefully called "God's providence" for fear of using the word *miracle.*

We all should believe that all things good come from God. This, of course, includes the *providence* of God. However, God's providence does not include miracles (acts of God). A square can be a rectangle, but a rectangle can't be a square. That is to say that providence can be considered miraculous, as it certainly is, but miracles cannot be considered to be providence without stealing God's glory and robbing God of due praise.

Providence for the world is "the rain falls on the just and the unjust." Providence for the believer is "give us this day our daily bread." God's sovereign will and God's covenant are "God will provide." That is *provide-ence.*

Miracles are "God in motion," not God's *plans* in motion. God has promised to preserve the Word and protect the believers. How can God act without our calling it an act of God? If there are no miracles (acts of God) in our daily lives, why should we even pray?

Wouldn't "Signs and Wonders" Help?

Many "signs and wonders" were performed by Jesus, the apostles, and those chosen by the apostles by the "laying on of hands." The "signs and wonders" of Sunday school were mostly turning water into wine and multiplying food, like the loaves and fishes. Other "signs and wonders" were performed multiple times that we have record of—and many other times that we don't know about. These "other" miracles included acts of healing and even literally returning the dead to life. John 21:25 (the last verse of the book) reads, "And there are also many other things which Jesus did, the which, if they should be written every one, I suppose that even the world itself could not contain the books that should be written. Amen."

God made this point when He told the rich man in Luke 16* that one more miracle would not change anything. It's true, you know. People who are disposed to a sinful life cannot be changed without a change in their personal conscience. They will rationalize even the most miraculous happening with some physical reason that makes sense to them and will turn back to "wallowing in the mire."

* See chapter 26, "Lazarus and the Rich Man" for greater detail.

28

The Armor of God

Armor means war. Indeed, warriors wear armor. Diplomats and negotiators do not. Think on that.

If you truly do not think of putting on the armor of God when you get out of bed—while you're saying your "good morning" prayer to God—you need to look at your priorities. If you get started on your day without either, you are unprepared for what will unfold before you.

First Line of Defense

The believer is God's first line of defense. That's what the armor of God is about: *defense*. I interject here a verbatim excerpt from the opening of *Letter to a Christian Nation*, a book written by Sam Harris, one of the more contemporary flag-bearers of humanism.

As I've said before, in this new age of communication where even the smallest voice can gain an audience, we must stand firm with the whole, singular truth of the Scripture. In the excerpt that follows, any emphasis, italics, or bracketed commentary is my own added emphasis.

> You believe that the Bible is the word of God, that Jesus is the Son of God, and that only those who place their faith in Jesus will find salvation after death. As a Christian, you believe these propositions not because they make you feel good, but because you think they are true. Before I point out some of the problems with these beliefs, I would like to acknowledge that there are

many points on which you and I agree. *We agree, for instance, that if one of us is right, the other is wrong. The Bible is either the word of God, or it isn't. Either Jesus offers humanity the one, true path to salvation (John 14:6), or he does not. We agree that to be a true Christian is to believe that all other faiths are mistaken, and profoundly so. If Christianity is correct, and I persist in my unbelief, I should expect to suffer the torments of hell.*

Worse still, I have persuaded others, and many close to me, to reject the very idea of God. They too will languish in "eternal fire" (Matthew 25:41). [I think Sam meant to cite verse 46.] If the basic doctrine of Christianity is correct, I have misused my life in the worst conceivable way [unpardonable sin]. I admit this without a single caveat. The fact that my continuous and public rejection of Christianity does not worry me in the least should suggest to you just how inadequate I think your reasons for being a Christian are.

Of course, there are Christians who do not agree with either of us. There are Christians who consider other faiths to be equally valid paths to salvation. There are Christians who have no fear of hell and who do not believe in the physical resurrection of Jesus. These Christians often describe themselves as "religious liberals" or "religious moderates." *From their point of view, you and I have both misunderstood what it means to be a person of faith.* There is, we are assured, a vast and beautiful terrain between atheism and religious fundamentalism that generations of thoughtful Christians have quietly explored. According to liberals and moderates, faith is about mystery, and meaning, and community, and love. People make religion out of the full fabric of their lives, not out of mere beliefs.

I have written elsewhere about the problems I see with religious liberalism and religious moderation. Here, we need only observe that the issue is both simpler and more urgent than liberals and moderates generally admit. *Either the Bible is just an ordinary book, written by mortals, or it isn't. Either Christ was divine, or he was not. If the Bible is an ordinary book, and Christ an ordinary man, the basic doctrine of Christianity is false. If the Bible is an ordinary book, and Christ an ordinary man, the history of Christian theology is the story of bookish men parsing a collective delusion. If the basic tenets of Christianity are true, then there are some very grim surprises in store for*

> *nonbelievers like myself.* You understand this. At least half of the American population understands this. So let us be honest with ourselves: *in the fullness of time, one side is really going to win this argument, and the other side is really going to lose.* (Sam Harris, *Letter to a Christian Nation*, circa May, 2006)

This humanist makes the case better than most. The problem is not with God. The problem is not with God's plan of salvation. The problem is not with believers. The problem *is* with the adulteration of the Word! The problem *is* with man's ever-changing definition of Christianity!

Humanists intentionally confuse the context, and thereby the true meaning, of the Word. Notice, however, that in order to have any argument at all, the humanist must study the Word. That is the beauty of the Word. It must be searched, even by detractors.

Those same humanists point to the disunity of the message of Christianity as the main reason not to believe any of it. The real problem is with the lack of understanding on their part. They have not asked for interpretation, and no one has offered.

As we said at the outset, we'll not deride anyone for believing this way. Our discussion of humanism, specifically, will not continue further—except to thank the humanists for pointing out where the real problems are.

The Real Problem

We must point out here that there are going to be detractors of the truth. However, what has been identified very plainly above is that the real problem is *true faith*, or more precisely, the lack thereof.

In the preface of this book, we saw that one must decide what to do with the truth. I will repeat it here to make the point.

In every Bible study, the choices are:

- Adjust my beliefs as I increase in understanding.
- Adjust or "jigsaw" Scripture to better fit my existing belief (which, by the way, takes a lot more time and effort).

- Ignore the passages and study around them (Occam's Broom).
- Start a new religion that discounts the difficult passages. (This is more common than you'd think.)

The humanist reminds us that there are those who call themselves "religious liberals" or "religious moderates." These have chosen to ignore some Scripture and to "jigsaw" other Scripture in order to feel that it fits better with the worldly worldview. I heard the following first (I think) from Shane Idleman: "The church does the most good for the world when it is least like the world."

It's human nature to respect a person who has a firm stance on any issue. This is why vacillating politicians are often called liars—as are many so-called Christians. If the Word of God has not changed, how can the stance of Christians today be any different from those of the first century?

What About the Armor of God?

You're right. That is our discourse here. The previous was another of those "I said all of that to say this" preambles. Our real discussion here is the adulteration of God's truth. Let's look at the Scripture in Ephesians 6:10–18. Paul was exhorting the Ephesians to a stronger faith with even greater works in an already strong church. At the end of his letter, he wrote,

> Finally, my brethren, be strong in the Lord, and in the power of his might. Put on the whole armour of God, that ye may be able to stand against the wiles of the devil. For we wrestle not against flesh and blood, but against principalities, against powers, against the rulers of the darkness of this world, against spiritual wickedness in high places. Wherefore take unto you the whole armour of God, that ye may be able to withstand in the evil day, and having done all, to stand. Stand therefore, having your loins girt about with truth, and having on the breastplate of righteousness; And your feet shod with the preparation of the gospel of peace; Above all, taking the shield of faith, wherewith ye shall be able to quench all the fiery darts of the wicked. And take the helmet of salvation, and the sword of the Spirit, which is the word of God.

If we dig a little into this passage, we find some things that many have not seen.

First, note that Paul tells us that we are not fighting against men. We are fighting "against principalities, against powers, against the rulers of the darkness of this world, against spiritual wickedness in high places."

Ours is spiritual warfare. We need to realize that we are not fighting people who espouse the "ways of the wicked"; this is only the symptom. We are fighting Satan and sin and against the powers that come with them; this is the disease.

Second, and perhaps more importantly, Paul says that we *wrestle*. Paul was an athlete, and he knew what he was writing. Wrestling is perhaps the most close-contact conflict one can realize. It is sweaty. It is constant. It is grappling for position, and it will not end until one opponent is pinned to the ground! There is nothing casual about our fight.

Let's look at the armor itself.

The Belt	Truth
The Breastplate	Righteousness
The Foot Armor	The Gospel of Peace (Good News of Peace with God)
The Shield	Faith (above all)
The Helmet	Salvation
The Sword of the Spirit	The Word of God

The *belt of truth* is used to "gird the loins." It is used to keep the usually longer and flowing robes up between the legs and around the waist like a loincloth so one can maneuver and won't stumble over one's own clothes. Some say how tight it was depended on the reason for it—like an athletic supporter as opposed to just avoiding a nuisance.

The *breastplate of righteousness* is used to ward off direct shots to the body, the center of life and home of the heart.

The *foot armor of the gospel* protects the feet. If the feet are injured, the person can't even move to dodge or answer an attack.

The *shield of faith* is mobile and can protect any part necessary. It can especially protect against arrows (fiery darts).

The *helmet of salvation* protects the head. Without the head, the body is useless.

The *sword of the Word* is the "business end" of a warrior, used to injure an attacker.

As I was beginning this work, I nearly named this book after this passage. I thought to title it with one word: *Stand*. Three times in this short passage, Paul told us to *stand*. In verses 13–14, Paul said it twice, back to back: "Wherefore take unto you the whole armour of God, that ye may be able to withstand in the evil day, and having done all, to *stand. Stand therefore …*"

"The evil day," by the way, has no special meaning other to than to say that there are going to be days when you will have to depend on your armor and hush those who would adulterate the Word and/or the truth.

Remember that Paul, by avocation, was an athlete. The word *stand* used to convey Paul's meaning is translated to "stand still and firm," like a wrestler about to get hit. That is a defensive stance.

The soldier we envision is not advancing. He is defending what he has been charged to protect, and he is not giving ground! Nor will he, to the best of his ability, let anything get past him to harm what he is protecting. One can also envision that he is ready to strike with his sword, but only if necessary.

Without fail, defending the Word is far different from what we discussed earlier about forming a defense for what we want the Scripture to say (*eisegesis* rather than *exegesis*). Remember that the *belt of truth* is to be about our waist.

Jesus was tempted by Satan himself. That single fact proves Jesus' readiness to "stand against the wiles of the Devil." In each and every instance that Jesus was "attacked," He answered wisely and used the Scripture judiciously. Jesus "struck" Satan with the sword of the Word by saying "it is written" in every answer to Satan's tests. Notice that Jesus stopped after He quoted the Scripture; that was enough. Jesus offered no theological discussion or fancy explanation. Jesus struck soundly with the *sword of the Spirit*, the Word of God.

That brings us to the next proof of Paul's meaning. Out of all the armor of God, the sword is the only offensive weapon. The armor of God is for protection—for defense–with the exception of the sword. The sword, if used judiciously, can be used to fend off attackers without leaving one's post.

That's what this passage is all about. Paul is *not* talking about evangelism. Paul is *not* talking about gaining ground in any way. Paul is talking about defending the truth.

Paul, in his inspired message, is "posting" us in positions around the truth of God's Word. We are charged with protecting "the truth, the whole truth, and nothing but the truth."

Aren't we doing that? In many ways, yes. In far too many ways, the answer is a resounding *no*!

The humanist excerpt earlier made it clear that those outside Christianity see believers as two-faced, wishy-washy people who wish to "fit in" rather than stand firm. Hopefully, we can all point to someone we know who will not "give an inch" on matters of faith—and life.

The most contemporary public example is Ronald Reagan. Even his staunchest political enemies voted for him, because they knew where he stood on virtually every issue. Reagan didn't wave his faith like a banner, but *everyone* considered him to be a man of integrity who would stand behind whatever he said—not with impunity but with conviction.

Religious Fundamentalism

Religious fundamentalism has become a "buzzword phrase" meant to be demeaning and slanderous among those outside Christianity. In fact, it has become used more and more by Christian moderates and religious liberals as well—also to demean and slander.

The problem lies in the fact that many consider the "umbrella" of the words *religion* and *religious* to encompass all people who feel they have some deity or "higher power." In this work, we have discussed the only way to salvation, and the many ways that humankind has decided are better, more convenient, or easier to believe.

In the introduction to this book, I said this about truth: "The largest single argument against defensive behavior is the simple fact that truth needs no defense, nor does it need a defender. Yes, there are those who would detract from the truth, and those who would listen to those detractors. This does not change the truth. We will see, as Lancelot said, "But at the length truth will out."

It is not contradictory to say, "the truth needs no defender," and also to say, "we must defend the truth." In this chapter, we have shown that we must defend what is the truth from those who will distort it to suit themselves. The truth is the truth; it needs no defense. The distortions of those who would have us believe other things and do things counter to the teachings of Jesus are what we must defend against.

We must remember what we have seen previously. Satan wants us to be faithful in *wrongful* faith even more than he wants us to curse God. Our zealous pursuit of the wrong path is to the greatest sorrow of God. We're not told to "attack" anyone, but we're told—with no uncertain words—that we are to defend the truth with the strength of warriors.

Hereby, we assure those "with ears to hear" that modern religious fundamentalism is miles away from a true faith in Christ. Make no mistake, however. There are fundamentals—God-given foundations—that cannot be altered. Herein, we have dealt with the true fundamentals of Christianity, and every reader has now heard the truth, the very *simple* truth given to us by Jesus, the Christ.

Detractors, at this point, are probably saying, "These/Those/They don't agree with you." We can't help that, except by praying for fertile fields in which to plant the seed.

I repeat the words of humanist Sam Harris, "So let us be honest with ourselves: in the fullness of time, one side is really going to win this argument, and the other side is really going to lose."

29

God's Glory

"Glory is praise." That's one option, but it's not *God's* glory.

For the most part, we use the term *glory* to indicate praise simply because everyone else does. The truth is that the glory of God is a "thing" with physical properties.

The glory of God is, quite literally, the brilliance of God. It exists because God is. The purity of God is radiant. From a human aspect, to look upon the actual glory of God is tantamount to looking at the sun. The glory of God is both evidence and manifestation of righteousness, goodness, and purity on a scale we cannot fathom.

When God said, "Let there be light," He allowed His goodness and, thereby, His glory to pervade His creation, and it was illuminated by it. At that point in the story of creation, there was no sun; that wasn't created until the fourth day. The glory of God was the only light. When we're told to "walk in the light as He is in the light," we are not being given some cute metaphor. We are told to walk in the light of God's glory, the light of God's purity.

The psalmist said in Psalm 89:15, "Blessed is the people that know the joyful sound: they shall walk, O LORD, in the light of thy countenance."

There are other Scriptures that give us direction to this thought, but you can see the point. Have you heard someone say something like, "That's so cute it hurts"? To the human perception, God's purity is visible in our world in the form of powerfully pure light—painful to look at, but wonderfully beautiful to perceive.

The Confusion

The Hebrew word, *kâbôd* (kaw-bode'), has been translated to many words in the King James translation. Both it and the root word *kābēd* (kaw-bad') are used primarily to indicate weight, as in "his word carries more weight." This must have been taken to mean that "He carries more weight and therefore is worthy of praise (or honor)." The former is understood in a good way (famous), and the root is understood in a bad way (infamous).

Our "good" word, *kâbôd*, is translated 156 times to the word *glory*. It is also translated 32 times to the word *honour*. One can see where there might be some confusion. There are a few other words that translate to either glory or honour as well.

Hebrew is a language of description. Hence, names are more a description of a person than a way to call them for supper. However, those things that could not be described in accurate terms often fell to lesser words that didn't do justice to the description. We must always remember that these things of the Bible were written by and to people who didn't know or understand even the simplest science that we take for granted in this era.

Even so, more modern works have failed in our translations to understand the physical aspects of God's glory. In a sense, one might say—as we do so often that "there are no words" to describe it. However, to show a difference between the other uses of the word *glory* and the *glory of God*, we might do better to speak of the glory of God as *divine glory*.

Physical Example

When the people grumbled in Exodus 16, we see in verse 10 that a cloud appeared and "the *glory of the LORD* appeared in the cloud."

They went from Rephidim through the Sinai Desert to Mount Sinai. This, of course, was where God gave us the Ten Commandments and the rest of the Mosaic law. Upon their arrival, in chapter 19, the people were commanded to prepare to meet God on the "third day hence." God decided that the people needed absolute proof that Moses was not supernatural and that He, God, was God Almighty.

God descended to the mountain in a cloud of smoke, fire, lightning, and thunder. Notice, by the way, that throughout the Bible the voice of God is likened to thunder—awesome and due respect because of its natural exhibition of power.

The people told Moses that he should go talk to God and then return with whatever God said, because they were afraid of God speaking directly to them. We can see obvious modern parallels, but we'll not chase those rabbits here.

Therein, God began His covenant with the people and the grandest of all promises, which is still alive today. In Exodus 23:20, God promised that if we remain within His will, He will "send an Angel before thee, to keep thee in the way, and to bring thee into the place which I have prepared." The people really knew nothing of the Holy Spirit, but they understood angels.

Moses wrote the law in the "book of the covenant," and on the morning of Exodus 24, he built an altar and followed all of God's commands. Moses, Aaron, Nadab, Abihu, and seventy elders went toward the mountaintop. "And they saw the God of Israel: and there was under his feet as it were a paved work of a sapphire stone, and as it were *the body of heaven in his clearness*" (v. 10, emphasis added).

When God came, He appeared awesome and fearful to make sure that the people knew that none of the happenings were of humanity's making and that God's power and command were truly evident. However, having made His point—and the covenant with Moses—God called Moses up the mountain to get the laws on tablets so they could be remembered and taught—word for word—as they had been given by God.

God's power was understood, and now His purity could be shown as well. In Exodus 24:15–17, the scenario unfolds. "And Moses went up into the mount, and a cloud covered the mount. And the *glory of the LORD* abode upon mount Sinai, and the cloud covered it six days: and the seventh day he called unto Moses out of the midst of the cloud. And the sight of the *glory of the LORD* was like *devouring fire* on the top of the mount in the eyes of the children of Israel"

A "devouring fire" was the brightest light that any person of that era could think of. A raging fire was the most brilliant and awesomely powerful light of that time.

In the middle of the remaining instructions of the book of Exodus, there is another citation of *glory*. God said that when He came to dwell in the tabernacle, "there I will meet with the children of Israel, and the tabernacle shall be *sanctified by my glory*" (Exodus 29:43, emphasis added).

Here we see another major point. There is now no doubt that divine glory is a real thing. We now also see that divine glory, filled with the power of God, actually works to sanctify both the people and things it touches.

In our modern times, do we not sanitize things simply by putting them in ultraviolet light? How much more would something be sanctified by being in God's glory?

More Proof

Just like other humans, Moses was concerned about two things. First, Moses wanted "a little something" that would prove that he had found favor in the eyes of God. Second, He wanted something that would prove, when he went back to the people, that God was with them. Moses sought to view the divine glory. Until that point—and thereafter as well—God's glory had been a light "veiled" by cloud.

The reason for this discussion between Moses and God was that Moses had already been given two tablets, but he had broken them at the sight of the sin of the people. In the often overlooked passage of Exodus 33:16–23, Moses posed his concerns, and God responded with the best He could do and still allow Moses to "live to tell the tale." Moses asked,

> For wherein shall it be known here that I and thy people have found grace in thy sight? is it not in that thou goest with us? so shall we be separated, I and thy people, from all the people that are upon the face of the earth. And the LORD said unto Moses, I will do this thing also that thou hast spoken: for thou hast found grace in my sight, and I know thee by name. And he [Moses] said, *I beseech thee, shew me thy glory.* And he [God] said, I will make all my goodness pass before thee, and I will proclaim the name of the LORD before thee; and will be gracious to whom I will be gracious, and will shew mercy on whom I will shew mercy.

God was saying that only He would decide what happened, but He wanted to comply with Moses' request, because Moses had found favor in the eyes of the LORD. "And he [God] said, Thou canst not see my face: for there shall no man see me, and live. And the LORD said, Behold, there is a place by me, and thou shalt stand upon a rock: And it shall come to pass, while my glory passeth by, that I will put thee in a clift of the rock, and will cover thee with my hand while I pass by: And I will take away mine hand, and thou shalt see my back parts: but my face shall not be seen."

God told Moses that he would have to get behind "a rock beside me" that would shade him from the searing brilliance of God's *divine glory.* God Himself would shade Moses with His hand while He passed by. After God had passed, He would remove His hand so that Moses could see God "going away" or "at a safe distance." Remember that Moses could only slightly envision God's divine glory based on his minimal experience at the burning bush.

Moses had set up a base camp a little ways down the mountain where Joshua, his minister, waited. God said that Moses was to return to the mountaintop the next day and prepare himself by getting behind "that rock," and that He (God) would give Moses another set of tablets and would afterward pass by him to show him His glory. God did so, and it confirmed the covenant in the first part of Exodus 34.

Indwelling of Divine Glory

In Exodus 34, Moses came down from the mountain and returned to the people with tablets in hand. Moses was not aware that his own face shone with divine glory because of his earlier proximity to it and, of course, to God Himself.

Let me give you an idea of the "translation barrier" here. The glory that shone from Moses' head and face was written as *qāran*, which literally means "horns." Of course, the people were trying to describe the beaming radiance of what we have come to call an "aura." Through the years, artists have depicted it in various ways, like a halo or some such. The closest thing that the ancient Hebrews could use for the "beams" of that radiance (like a spotlight) was "horns." In fact, medieval sculpture and art is shown using a literal interpretation of the Scripture—with Moses actually having horns.

There is little doubt that the physical appearance of Moses was equal to the appearance of Jesus at His transfiguration thousands of years later. In Matthew 17:2, we're told that Jesus "was transfigured before them: and his face did shine as the sun, and his raiment was white as the light."

Aaron and the "rulers of the congregation" were afraid to approach Moses because of the brilliance of the divine glory that was in Moses. This glory was certainly *visible and discernable.*

Just as God cannot look upon sin, sinful people, apparently, cannot look upon the glory of God—or are certainly fearful of doing so. While Moses spoke to the people, he wore a veil to shade the brilliance of the glory. We can have little doubt that the people were concerned about their very lives after the Levites killed three thousand men for worshipping the golden calf. We're told over and over that sin runs from the light.

In Exodus 34:33–35, we read the story. "And till Moses had done speaking with them, he put a vail on his face. But when Moses went in before the LORD to speak with him, he took the vail off, until he came out. And he came out, and spake unto the children of Israel that which he was commanded. And the children of Israel saw the face of Moses, that the skin of Moses' face shone [as with horns, beams of light]: and Moses put the vail upon his face again, until he went in to speak with him [God]."

New Testament Example

Is it a mistake to say that Jesus had not been "glorified" before His death? John 7:37–39 says, "In the last day, that great day of the feast, Jesus stood and cried, saying, If any man thirst, let him come unto me, and drink. He that believeth on me, as the scripture hath said, out of his belly shall flow rivers of living water. (But this spake he of the Spirit, which they that believe on him should receive: for the Holy Ghost was not yet given; because that *Jesus was not yet glorified*" (emphasis added).

The passage plainly says that the Holy Ghost was not yet given (as it was later on the day of Pentecost), because Jesus was not yet glorified. Many people say that this passage says that Jesus was not yet famous. That would be believable if it were not for the notation of the Holy Spirit. Jesus told us plainly in John 16:7, "Nevertheless I tell you the truth; It is expedient for you that I go away: for if I go not away, the Comforter will not come unto you; but if I depart, I will send him unto you."

To "be glorified" is an act, not a simple figure of speech. To be specific, it is an act of the purity and goodness of God. We have seen that glorification is attained by direct contact with the divine glory of God Almighty, as it was with both Moses and Jesus. For most believers, glorification will come at death/judgment.

Which Is Correct?

This is another thing that will neither get you into heaven nor keep you out. Our endeavor throughout this study is understanding. To say, "Give God the glory" is quite correct if you mean "praise God." Even though we really can't give something we don't have, it's still simply a matter of semantics.

Understanding that there is a difference between praise glory and divine glory is the thrust of this chapter. Being correct or incorrect doesn't enter in, unless you now try to deny that divine glory exists. That would be foolish.

30

Continual Cleansing

The Original Source of Thought

Nowhere in the Bible is found the phrase "continual cleansing" or "continually cleans" or "as soon as you sin" or any other such. This is another of those transliterated thoughts that arise from interpretations of the Scripture to better or more comfortably fit humanity's understanding and personal life.

The doctrine of *continual cleansing* comes from a single verse of the New Testament. We read in 1 John 1:7, "But if we walk in the light, as he is in the light, we have fellowship one with another, and the blood of Jesus Christ his Son cleanses us from all sin."

The point of continual cleansing in that verse is this: "the blood of Jesus Christ his Son cleanses us from all sin." That means, considering rules of grammar, that the blood keeps cleansing. That much is absolutely correct. In Romans 9:10, we read, "Knowing that Christ being raised from the dead dieth no more; death hath no more dominion over him. For in that he died, he died unto sin *once*: but in that he liveth, he liveth unto God" (emphasis added).

Jesus died once, and that perfect sacrifice need never be repeated. We all agree on that. However, people continue to throw hypothetical scenarios at this and other points of Scripture to such a degree that only confusion remains. As I said in the introduction, *ad hoc* hypotheses will find no home here.

God can handle anything, no matter what it is. God can—and will—render judgment instantly on things about which we could spend a lifetime debating and asking "what if." God knows where He stands on every issue. We cannot presume to know the mind of God. More importantly, we should never presume that we might be capable of same.

We are given the Holy Scripture, and with the Holy Scripture we will remain.

One Extreme View: Instant Forgiveness

The first "extreme" basically argues that God is continually cleansing us—whether or not we acknowledge our sins. Basically, it says that once someone becomes a Christian, the blood of Jesus is continually cleansing the person from all sins, regardless of what he does. This is one proof used by the believers of the "once saved, always saved" theology.

Hypothetically, this view argues that I can "spend my inheritance on riotous living" with no worries about my salvation. Without further example, it is saying, "I can [you pick the sin], and it disappears from my permanent record as soon as I do it."

The *instant forgiveness* slant on continual cleansing disregards the context of the original passage. The complete passage is 1 John 1:5–10.

> This then is the message which we have heard of him, and declare unto you, that God is light, and in him is no darkness at all. If we say that we have fellowship with him, and walk in darkness, we lie, and do not the truth: *But if we walk in the light*, as he is in the light, we have fellowship one with another, and the blood of Jesus Christ his Son cleanseth us from all sin. If we say that we have no sin, we deceive ourselves, and the truth is not in us. If we confess our sins, he is faithful and just to forgive us our sins, and to cleanse us from all unrighteousness. If we say that we have not sinned, we make him a liar, and his word is not in us. (emphasis added)

First and foremost, no cleansing of any sort is blindly promised to Christians or others; it is conditional. John says the condition is this: "if we walk in the light."

To suggest in any way that a Christian can run roughshod over the moral will of God without recompense of any sort is, for lack of a stronger word, ludicrous. Many, at this point, say that a true Christian wouldn't do such things. We all certainly wish not. However, saying that then says that the severity of sin has a "breaking point" at which continual cleansing no longer applies. We must realize that God sees any and all sin to be sin, period.

This point is that we must not only become Christians but must also do our best to remain Christians—in word and deed—before we can even think of forgiveness on any scale. This is not meant to seem legalistic but to point to *living a right life*, which is the very simple requirement given to us by Jesus Himself.

Another thing suggested by *instant forgiveness* is that if a Christian's sins are forgiven as they are committed—the instant they are committed—a continual state of sinlessness is attained. That being the case, a person's conduct again is irrelevant to his salvation. John contradicts that in verse 8: "If we say that we have no sin, we deceive ourselves, and the truth is not in us."

Another Extreme View: Detailed Confession

The polar opposite of instant forgiveness is *detailed confession*. There are legalists out there who believe that one must enumerate and confess, with as much detail as possible, each and every sin that has been committed. This actually strains most imaginations. The principle thought here is that if we do not confess it, it will not be forgiven. In the larger sense, that is true, but not in the sense of this argument.

The first very real problem is that we are human. Imperfect humans have imperfect memories. This would mean that we'd have to spend most of our time remembering, recording, or writing down all our sins, with little time to do anything else. It might be productive, however, we wouldn't have time to sin in the first place, eh?

The second very real problem is also a result of our being human. We can "offend thy brother" or "cause thy brother to stumble" and not even know it. However, to "offend thy brother" or "cause thy brother to stumble" is a sin by the perception of others at the very least. How can we remember a sin if we don't know we've committed it in the first place?

On both counts just listed, we must realize that without a deep lifelong communion with God Almighty, we won't come to a realization of a life of true righteousness. Our life will become "cleaner" as we go through it with God, but we will rarely, if ever, be able to "police" our lives to the point of sinlessness. David was speaking of the beauty of the law when he wrote in Psalm 19:12, "Who can understand his errors? cleanse thou me from secret faults."

David was asking God's help and forgiveness for things of his daily life, but David was saying in this particular verse that he may have sinned and didn't realize it. He was also asking for forgiveness of unknown sins.

Again, there are hypothetical scenarios we can apply here, but you know how we feel about that.

Confession in the True Spiritual Sense

Paul wrote in Romans 3:23, "For all have sinned, and come short of the glory of God." God inspired Paul to write that. Do you think that God doesn't know it? Our confession is a confession of our sinful state. Forgiveness is afforded to all those who have followed the examples and teachings of Jesus.

Our confession is in asking forgiveness for "missing the mark," not for any specific sin. Certainly, we can ask for forgiveness for any specific action, but enumeration is not necessary. God knows already. God forgives us because we know we need forgiveness, not because of any specific action.

After a while, though, you'll begin to notice areas of sin in your life. As you ask for forgiveness, you may need to ask for strength, courage, and other attributes necessary to bolster those weak spots, as did David.

The Bottom Line

Living a right life within the will of God will see you in prayer often. You will have opportunity to ask forgiveness in your closet. You can utter a quick prayer as you're walking across the yard or driving to the store or doing anything that allows your mind a free moment. "Forgive me" should be on your lips constantly. If so, you are "walking in the light" and have no fear of not receiving forgiveness in whatever quantity you need.

The simplicity of the passage can be expressed this way: "The blood of Jesus Christ his Son cleanseth us from all sin"—continuously, *if we also continuously ask for forgiveness*, and thereby we remain in a "saved" (not sinless) state.

The study in this chapter is purely applied to forgiveness of our confessed sinful state. We have addressed the need for living a right life elsewhere in this work on numerous occasions.

31

The Prodigal Son

The "Why" of the Story

Most everyone has heard the story of the Prodigal Son. *Prodigal*, by the way, does not mean "runaway," "defiant," or any such. *Prodigal*, by definition, means "spending money or resources freely and recklessly; wastefully extravagant." You'll also note that the word is not used anywhere in the King James Version or near translations.

The story is told by Jesus as further emphasis on the feeling in heaven over the salvation of a single soul. We often call Luke 15 the "lost and found" chapter. Jesus first told the parable of a shepherd who recovered his lost sheep and a woman who recovered a lost coin. Jesus was telling us that with the salvation of a single soul, all of heaven stops to rejoice. Your soul is that important to God.

The Story

The parable of the prodigal son is told to us in Luke 15:11–32.

> And he [Jesus] said, A certain man had two sons: And the younger of them said to his father, Father, give me the portion of goods that falleth to me. And he divided unto them his living. And not many days after the younger son gathered all together, and took his journey into a far country, and there wasted his substance with riotous living.

And when he had spent all, there arose a mighty famine in that land; and he began to be in want. And he went and joined himself to a citizen of that country; and he sent him into his fields to feed swine. And he would fain have filled his belly with the husks that the swine did eat: and no man gave unto him.

And when he came to himself, he said, How many hired servants of my father's have bread enough and to spare, and I perish with hunger! I will arise and go to my father, and will say unto him, Father, I have sinned against heaven, and before thee, And am no more worthy to be called thy son: make me as one of thy hired servants.

And he arose, and came to his father. But when he was yet a great way off, his father saw him, and had compassion, and ran, and fell on his neck, and kissed him. And the son said unto him, Father, I have sinned against heaven, and in thy sight, and am no more worthy to be called thy son.

But the father said to his servants, Bring forth the best robe, and put it on him; and put a ring on his hand, and shoes on his feet: And bring hither the fatted calf, and kill it; and let us eat, and be merry: For this my son was dead, and is alive again; he was lost, and is found. And they began to be merry.

Now his elder son was in the field: and as he came and drew nigh to the house, he heard music and dancing. And he called one of the servants, and asked what these things meant. And he said unto him, Thy brother is come; and thy father hath killed the fatted calf, because he hath received him safe and sound.

And he was angry, and would not go in: therefore came his father out, and intreated him. And he answering said to his father, Lo, these many years do I serve thee, neither transgressed I at any time thy commandment: and yet thou never gavest me a kid, that I might make merry with my friends: But as soon as this thy son was come, which hath devoured thy living with harlots, thou hast killed for him the fatted calf.

And he said unto him, Son, thou art ever with me, and all that I have is thine. It was meet that we should make merry, and be glad: for this thy brother was dead, and is alive again; and was lost, and is found.

The First Lesson

Notice that a good number of the parables of Jesus begin with all things equal. This is one of those. The saved are all blessed with many things we would not have if we lived "outside the family." The son we call "prodigal" was exactly that. In verse 13, we see that the son took what he had been given and not only left the family but "wasted his substance with riotous living."

Jesus showed us how the son fell to the depths of degradation. Ultimately, the son was relegated to tending the swine, and all he had to eat was the garbage that was fed to the pigs. Living with swine seems ugly enough, but realize that swine were considered unclean by the Jews. Not only was the son living with "unclean" people but with the unclean animals. All he had to eat was what was given to these same unclean animals. To the Jews of the day, this was a "fate worse than death."

We touched on this when we talked about God's discipline.* Realize, again, that nothing bad comes from God. However, realize that when God "steps back," or when we remove God from our lives by "leaving the family," "not good" things begin to happen. This is simply the occasion of no longer receiving God's blessing of protection or even advice. This discipline is exhibited by the son's predicament. The son was simply learning from his own mistakes.

While not applicable here, we can now understand that when we're told that "God hardened his heart," this simply means that God stopped intervening with a person's thoughts. That person's heart invariably turns to sin and the thoughts that come with it, and his heart "hardens" against God.

The son left the family and, left to his own devices, wasted his life. In verses 17–18, the son "came to his senses" and realized that even the servants of his family had more than enough to eat, just as the son himself had had before he left. The son decided to return home. There's a reason we call horse training "breaking a horse." Remember the "boot camp" comparison?

---

* See chapter 22, "Testing, Testing: Is That You, God?," specifically, our own failings.

A tacit lesson is this: to leave the family of God is to leave the umbrella of God's protection and blessing. We will invariably turn to sin, because there is nowhere else to turn.

A separate and very important thought is that the prayers of those who remain in the family will still be heard by God, of course. If even one of those faithful ones earnestly and fervently pray intercessory prayer for the person who has left, God will look after the person enough to at least keep him alive until he comes to his senses. I, personally, have seen this in action and have heard other stories with the same result.

The Second Lesson

The second lesson is about unconditional, forgiving love and begins with verse 20.

The son returned home. His father was obviously looking down the road whenever he could in anticipation of seeing his son. On this particular day, the father's wish was granted. It would probably be better to say that his prayers were answered. The father did not wait for the son to get closer but ran down the road to meet him.

The son told his father that he was not worthy to be a family member but that he wished his father would let him become "as one of your hired servants." The father didn't even answer the son but started ordering the servants to reinstate the son and celebrate his return. In verse 24 we're told that the father said, "'For this my son was dead, and is alive again; he was lost, and is found.' And they began to be merry."

Notice also that when we say *unconditional love*, we are speaking of the son returning to the father's unconditional love of acceptance and forgiveness. The love was at home, waiting, but the son had to go and get it. We must understand that forgiveness only comes to those who humbly go to the Father and ask for it. Joy fills heaven at that point, but not before.

The Third Lesson

This is a very real lesson that is lost in most renditions of this parable. The story continues in verse 25. The son who did not leave home was working in the field. He heard the commotion and asked one of the servants what was going on. In verse 27, he was told, "Thy brother is come; and thy father hath killed the fatted calf, because he hath received him safe and sound."

The celebration was for his long-lost brother who had come home again. Instead of being happy, the elder brother became angry, probably out of jealousy. He would not even come in to greet his brother or take part in the celebration.

The father came to that elder son and "intreated him" to come in. He told his father in verses 29–30, "Lo, these many years do I serve thee, neither transgressed I at any time thy commandment: and yet thou never gavest me a kid, that I might make merry with my friends: But as soon as this thy son was come, which hath devoured thy living with harlots, thou hast killed for him the fatted calf."

The elder son who had remained was applying the relativism yardstick that we studied in chapter 15 and elsewhere. We who read this story get so lost in the wonderful forgiveness of the father that we neglect the selfish jealousy of the elder son. How many times has the church membership failed to share the forgiveness granted by God with those whom it has deemed "not worthy?" Haven't those who returned home also been forgiven? Realize that these things too are counted toward the righteousness of the believers.

Look back at the parable of the workers in the vineyard, and see that this is not a point that is lost on God.[†] We would do well to also read the parable of the unmerciful servant in Matthew 18:23–35.

As members of God's church, we must remember that we are working for God, not the other way around. I have no doubt that lifelong members of the church who have lived lifelong righteous lives will probably receive a few more jewels for their crowns. However, *all* the faithful will be in heaven to see it.

Another very important thought here is that members of the church, like the elder son, all too often do not recognize the blessings of being "in the family." The remaining son was working in the field. Members of the church are, hopefully, also working in the field. Their common problem is that they both see being in the family as work without reward. This point of view deserves introspection by each and every one of us.

---

† See chapter 1, "There Are Minimum Requirements?," the section titled, "'It's My Money,' Says Jesus."

In verse 31, we read, "And he [the father] said unto him, Son, thou art ever with me, and all that I have is thine."

Remember the words of Jesus in Matthew 7:7–8 where God the Son told us the same thing in other words: "Ask, and it shall be given you; seek, and ye shall find; knock, and it shall be opened unto you: For every one that asketh receiveth; and he that seeketh findeth; and to him that knocketh it shall be opened."

The Theme of Luke 15

We mentioned the shepherd with a lost sheep and the woman with a lost coin whose stories are in this same fifteenth chapter of Luke. The Prodigal Son has separate lessons, but the theme of this entire chapter of the Bible is "lost and then found."

The story of the shepherd speaks directly to the church in relation to the lost. From His own lips, Jesus told us in verse 7, "I say unto you, that likewise joy shall be in heaven over one sinner that repenteth, more than over ninety and nine just persons, which need no repentance."

This is not that God loves the church less; that can never be. However, one saved soul is another victory over Satan, as well as another soul saved from eternal damnation. This is what we call a win-win situation. This should be reason for both earth and heaven to rejoice. We see, by what Jesus said, that heaven rejoices. The Christ's church here on earth should do no less. This is fruition of God's will (2 Peter 3:9).

32

The Shrewd Steward

A Difficult Passage

If you ask students of the Bible which passage they would consider most "difficult," most of them will choose the parable of the shrewd (unfaithful) steward more than any other. This parable immediately follows Luke's "lost and found" chapter.

This is one of the most seemingly contradictory passages in all of the Holy Scripture. It seems not only to contradict itself, but to contradict the teachings of Jesus. Add to it the fact that Jesus was telling the story, and most people simply say, "It's not for us to understand," and then move on. But we won't.

With this passage in particular, it is important to note that the language of translation does not truly match the meaning of the original—at least not in a modern sense of the English language. Translation of *thought* is difficult, at best, when a person tries to "put it into words."

Any teacher will tell you that teaching a *concept* is far more difficult than simply presenting facts. Concepts require genuine understanding, whereas facts can be taken at face value.

The passage itself follows directly on the heels of the parable of the prodigal son. It actually has a place here, in that its overall thrust is to be careful not to misuse the blessings of God, i.e., to be good stewards of what we are given. The story in Luke 16:1–9 reads thus:

> And he [Jesus] said also unto his disciples, There was a certain rich man, which had a steward; and the same was accused unto him that he had wasted his goods. And he called him, and said unto him, How is it that I hear this of thee? give an account of thy stewardship; for thou mayest be no longer steward.
>
> Then the steward said within himself, What shall I do? for my lord taketh away from me the stewardship: I cannot dig; to beg I am ashamed. I am resolved what to do, that, when I am put out of the stewardship, they may receive me into their houses.
>
> So he called every one of his lord's debtors unto him, and said unto the first, How much owest thou unto my lord? And he said, An hundred measures of oil. And he said unto him, Take thy bill, and sit down quickly, and write fifty. Then said he to another, And how much owest thou? And he said, An hundred measures of wheat. And he said unto him, Take thy bill, and write fourscore.
>
> And the lord commended the unjust steward, because he had done wisely: for the children of this world are in their generation wiser than the children of light.

That's the end of the story but not of Jesus' lesson.

First, let's realize that nearly all of the parables could be preceded with "The kingdom of God is like unto …" This parable is, at least partly, a real representation of the church and the kingdom of God. Jesus mixed this particular story with practical application as well.

The steward was caught wasting the rich man's goods by embezzlement, gambling, or who knows what. He was to "settle the account" and lose his position.

The steward began to run around, trying to "feather his bed" through even more subterfuge. A lie requires more lies to keep it from being exposed. A crime often requires more crime to keep it from being found out. This is not totally relevant to the heavenly side of the story, but it does show the futile efforts of men who believe the worldly attitude that "the end justifies the means."

The steward should have been working for his master all along. The steward simply compounded error with error in an effort to minimize the pain of his punishment.

The lord (the rich man) actually commended the steward for being so shrewd. This lord is not the Lord Jesus, as some have said. The point here is that even though the rich man was embezzled by the steward, the rich man could not help but commend his efforts to "soften his landing." The efforts were not justified, only duly noted in a worldly fashion.

This actually ends the story. Jesus gave commentary in verse 9.

Lesson #1: The Rest of the Story

In Luke 16:9, Jesus said, "And I say unto you, Make to yourselves friends of the mammon of unrighteousness; that, when ye fail, they may receive you into everlasting habitations."

Jesus was making the point that it seemed to Him that we can only hope to be as good at return on God's investment as humanity is with various worldly ways of making money. In the second half of verse 8, Jesus said, "For the children of this world are in their generation wiser than the children of light."

Jesus said "in their generation" to mean "with their kind," because the term "children of this world" was a Jewish usage that to them literally meant "Gentiles" or "other than we, the chosen people." Jesus was telling us to view and use their ways—to no person's detriment—because the worldly are so practiced at making money that they are even commended by the people they have misused.

I knew a Jewish man who had taken this to heart. He had one competitive price for making bids, another higher price for regular individual customers, and yet another still higher price for those "of the faith," since they tried to do business only with each other. He said that those of "the community" understood and all did the same. They were shrewd indeed.

Lesson #2: The Heavenly Interpretation

Let's set the cast of characters in this parable:

- a certain rich man = God
- the steward = saved believer
- His goods = blessings of God

View this parable as God accusing a so-called Christian of misusing the blessings received as a beneficiary of the covenant. Refer to the parables of Matthew 25.* Other examples can be cited, but suffice it to say that God expects His blessings to be used for the benefit of benevolence, and thereby evangelism.

Some say that the steward was found out (judgment) and had lost his job (salvation). If this were the judgment, there would be no ability to "fix" the situation. Notice that the steward did not attempt restitution but sought relief elsewhere.

This parable is actually showing us a person who needs discipline before judgment. We see this plainly when we look at chapter 22†. The lesson stands on its own merit, which we saw also in Matthew 25.

The story then turned into a lesson on another passage. "Behold, I send you forth as sheep in the midst of wolves: be ye therefore wise as serpents, and harmless as doves" (Matthew 10:16).

One additional note is that the story also shows the fact that the steward was thinking only of himself. He wanted to be taken in by those for whom he had "cooked the books." Jesus called actions like that "seeking earthly treasures." As we discussed elsewhere, those acting as such will receive an earthly reward, but that is it. The steward could have arranged restitution and might have even been reinstated, but he was thinking only of his immediate comfort, and he continued down his own crooked path.

We can put this story in terms of a believer in the church. The believer can seek forgiveness and do what is right by those he has harmed, or he can believe that he has no recourse other than to turn to his friends of the world and leave the church behind.

The only other thought here is that some see verse 9 to mean that you should take ill-gotten gains and give them benevolently so that the poor can vouch for you in heaven. This is simply not the case. Ill-gotten gains are covered in the law (Leviticus 6): they are to be returned, or restitution is to be made.

---

* See chapter 19, "Benevolence = Love," the section titled "It's That Important?"

† See chapter 22, "Testing, Testing: Is That You, God?," "Scenario #2: God Judges and Seeks Retribution."

The Bottom Line

The point of the parable of the Shrewd Steward is actually simpler than most people make it. Jesus was telling us again, just as He did in Matthew 25, that we will lose our position—both in life and at judgment—if we misuse the blessings of God and do not work for the Lord. Verse 9 of the parable is perhaps the most confusing part of this lesson. Jesus said, "And I say unto you, Make to yourselves friends of the mammon of unrighteousness; that, when ye fail, they may receive you into everlasting habitations."

Jesus was saying that we should do our best to make a living for God, that we should do all we can to make as much as we can so we can do more for God. We are to take God's blessings and multiply them. Jesus also was saying that we need to use worldly means—honestly, of course–because men of worldly finance are very careful and prudent with their money. We should watch how they work. They are better at it than "the children of light."

When Jesus said, "when ye fail, they may receive you into everlasting habitations," He was speaking of the angels of heaven receiving us when we die, because we were benevolent with our gains. We were working for the Lord.

PART VI

In a Nutshell

This section might well have been titled "Summaries." It contains a few more chapters that manifest the propulsion and flow of thought that both carried this work to print and will carry the reader to a greater understanding. In this section, we will focus on:

- "This Study": a synopsis of the spirit of unity in which this work was written
- "The Covenant": an overall understanding of why we must know absolute truth
- "Bull's Eye Theology": a visual representation of the spiritual ideal
- "The Christian Life": how to reach the ultimate goal, in a nutshell.

33

THIS STUDY

Ransom Note Religion

This is a phrase I coined to illustrate the cut-and-paste approach to the Holy Bible—the Word of God—that a great many people have both attempted and accomplished throughout the years, both before and after the Christ walked the earth. I follow here with an example we've all seen:

Ransom **notes cut** ***from*** **different** ***magazines*** that **MAKE** *complete sentences, but* **LACK** real **cohesive** *continuity.*

When you view the "ransom note" above, you have to read each word individually and then force your mind to make it into a complete sentence. That is what this study has sought to clarify.

The "ransom note religion" is what Jesus sought to dispel with His teaching and example. This study has merely sought to clarify some of the areas of biblical interpretation where humankind has decided that "this" or "that" would

- sound better
- look better
- be easier to understand
- be easier to perform

if we just

- tweaked it a little bit
- completely changed it
- simply eliminated it

As we noted at the outset, there are areas that some people may consider important and other areas that are totally irrelevant to the soul's salvation. Our point in those areas is to point out error in believing something to be unimportant when it is vital, and vice versa.

This study has been drawn *totally* from the Bible. We have sought no "scripture" given by any outside source of tradition or "recitation" or any other works of people that assume the authority that rightfully belongs only to God. The Holy Scripture alone is quoted as the final authority and Scripture alone is used to interpret or clarify any of the Holy Scripture used herein, either by cross-reference or by returning to the original language.

What's the Point?

I hope that by now the reader has digested this study from beginning to end. If you have not, please do. My point in this study is for the reader to see the great continuity of Scripture and God's covenant with humanity, and not only continuity but a cohesiveness that proves that no other source has the authority of the Holy Bible.

The word *congruent* comes to mind. Two things are congruent when they are an exact match when one is laid upon the other. A precise "tracing" is congruent. Two angles from different structures that are exact matches are congruent. The Scripture, history and underlying story of the Bible is invariably unchanged from beginning to end.

No other source of any "religion," past or present, has survived intact through centuries, let alone millennia. Every "doctrine" known to man, other than the Bible, has been revised, altered, forgotten, or otherwise proven to be man-made. God never changes, and neither has His Word. In Matthew 24:35, Jesus said, "Heaven and earth shall pass away, but my words shall not pass away."

One must study the Word of God, and *only* the Word of God, to expect the benefit of the covenant with God.

What About Bible Commentaries?

The Scripture, when applied to Scripture, interprets itself. There are many who say that it is wrong to even consult commentary to help understand Scripture. This is a double-edged sword. Bible commentary, in and of itself, is not wrong. Even this work, in a sense, is another Bible commentary.

There are three major considerations that one must remember when using Bible commentary.

1. *We all need to be taught.* The Scripture shows us a great example in the story of Philip and the eunuch recorded in Acts 8:30–31. "And Philip ran thither to him [the eunuch], and heard him read the prophet Esaias, and said, Understandest thou what thou readest? And he [the eunuch] said, *How can I, except some man should guide me?* And he desired Philip that he would come up and sit with him" (emphasis added).

   It is not some kind of spiritual weakness to admit you don't understand something from the Scripture. In fact, it exhibits a strength that God seeks in us. There is weakness, however, in not seeking the understanding and simply accepting the views of someone else. The saved can pray for the Spirit to help with the understanding. The unsaved can seek salvation, and then much will be revealed.

2. *The commentary must be scripturally sound.* I once knew a man who said he was going to make his own translation/interpretation of the Bible. He was going to interpret the Bible from, as he put it, the "skinhead" point of view.

   That sounds rather silly when you think of it, but this is the problem with Bible commentary. If the commentary is opinion rather than interpretation, it is not worthy of your time and should be avoided. Those are a "left-handed" attempt to persuade others to the writer's point of view. Decidedly, the only point of view that is relevant is that of God Almighty.

If the commentary uses the Scripture to interpret the Scripture, it is viable. If the commentary uses other references but speaks only of the Scripture of the Bible for authority of the interpretation, it is still worthy of study.

That is, a Bible commentary may refer to other sources, but if it declares those other sources to be more than a reference—if it declares a source other than the Bible to be additional "scripture"—it is as we said above. It is attempting to persuade you to look to something other than the Bible and to see it as also having the authority of God.

3. *Ultimately, it's up to you.* Allow me to point once again to the Scripture. In 2 Timothy 2:14–15, we read, "Of these things put them in remembrance, charging them before the Lord that they *strive not about words to no profit, but to the subverting of the hearers*. Study to shew thyself approved unto God, a workman that needeth not to be ashamed, rightly dividing the word of truth" (emphasis added).

   Simply put, Paul told Timothy not to get into discussions (hypothetical, etc.) about things that only serve to confuse. Rather, Timothy was to study the Word. Let me put it another way: *Don't worry about revelation. Worry about salvation.* In Acts 17:11, we read a testimony. "Now the Bereans were of more noble character than the Thessalonians, for they received the message with great eagerness and examined the Scriptures every day to see if what Paul said was true."

   This seems self-explanatory. The people of Berea received the message "with great eagerness," but they did not simply accept what was said. They investigated for themselves to prove what was the truth. The point here is that the Bereans not only "examined the Scriptures" but that they also did not refer to any other source as an authority for determining what the truth was.

   In Philippians 2:12–13, Paul told the believers, "Wherefore, my beloved, as ye have always obeyed, not as in my presence only, but now much more in my absence, work out your own salvation with fear and trembling. For it is God which worketh in you both to will and to do of his good pleasure."

It was always evident that Paul had a warm spot in his heart for the church at Philippi. Paul's admonishment to the church there was to "work out your own salvation with fear and trembling." Paul alluded to "private worship." He was saying that the right life was a continuing process and that we should always seek God's guidance with submission and willingness.

34

The Covenant

The Wording Is Beautiful

"But this shall be the covenant that I will make with the house of Israel; After those days, saith the LORD, I will put my law in their inward parts, and write it in their hearts; and *will be their God, and they shall be my people*" (Jeremiah 31:33, emphasis added).

"*And they shall be my people, and I will be their God*: And I will give them *one heart,* and *one way*, that they may fear [respect] me for ever, for the good of them, and of their children after them: And I will make an everlasting covenant with them, that I will not turn away from them, to do them good; but I will put my fear in their hearts, that they shall not depart from me. Yea, I will rejoice over them to do them good, and I will plant them in this land assuredly with my whole heart and with my whole soul" (Jeremiah 32:37–41, emphasis added).

The beauty of God's covenant with humanity glows with God's glory. God makes the way simple: one heart and one way.* Those who enter the covenant with God will see their own good and even the good for their children. God will not turn away. God often reiterates, even here, that He will do the believers good. Our side of the agreement is to respect and revere God and not depart from Him. God emphasizes that He will happily do the believers good, *with His whole heart and His whole soul.*

---

* See part I.

God says that He is wholly invested in the covenant and in the people who choose to enter the covenant with Him. What a promise! None can compare.

Different Worlds

The one thing that most people do not realize about the Christian life on earth is the fact that we are talking about operating on different "planes of existence." Becoming a true Christian by God's plan of salvation is, according to God, the only way to be saved.

Without going into the stories, Jesus made that point plainly on two recorded occasions. "And he said unto them, Ye are from beneath; I am from above: *ye are of this world; I am not of this world*" (John 8:23, emphasis added).

"Jesus answered, *My kingdom is not of this world*: if my kingdom were of this world, then would my servants fight, that I should not be delivered to the Jews: but now is my kingdom not from hence" (John 18:36, emphasis added).

On both occasions—to the accusing Pharisees and to Pilate—Jesus said that both He and His kingdom were not of this world. Jesus told Pilate that He was a king and that everyone "that is of the truth" would understand what He meant.

What Jesus meant, and what we understand, is that there is an "earthly kingdom" and a "heavenly kingdom." Some might say an "earthly realm" and "heavenly realm."

Citizenship

The point is that when you become a citizen of the kingdom of God, you are no longer a citizen of "the world." There is no dual citizenship as there is in our human world, the earthly kingdom. At the point of becoming part of the kingdom of God, we become missionaries to the world; we become *visitors in a strange land*, going about doing the good of God's love. In John 12:25, Jesus told us, "He that loveth his [worldly] life shall lose it; and he that hateth his life in this world shall keep it unto life eternal." (Remember that the word *hate* in biblical times meant "like less" or "respect less.")

We won't belabor the point here, but we *are* making the point that there are two separate "planes," our earthly realm and our spiritual realm.

Two Kingdoms

On more than one occasion, Jesus said words to this effect when He told the disciples and us, "All authority in heaven and on earth has been given to me" (Matthew 28:18).

That is to say that Jesus has dominion, not that Jesus is ruler of the earth. Satan, since the sin of Adam, has been the "prince of the power of the air" (Ephesians 2:2). To the people of biblical times, the air (beneath heaven) was where the evil spirits dwelled.

At the time of Adam's sin, God "walked away" from the world and turned His attention to His reason for creating the universe: humanity. God has placed limits on Satan, but beyond that, as far as God is concerned, the earth is on autopilot. God set the universe in motion, and "the rain falls on the just and the unjust."

Humanity became God's only real concern. In this study, we've been all over the proof of that one, lone fact. God set Himself on a "mission" to return humankind to the original sinless state in which he created Adam.

At this point of thought, one very often hears, "If that's true, then why didn't God just wave His hand and make it so?" The reasoning is as simple as every parent-child relationship. In order for humanity to return to a sinless state, he has to learn from his own mistakes or those of others. Adam, and all of us, have to know what is right and *want* to return to that right state of mind.

Just like we humans do, God wants to spend His time on people who want to spend their time on Him. God could "make it so," but yes-men and fake friends are no friends at all.

God Abandoned His Creation?

No, He only abandoned some of it. God left the earth to Satan, but God did not leave His people to Satan. However, God, over time, came to realize that only some—not all—of His children would want to be with Him and to live a right life. Some of God's children, no matter what He did, simply were going to live and love a life of sin and degradation. Things finally got to the point where God decided to simply start over with only one righteous man: Noah.

God has proven—over and over and over—and Jesus stated—over and over and over—that the way our sovereign God fixes an "illness" is to cut away the bad parts. "Every tree that bringeth not forth good fruit is hewn down, and cast into the fire" (Matthew 7:19).

Your understanding will be more complete if you think on these things while reading the book of Jeremiah.

The Chosen People—Again

We did a good study on "the chosen" in chapters 1 and 14. We'll not go into it here again except to say this. To believe that "the chosen people" are any people other than the members of God's family–adopted brothers of the Christ through God's plan of salvation—is error. It's okay to read that again.

There are those who have not considered "the change of the chosen," as we did in chapter 7. These people still consider the Jews—and especially Israel—to be the "chosen people." Others believe that to be "chosen" is a decision not left to us. Still others believe they can shortchange the plan of salvation. These people are wrong, and we've already proven it biblically.

Our point here is that God considers those outside His family to be "culls." The word *cull* is rarely, if ever, used to mean a good thing. For the most part, a cull is something cut out or removed, like a bad apple. These people, by their own decision—or lack of decision—are "outsiders" for two reasons, one leading to the other:

1. They do not belong to God's family and will not belong until God adopts them.
2. They are condemned until they obey (follow) Jesus and God then adds them to the family.

In John 3:18, we read the judgment: "He that believeth on him is not condemned: but he that believeth not is condemned already, because he hath not believed in the name of the only begotten Son of God."

We earlier spoke of the song "Free Will" by the group Rush, in which Geddy Lee sings, "If you choose not to decide, you still have made a choice." We must realize that, concerning God, to remain neutral is to remain lost.

The point here is that God considers and takes care of "the chosen people."† God considers the chosen people to be those who choose to follow the example and instruction of Jesus according to God's long-standing covenant agreement.

The beautiful visage of God's covenant is in Deuteronomy, chapters 6 through 11. Read the full account there. Here we show the "purpose" with Deuteronomy 7:9: "Know therefore that the LORD thy God, he is God, *the faithful God*, which keepeth covenant and mercy *with them that love him and keep his commandments* to a thousand generations" (emphasis added).

God Keeps a Ledger

We discussed it before but will reiterate it here. Until you accept God's invitation and become an adopted brother of the Christ, your name is not written in the Book of Life. The Book of Life is simply a list of those who get to see judgment.

The judgment of the Christ is based on your life *after* you have become a Christian—that is, after you have shown that you have followed Jesus to the grave and desired a new life through living by His example.

Why a record only after baptism? We are all sinners and (again, with the exception of those who have never heard the gospel message) everyone who has not manifested his faith through God's plan of salvation—including baptism by immersion—has not finished the requirements for entering the new covenant with God.‡ Those persons continue to be unsaved sinners. Their records are not kept, because they are not citizens of God's kingdom.

This is why intercession is so important. Without the intercessory prayer of the "saved sinners" of God's church, God will not hear the prayer of the sinner, and that person cannot and therefore will not be saved.

---

† A very real example is the "144,000" in chapter 25 on Revelation in the section titled, "One Big Human Misconception."

‡ See part I.

God's desire is that the Book of Life be filled with every name of every person who lives on this earth. This should also be the desire of every Christian as well. Don't be confused about this; it is not a membership drive. It is a desire that all humankind will have the perfect love of God and manifest it to the other members of the "fellowship of man."

God wishes for the Book of Life, His ledger, to be large—much larger than it will ever be. However, God will not abide those who do not wish to be true to His Word. God says of the people listed in the Book of Life, "They will be my people and I will be their God." The benefit is unfathomable.

God, by His sovereignty, is the God of all. This will be proven by the judgment. In Isaiah 45:23, God said, "I have sworn by myself, the word is gone out of my mouth in righteousness, and shall not return, That unto me every knee shall bow, every tongue shall swear."

This is repeated in Romans 14:11, and it is not the only New Testament reference: "For it is written, As I live, saith the Lord, every knee shall bow to me, and every tongue shall confess to God."

This Offer Is for a Limited Time Only

We've all heard something to that effect in modern advertising. The point is that while God's salvation is unlimited—until death—and every human is invited to answer His invitation, the benefit of knowing God while on this earth is limited to those who answer with a heartfelt "I do" and become "married to the Master."

For each of us, God's offer is limited to our own lifetime. The offer of the covenant with God is only a benefit to the saved souls whose names are written in the Book of Life.

The covenant is between God and His chosen people. God has been, is, and will continue keeping His covenant. The fact we show here is that all those who think that God is looking after them while they have not been saved are—and most certainly will be—sadly mistaken and disappointed for eternity.

35

Bull's-Eye Theology

This is a very simple and visual example of what God is getting at. It is our hope here that you get an idea of the true focus and purpose of God's plan for a right life by seeking the path of "the footsteps of Jesus." No one knows where this beautifully simple idea came from, except from God. Paul Faulkner showed it to me.

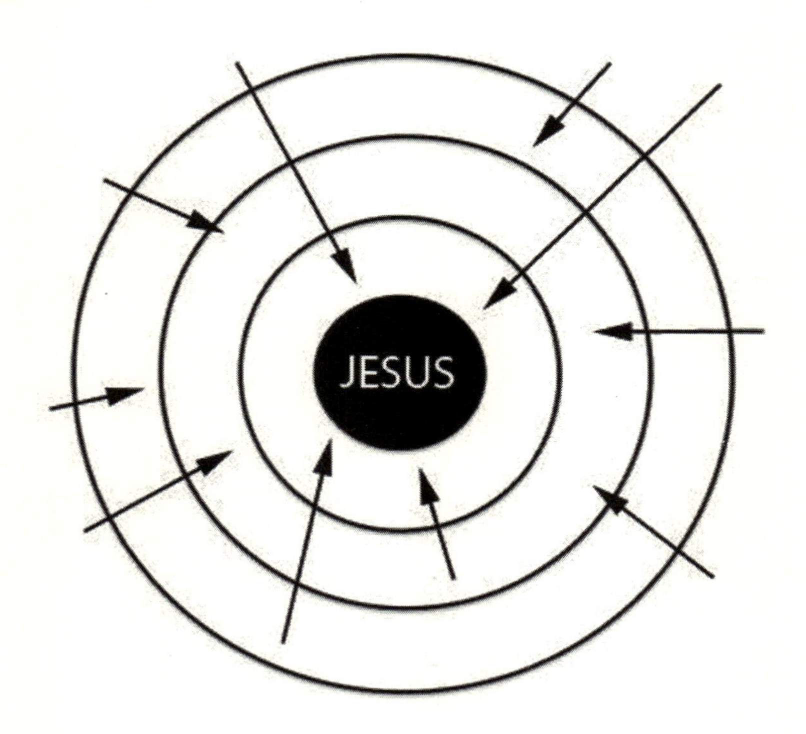

As we begin our spiritual journey, we enter the target's area. That is, we believe and begin to see the examples of Jesus as instruction rather than a bunch of good stories.

With any target, the idea is to come as close to the bull's-eye as we can. In the case of "bull's-eye theology," the realization is that anywhere outside the bull's-eye shows room for improvement.

We discussed this when we spoke of sin earlier, but it seems to apply very well here as well. The Greek (New Testament) word for *sin* is *hamartia*, which comes from a root word, *hamartano*. It is a sporting word that means "miss the mark and not share in the prize."

All of us will start from different points around the target–from the left, the right, north, south, and all points in between. Some will start from closer to the target than others. We are all different. We all come from different backgrounds, and we certainly have different levels of belief.

This is not a "secret passage" or anything like that. This is merely a visual idea of a world of spiritual life.

As we have seen elsewhere in this study, we need to continue to get closer and closer to Jesus Himself and to His examples of how to live and how to love. Our journey is never-ending. As we get closer to a "right life," we'll continue to see more to do and room for improvement.

The thing to remember is that the unsaved are missing the target completely. In fact, until they shake hands with Jesus, the unsaved can't even see the target—or know that the target exists. It's up to each and every believer to introduce them to God by word and deed. The Holy Spirit will help us; we have that promise. If each of us continues to "strive for perfect love," the world will see, and they will like what they see. Others will begin to seek the target and then Jesus.*

The Target Stays the Same

As we've already discussed, a great many people have painted their own bull's-eye on a target of their own making. This is error. However, a lot of people look at the target example and say that it proves that everyone seeks Jesus in his own way.

---

* We discuss this point directly in chapter 3, "That's Not the Way I Heard It," in the section titled segment, "But *They* Said ..."

This is very true. The rub is that some are seeking the bull's-eye when they haven't even seen the target yet. Note that while there may be different paths to the target, there is only one way to the bull's-eye.

We started with using the target as an example of being a baptized believer. Let's look at the target as referring to all the "seekers" of the world, as some would have it. The bull's-eye becomes salvation, and the seekers are coming from all the compass points in an attempt to gain that salvation. The point is that Jesus is still at the center; there is no other way. Jesus makes one statement that says it all in John 14:6: "Jesus saith unto him, I am the way, the truth, and the life: *no man cometh unto the Father, but by me*" (emphasis added). People only find the truth when they follow *the way* to the truth.

Benefit of the Bull's-Eye

Let's look again at the target. Most people don't realize it, but as we are seeking the truth and heading toward the bull's-eye, we are all getting closer to each other as well.

Even from a world-wide perspective, if we all strive to get closer to Jesus as the bull's-eye, we will continually get closer to one another!

As we get closer together, differences disappear, borders blur, fences fall.[†] However, this wonderful thing happens only if we are all aiming at the same bull's-eye on the same "target of truth."

[†] Please read the fourth chapter of 1 John. If you've read it before, read it again.

36

The Christian Life

It's So Hard, They Say

I hear even preachers of the church say things from the pulpit like, "Living a Christian life isn't easy" and "a Christian life is not only hard, but you'll be persecuted for it." Thoughts like these make you wonder why anyone would even want to try it.

Remember the yardsticks?* These folks who tell us that the Christian life is hard have a picture of a high-jump bar (or some other "legalistic" type of thought) as a vision of a certain goal that must be attained and then maintained. Unfortunately, a majority of so-called Christians feel this way.

With language like that coming from the ones who are supposed to know so much more about it than the rest of us, how can we be expected to be Christians in any form of the biblical example we've seen?

There is no "goal" in Christianity other than heaven.† The real satisfaction of the Christian life, however, is not in simply being saved. Being saved is an inspiration and a joy greater than any other. We've seen that the angels in heaven rejoice over one saved soul. However, salvation is truly only the birthplace of the Christian life. The Christian life is service and love, and that is achieved through a personal relationship with God. God alone decides when you will retire from that "job."

---

* See chapter 15, "Sin: Do This, Don't Do That," and the section titled "Righteousness vs. Relativism and Pragmatism.", Section 15a

† See part I.

Legalism

The word *legalism* is defined in one place as "excessive adherence to a law or formula." Another defines it as "strict adherence to the law, especially the stressing of the letter of the law rather than its spirit."

Legalism arises when we start to explain or clarify one law by invoking another. That is to say that if the law calls for "red," three more laws are made: one to qualify what *can* be classified as red, another to qualify what shades of color *are* red, and yet another to express what is *not* red.

We spoke of the Pharisees of Jesus' time who had defined what was "unclean" (by law, the things that could not be consumed) by going all the way down to a gnat. Their law stated that one had to filter at least ceremonial wine (and better, all wine) through a fine cloth to make sure that a gnat was not in it to avoid its consumption.

Legalism in today's church is Satan's "gift that keeps on giving." We, God's children, have decided not only the *what* but the *how* of what is pleasing to the Father. We then apply the yardstick of our own making to others of the faith to see how they "measure up."

Legalism is wrong, but the law, as given by God, is very much a right guide for life. Those who see or have seen the law as a guide rather than a religion have found "grace in the eyes of God."

In our discourse on Judaism, we spoke of the law as "guardrails." Those who saw the law as such and lived within the law (between the guardrails) lived a right life of faith. The "faith hall of fame" in Hebrews 11 tells us of some individuals who did this, and mentions others in a noninclusive list.

If a Christian lives with legalism, heaven will often appear unattainable.

By the plan of the Godhead, Jesus destroyed all aspects of legalism. We spent a great deal of time explaining this earlier in part II. A right life of benevolence and love is all that is required.

Society

Allowing society to lead and establish law is not the same as letting the majority establish law, and it certainly does not consider what may be truth. Relativism has made present-day law a matter of opinion. While it is not a majority view, a pervasive thought in our modern times is "I need only to obey the laws that I think are good for me."

There exists a human trait that parents use all the time. When we tell someone that he can't do something, we'll see just how quickly he will do it. "Morality" laws most certainly have that effect. The laws on the prohibition of alcohol in the 1920s and early 1930s are a case in point.

There is one irrefutable fact of law: no government *can* legislate morality. Morality is a taught-and-learned base of a society. The problem with our society, as in times past, is that even the word *morality* has become a relative term. Therefore, there are those nowadays who have construed the intent of some laws to mean something else entirely. Now, society says that no government *may* legislate morality.

The relativist attitude that has quite successfully infiltrated our judicial system has now also infected our society's legislative process. There is now a tendency toward allowing lawbreakers to dictate legislation. A prominent example is the legalization of marijuana, an issue not unlike the laws of alcohol prohibition. The idea is that if people break the law enough to be a problem to law enforcement—especially if the lawbreakers are lawmakers—the law should be removed, or at least changed to be more lenient to be removed later.

In recent times, things like the Defense of Marriage Act (DOMA) have incited very vocal minorities to give a "call to arms," and those minorities are backdoor-ing legislation by swaying individual judges to rule counter to the laws' intents.

No matter how it happens, the idea that "no morality legislation is allowed" is becoming acceptable and, in some cases, preferable. As mentioned earlier, the problem compounds itself when the lawbreakers decide which laws to change or disallow.

This should concern all of us, but it should hold no sway over the mind of a Christian.‡ The problem in the Christian world is the thought that something is okay as long as it doesn't affect us, which is now becoming a common idea in many pulpits and, even more, within the Christian populace.

The laws based on "separation of church and state"—which were once, in the words of Jefferson, "a *wall* of separation *between* church and

‡ Refer to chapter 28, "The Armor of God."

state" designed to protect freedom of religion—have now been totally construed to mean "nothing of God is allowed." Freedom *of* religion has now been changed to freedom *from* religion by even the highest office of our American government.

All people, whether Christian or not, tend to use the yardstick manufactured by society to measure the propriety not only of a person's actions but of his thoughts.

There is a pendulum effect in most societies based on freedom. We need to pray that the pendulum of morality will begin swinging the other way—soon. In this day of instant communication, where even the smallest voice can gain an audience, we must speak of these things. Morality is the application of one's character and conscience, for good or bad. In more and more cases in this world of relativism, personal morality is both decided and adopted from a social network or the evening news.

Make no mistake: liberty is not freedom. Liberty is granted by freedom. Freedom is equally available to all, and every person has an equal amount. Liberties (rights) end at the borders of another's liberties. Liberties have boundaries. When one person's liberties are held to be more important than another's liberties, freedom is diminished.

What's the Point?

If a Christian has any amount of relativism inside, Christianity *will* be difficult.

Relativism applied through legalism makes people look at the wrong yardstick. Legalism uses the yardstick of "what I think is right" to compare itself to the lives of others. Legalism demands that everyone live up to "my standard." This is wrong, in and of itself.

Jesus spoke of this when He said that we would have no hope of heaven if we did not exceed the righteousness of the Pharisees. During His last week before the crucifixion, Jesus finally decided that the temple leaders would not change yardsticks from their self-manufactured standard to the standard of the example of His life and His simple commandments. Jesus, the judge of all, then told them in Matthew 21:43, "Therefore say I unto you, The kingdom of God shall be taken from you, and given to a nation bringing forth the fruits thereof."

Legalism was wrong when Jesus walked the earth (and long before). How can we think legalism is right today?

Relativism applied through society also makes humanity look at the wrong yardstick. Society uses the yardstick of "what is right for me" and applies it for comparison as well. However, if the comparison makes a person feel better, that's great. If the comparison makes a person feel "not so good" or makes him feel that he is in a minority position, he will simply label the other position as blatantly wrong or as a "bullying" attempt to oppress him for his views.

"Live and let live" has become the anthem of society. However, society is moving ever further from the middle of the road and is coming to believe that if any minority's position "feels oppressed," the other positions should be squelched or even removed from society completely.

Tolerance no longer means to live and let live. Tolerance has now been redefined to mean that one must accept, and even embrace, disagreeable thoughts and/or behavior.

Bob Dylan said, "You don't need a weatherman to know which way the wind blows." I quote him here because a Christian mind-set that truly believes in right and wrong can see that the ship of our society has begun to list hard to port and has begun to take on water.

The larger understanding here is this: if society decides to be at odds with God, don't gamble with your soul. If you have no faith, look to history. History has proven that there is no contest. Christians are called to be *in* the world but not *of* the world. John wrote to us in 1 John 2:15, "Love not the world, neither the things that are in the world. If any man love the world, the love of the Father is not in him."

The Bottom Line

Jesus was expressly addressing the legalism of the temple leaders and their vain attempts at designing their own way to salvation when He said, "Come unto me, all ye that labour and are heavy laden [under *their* law], and I will give you rest. Take my yoke upon you, and learn of me; for I am meek and lowly in heart: and ye shall find rest unto your souls. For *my* yoke is easy, and *my* burden is light" (Matthew 11:28–30, emphasis added). When

Jesus said, "My yoke is easy," He was referring to His simplification of the definition of a "right life."

After Moses, there were approximately 613 commandments to which the temple leaders had added many more "explanatory laws." The real problem of the temple leaders was that they were not real students of the Word but were worshippers of the law and not God.

David had already simplified the law to about fifteen commandments. Micah reduced the number even further to three commandments in Micah 6:8.

Jesus showed and told all who met Him that *God desires mercy and not sacrifice*, which was what Scripture had recorded long ago. In Matthew 22, a lawyer tested Jesus, asking, "Which is the great commandment in the law?"

At that point, Jesus simplified the law to "1a and 1b,"[§] one single command of love and its priorities. In Matthew 22:37–40, we read, "Jesus said unto him, Thou shalt love the Lord thy God with all thy heart, and with all thy soul, and with all thy mind. This is the first and great commandment. And the second is like unto it, Thou shalt love thy neighbor as thyself. On these two commandments hang *all* the law and the prophets" (emphasis added).

This makes Christianity so very simple—and easy! Love God, and love your neighbor—and every decision of your life is made for you. You'll always do the right thing. It's like *The Perfection of Society for Dummies*!

So, What Is a Christian Life?

Jesus gave us the perfect example of a Christian life. He told us how to be blessed in the first twelve verses of the fifth chapter of Matthew—and not only there. All of Jesus' instruction is filled with acts of love.

What I've found to be a basic tenet of life itself is that if we—believers or not—want more of *anything* in this life, we should at least share what we have—or better yet, simply give it away.

If you want more love, give your love to everyone.
If you want more fear, spread fear wherever you go.

§ Ravi Zacharias in *The Loss of Truth*, part 4 of 4.

If you want more friends, offer your friendship to all you meet.
If you want more hate, put yours on display.
If you want more of the Christ, share Him with everyone you possibly can.

Think of yourself as a container with an open top. If you pour in good, evil spills out and is lost. If you pour in evil, goodness spills out. The two never mix, much less homogenize.

I remember an old American Indian story. A tribal elder was teaching his grandson about life. "A fight is going on inside me," he said to the boy. "It is a terrible fight, and it is between two dogs. One is evil; he is anger, envy, sorrow, regret, greed, arrogance, self-pity, guilt, resentment, inferiority, lies, false pride, superiority, and ego. The other is good; he is joy, peace, love, hope, serenity, humility, kindness, benevolence, empathy, generosity, truth, compassion, and faith. The same fight is going on inside you and every other person." The grandson thought about it for a minute and then asked his grandfather, "Which dog will win?" The chief simply replied, "The one you feed."

This is it. Really, this is all the Christian life really is. After becoming a Christian:

- Love God first and foremost, and talk with Him often.
- Feed your "good dog" (Galatians 5:22–23). You are an example to someone.
- Decide in advance to do the right thing. Make up scenarios in which you might have problems, and decide what you will do if a particular situation arises. If that situation does occur, you will have decided your response in advance, and you will already know what is the right thing to do.
- Love your neighbor as yourself as taught in the Golden Rule (Matthew 7:12). Of course, because of your love, your light will shine, and you'll share Jesus just by being alive.

Living and Dying

Most of us can think of someone who has stood up for his belief in God, even to the point of death. The one thing I have found to be true about living and dying for God is that only those who truly live for God will ever be tested with death for their beliefs. Satan doesn't waste the big guns on small game.

At any rate, given both experience and study, I have come to realize that it is much easier to "be brave" amidst friends. It is also much easier to "believe" amidst friends. The thought I gleaned from that is this: your *character* determines how you live when no one is looking.

So many people make a big deal out of dying for Jesus. If you look at it, the moment of death is just that: a moment. Nearly anyone can be brave for just a moment. The long haul is in living for Jesus, not dying for Him.

Moses put it to the people in Deuteronomy 30:19. I put it to you now. "I call heaven and earth to record this day against you, that I have set before you life and death, blessing and cursing: therefore choose life, that both thou and thy seed may live."

Final Advice

1. Make every effort to dwell in the camp of true believers and to seek their fellowship and counsel. Remember that we're told in 1 Corinthians 5:33 that "evil associations corrupt good morals."

2. Think of the blessings of life. Consider them as your shadow. If you walk away from the light, you can never catch your shadow. If you walk toward the light, your shadow follows you wherever you go.

3. God cannot guide your steps if you are standing still.

PART VII

Appendixes

This is additional information for the diligent or the curious.

- "Appendix 1: Wisdom in Proverbs" contains wisdom—in the first, second, and third person—from Proverbs 7:1–9:12.
- "Appendix 2: Other Names of Jesus" is a listing of Scriptures that pertain to alternate names for Jesus.
- "Appendix 3: Pelagian Tenets" is proof of the Pelagian tenets, which were condemned by the Italian church.
- "Appendix 4: Crucifixion Time Line" is a time-of-day time line of Jesus' arrest, trial, and crucifixion.

Appendix 1

Wisdom in Proverbs

Solomon was thought to have been the wisest man who ever walked the earth—after he told God that his greatest wish was to gain wisdom. Solomon is also considered to be the author of Proverbs. The following passages from Proverbs 7:1–9:12 are a wise man's way of looking at wisdom.

Proverbs 7:1–27 (NIV)

1. My son, keep my words and store up my commands within you.
2. Keep my commands and you will live; guard my teachings as the apple of your eye.
3. Bind them on your fingers; write them on the tablet of your heart.
4. Say to wisdom, "You are my sister," and call understanding your kinsman;
5. they will keep you from the adulteress, from the wayward wife with her seductive words.

The writer of these proverbs, assumed to be Solomon, described in verses 6–27 how—without understanding and wisdom—one can be easily pulled by the "adulteress" away from a faithful life.

6. At the window of my house I looked out through the lattice.
7. I saw among the simple, I noticed among the young men, a youth who lacked judgment.

8. He was going down the street near her corner, walking along in the direction of her house
9. at twilight, as the day was fading, as the dark of night set in.
10. Then out came a woman to meet him, dressed like a prostitute and with crafty intent.
11. (She is loud and defiant, her feet never stay at home;
12. now in the street, now in the squares, at every corner she lurks.)
13. She took hold of him and kissed him and with a brazen face she said:
14. "I have fellowship offerings at home; today I fulfilled my vows.
15. So I came out to meet you; I looked for you and have found you!
16. I have covered my bed with colored linens from Egypt.
17. I have perfumed my bed with myrrh, aloes and cinnamon.
18. Come, let's drink deep of love till morning; let's enjoy ourselves with love!
19. My husband is not at home; he has gone on a long journey.
20. He took his purse filled with money and will not be home till full moon."
21. With persuasive words she led him astray; she seduced him with her smooth talk.
22. All at once he followed her like an ox going to the slaughter, like a deer stepping into a noose
23. till an arrow pierces his liver, like a bird darting into a snare, little knowing it will cost him his life.
24. Now then, my sons, listen to me; pay attention to what I say.
25. Do not let your heart turn to her ways or stray into her paths.
26. Many are the victims she has brought down; her slain are a mighty throng.
27. Her house is a highway to the grave, leading down to the chambers of death.

Proverbs 8:1–36 (NIV)

Solomon—if he is the author—begins speaking about wisdom—and even *as* wisdom in the first person in Proverbs 8:3. Notice that wisdom existed before creation (beginning with verse 22).

1. Does not wisdom call out? Does not understanding raise her voice?
2. On the heights along the way, where the paths meet, she takes her stand;
3. beside the gates leading into the city, at the entrances, she cries aloud:
4. "To you, O men, I call out; I raise my voice to all mankind.
5. You who are simple, gain prudence; you who are foolish, gain understanding.
6. Listen, for I have worthy things to say; I open my lips to speak what is right.
7. My mouth speaks what is true, for my lips detest wickedness.
8. All the words of my mouth are just; none of them is crooked or perverse.
9. To the discerning all of them are right; they are faultless to those who have knowledge.
10. Choose my instruction instead of silver, knowledge rather than choice gold,
11. for wisdom is more precious than rubies, and nothing you desire can compare with her.
12. "I, wisdom, dwell together with prudence; I possess knowledge and discretion.
13. To fear the LORD is to hate evil; I hate pride and arrogance, evil behavior and perverse speech.
14. Counsel and sound judgment are mine; I have understanding and power.
15. By me kings reign and rulers make laws that are just;
16. by me princes govern, and all nobles who rule on earth.
17. I love those who love me, and those who seek me find me.
18. With me are riches and honor, enduring wealth and prosperity.
19. My fruit is better than fine gold; what I yield surpasses choice silver.

20. I walk in the way of righteousness, along the paths of justice,
21. bestowing wealth on those who love me and making their treasuries full.
22. "The LORD brought me forth as the first of his works, before his deeds of old;
23. I was appointed from eternity, from the beginning, before the world began.
24. When there were no oceans, I was given birth, when there were no springs abounding with water;
25. before the mountains were settled in place, before the hills, I was given birth,
26. before he made the earth or its fields or any of the dust of the world.
27. I was there when he set the heavens in place, when he marked out the horizon on the face of the deep,
28. when he established the clouds above and fixed securely the fountains of the deep,
29. when he gave the sea its boundary so the waters would not overstep his command, and when he marked out the foundations of the earth.
30. Then I was the craftsman at his side. I was filled with delight day after day, rejoicing always in his presence,
31. rejoicing in his whole world and delighting in mankind.
32. "Now then, my sons, listen to me; blessed are those who keep my ways.
33. Listen to my instruction and be wise; do not ignore it.
34. Blessed is the man who listens to me, watching daily at my doors, waiting at my doorway.
35. For whoever finds me finds life and receives favor from the LORD.
36. But whoever fails to find me harms himself; all who hate me love death."

Then Solomon turned to "eat these words," saying that wisdom prepares a feast for all who seek her.

Proverbs 9:1–12 (NIV)

1. Wisdom has built her house; she has hewn out its seven pillars.
2. She has prepared her meat and mixed her wine; she has also set her table.
3. She has sent out her maids, and she calls from the highest point of the city.
4. "Let all who are simple come in here!" she says to those who lack judgment.
5. "Come, eat my food and drink the wine I have mixed.
6. Leave your simple ways and you will live; walk in the way of understanding."
7. "Whoever corrects a mocker invites insult; whoever rebukes a wicked man incurs abuse.
8. Do not rebuke a mocker or he will hate you; rebuke a wise man and he will love you.
9. Instruct a wise man and he will be wiser still; teach a righteous man and he will add to his learning."
10. "The fear of the LORD is the beginning of wisdom, and knowledge of the Holy One is understanding.
11. For through me your days will be many, and years will be added to your life.
12. If you are wise, your wisdom will reward you; if you are a mocker, you alone will suffer."

Appendix 2

OTHER NAMES OF JESUS

The study to which these Scriptures apply is in chapter 9, "The God We Call Jesus." These are Scripture references for various names, other than "Jesus,: for God the Son.

The Word

1 Samuel 15:10 (KJV): "Then came the word of the LORD unto Samuel, saying …"
2 Samuel 7:4 (KJV): "And it came to pass that night, that the word of the LORD came unto Nathan, saying …"
2 Samuel 24:11–12a (KJV): "For when David was up in the morning, the word of the LORD came unto the prophet Gad, David's seer, saying, Go and say unto David, thus sayeth the Lord …"
1 Kings 6:11 (KJV): "And the word of the LORD came to Solomon, saying …"
1 Kings 12:22 (KJV): "But the word of God came unto Shemaiah the man of God, saying …"
1 Kings 13:1 (KJV): "And, behold, there came a man of God out of Judah by the word of the LORD unto Bethel: and Jeroboam stood by the altar to burn incense." (Notice that is says "man of God," not "the Word of God." Man ate and failed, eaten by a lion.)
1 Kings 16:1 (KJV): "Then the word of the LORD came to Jehu the son of Hanani against Baasha, saying …"
1 Kings 17:2 (KJV): "And the word of the LORD came unto him, saying …"

1 Kings 17:8 (KJV): "And the word of the LORD came unto him, saying ..."

1 Kings 18:1 (KJV): "And it came to pass *after* many days, that the word of the LORD came to Elijah in the third year, saying, Go, shew thyself unto Ahab; and I will send rain upon the earth."

1 Kings 19:9 (KJV): "And he came thither unto a cave, and lodged there; and, behold, the word of the LORD came to him, and he said unto him, What doest thou here, Elijah?"

1 Kings 21:17 (KJV): "And the word of the LORD came to Elijah the Tishbite, saying ..."

1 Kings 21:28 (KJV): "And the word of the LORD came to Elijah the Tishbite, saying ..."

1 Chronicles 22:8 (KJV): "But the word of the LORD came to me, saying, Thou hast shed blood abundantly, and hast made great wars: thou shalt not build an house unto my name, because thou hast shed much blood upon the earth in my sight."

2 Chronicles 11:2 (KJV): "But the word of the LORD came to Shemaiah the man of God, saying ..."

2 Chronicles 12:7 (KJV): "And when the LORD saw that they humbled themselves, the word of the LORD came to Shemaiah, saying, They have humbled themselves; *therefore* I will not destroy them, but I will grant them some deliverance; and my wrath shall not be poured out upon Jerusalem by the hand of Shishak."

Psalm 33:6 (KJV): "By the word of the LORD were the heavens made; and all the host of them by the breath of his mouth."

Isaiah 38:4 (KJV): "Then came the word of the LORD to Isaiah, saying ..."

Jeremiah 1:2 (KJV): "To whom the word of the LORD came in the days of Josiah the son of Amon king of Judah, in the thirteenth year of his reign."

Jeremiah 1:4 (KJV): "Then the word of the LORD came unto me, saying ..."

Jeremiah 1:11 (KJV): "Moreover the word of the LORD came unto me, saying, Jeremiah, what seest thou? And I said, I see a rod of an almond tree."

Jeremiah 1:13 (KJV): "And the word of the LORD came unto me the second time, saying, What seest thou? And I said, I see a seething pot; and the face thereof is toward the north."

Jeremiah 2:1 (KJV): "Moreover the word of the LORD came to me, saying ..."

Jeremiah 13:3, 8 (KJV): "And the word of the LORD came unto me the second time, saying ..."

Jeremiah 14:1 (KJV): "The word of the LORD that came to Jeremiah concerning the dearth."

Jeremiah 16:1 (KJV): "The word of the LORD came also unto me, saying ..."

Jeremiah 18:5 (KJV): "Then the word of the LORD came to me, saying ..."

Jeremiah 24:4 (KJV): "Again the word of the LORD came unto me, saying ..."

Jeremiah 25:3 (KJV): "From the thirteenth year of Josiah the son of Amon king of Judah, even unto this day, that *is* the three and twentieth year, the word of the LORD hath come unto me, and I have spoken unto you, rising early and speaking; but ye have not hearkened."

Jeremiah 28:12 (KJV): "Then the word of the LORD came unto Jeremiah the prophet, after that Hananiah the prophet had broken the yoke from off the neck of the prophet Jeremiah, saying ..."

Jeremiah 29:30 (KJV): "Then came the word of the LORD unto Jeremiah, saying ..."

Jeremiah 32:6 (KJV): "And Jeremiah said, The word of the LORD came unto me, saying ..."

Jeremiah 32:26-27 (KJV): "Then came the word of the LORD unto Jeremiah, saying, Behold, I am the LORD, the God of all flesh: is there any thing too hard for me?"

Jeremiah 33:1 (KJV): "Moreover the word of the LORD came unto Jeremiah the second time, while he was yet shut up in the court of the prison, saying ..."

Jeremiah 33:19 (KJV): "And the word of the LORD came unto Jeremiah, saying ..."

Jeremiah 33:23 (KJV): "Moreover the word of the LORD came to Jeremiah, saying ..."

Jeremiah 34:12 (KJV): "Therefore the word of the LORD came to Jeremiah from the LORD, saying ..."

Jeremiah 35:12 (KJV): "Then came the word of the LORD unto Jeremiah, saying ..."

Jeremiah 36:27 (KJV): "Then the word of the LORD came to Jeremiah, after that the king had burned the roll, and the words which Baruch wrote at the mouth of Jeremiah, saying ..."

Jeremiah 37:6 (KJV): "Then came the word of the LORD unto the prophet Jeremiah, saying …"

Jeremiah 39:15 (KJV): "Now the word of the LORD came unto Jeremiah, while he was shut up in the court of the prison, saying …"

Jeremiah 42:7 (KJV): "And it came to pass after ten days, that the word of the LORD came unto Jeremiah."

Jeremiah 43:8 (KJV): "Then came the word of the LORD unto Jeremiah in Tahpanhes, saying …"

Jeremiah 46:1 (KJV): "The word of the LORD which came to Jeremiah the prophet against the Gentiles."

Ezekiel 1:3 (KJV): "The word of the LORD came expressly unto Ezekiel the priest, the son of Buzi, in the land of the Chaldeans by the river Chebar; and the hand of the LORD was there upon him."

Ezekiel 3:16 (KJV): "And it came to pass at the end of seven days, that the word of the LORD came unto me, saying …"

Ezekiel 6:1 (KJV): "And the word of the LORD came unto me, saying …"

Ezekiel 7:1 (KJV): "Moreover the word of the LORD came unto me, saying …"

Ezekiel 11:14 (KJV): "Again the word of the LORD came unto me, saying …"

Ezekiel 12:1, 8, 17, 21, 26 (KJV): "The word of the LORD also came unto me, saying …"

Ezekiel 13:1 (KJV): "And the word of the LORD came unto me, saying …"

Ezekiel 14:2, 12 (KJV): "And the word of the LORD came unto me, saying …"

Ezekiel 15:1 (KJV): "And the word of the LORD came unto me, saying …"

Ezekiel 16:1 (KJV): "Again the word of the LORD came unto me, saying …"

Ezekiel 17:1,11 (KJV): "And the word of the LORD came unto me, saying …"

Ezekiel 18:1 (KJV): "The word of the LORD came unto me again, saying …"

Ezekiel 20:2 (KJV): "Then came the word of the LORD unto me, saying …"

Ezekiel 20:45 (KJV): "Moreover the word of the LORD came unto me, saying …"

Ezekiel 21:1 (KJV): "And the word of the LORD came unto me, saying …"

Ezekiel 21:8 (KJV): "Again the word of the LORD came unto me, saying …"

Ezekiel 21:18 (KJV): "The word of the LORD came unto me again, saying ..."
Ezekiel 22:1 (KJV): "Moreover the word of the LORD came unto me, saying ..."
Ezekiel 22:17 (KJV): "And the word of the LORD came unto me, saying ..."
Ezekiel 22:23 (KJV): "And the word of the LORD came unto me, saying ..."
Ezekiel 23:1 (KJV): "The word of the LORD came again unto me, saying ..."
Ezekiel 24:1 (KJV): "Again in the ninth year, in the tenth month, in the tenth day of the month, the word of the LORD came unto me, saying ..."
Ezekiel 24:15 (KJV): "Also the word of the LORD came unto me, saying ..."
Ezekiel 24:20 (KJV): "Then I answered them, The word of the LORD came unto me, saying ..."
Ezekiel 25:1 (KJV): "The word of the LORD came again unto me, saying ..."
Ezekiel 26:1 (KJV): "And it came to pass in the eleventh year, in the first day of the month, that the word of the LORD came unto me, saying ..."
Ezekiel 27:1 (KJV): "The word of the LORD came again unto me, saying ..."
Ezekiel 28:1 (KJV): "The word of the LORD came again unto me, saying ..."
Ezekiel 28:11 (KJV): "Moreover the word of the LORD came unto me, saying ..."
Ezekiel 28:20 (KJV): "Again the word of the LORD came unto me, saying ..."
Ezekiel 29:17 (KJV): "And it came to pass in the seven and twentieth year, in the first month, in the first day of the month, the word of the LORD came unto me, saying ..."
Ezekiel 30:1 (KJV): "The word of the LORD came again unto me, saying ..."
Ezekiel 30:20 (KJV): "And it came to pass in the eleventh year, in the first month, in the seventh day of the month, that the word of the LORD came unto me, saying ..."
Ezekiel 31:1 (KJV): "And it came to pass in the eleventh year, in the third month, in the first day of the month, that the word of the LORD came unto me, saying ..."

Ezekiel 32:1 (KJV): "And it came to pass in the twelfth year, in the twelfth month, in the first day of the month, that the word of the LORD came unto me, saying ..."

Ezekiel 32:17 (KJV): "It came to pass also in the twelfth year, in the fifteenth day of the month, that the word of the LORD came unto me, saying ..."

Ezekiel 33:1 (KJV): "Again the word of the LORD came unto me, saying ..."

Ezekiel 33:23 (KJV): "Then the word of the LORD came unto me, saying ..."

Ezekiel 34:1 (KJV): "And the word of the LORD came unto me, saying ..."

Ezekiel 35:1 (KJV): "Moreover the word of the LORD came unto me, saying ..."

Ezekiel 36:16 (KJV): "Moreover the word of the LORD came unto me, saying ..."

Ezekiel 37:15 (KJV): "The word of the LORD came again unto me, saying ..."

Ezekiel 38:1 (KJV): "And the word of the LORD came unto me, saying ..."

Daniel 9:2 (KJV): "In the first year of his reign I Daniel understood by books the number of the years, whereof the word of the LORD came to Jeremiah the prophet, that he would accomplish seventy years in the desolations of Jerusalem."

Jonah 1:1 (KJV): "Now the word of the LORD came unto Jonah the son of Amittai, saying ..."

Jonah 3:1 (KJV): "And the word of the LORD came unto Jonah the second time, saying ..."

Micah 1:1 (KJV): "The word of the LORD that came to Micah the Morasthite in the days of Jotham, Ahaz, and Hezekiah, kings of Judah, which he saw concerning Samaria and Jerusalem."

Zephaniah 1:1 (KJV): "The word of the LORD which came unto Zephaniah the son of Cushi, the son of Gedaliah, the son of Amariah, the son of Hizkiah, in the days of Josiah the son of Amon, king of Judah."

Haggai 2:1 (KJV): "In the seventh month, in the one and twentieth day of the month, came the word of the LORD by the prophet Haggai, saying ..."

Haggai 2:10 (KJV): "In the four and twentieth day of the ninth month, in the second year of Darius, came the word of the LORD by Haggai the prophet, saying ..."

Haggai 2:20 (KJV): "And again the word of the LORD came unto Haggai in the four and twentieth *day* of the month, saying ..."

Zechariah 1:1 (KJV): "In the eighth month, in the second year of Darius, came the word of the LORD unto Zechariah, the son of Berechiah, the son of Iddo the prophet, saying ..."

Zechariah 1:7 (KJV): "Upon the four and twentieth day of the eleventh month, which is the month Sebat, in the second year of Darius, came the word of the LORD unto Zechariah, the son of Berechiah, the son of Iddo the prophet, saying ..."

Zechariah 4:6 (KJV): "Then he answered and spake unto me, saying, This is the word of the LORD unto Zerubbabel, saying, Not by might, nor by power, but by my spirit, saith the LORD of hosts."

Zechariah 4:8 (KJV): "Moreover the word of the LORD came unto me, saying ..."

Zechariah 6:9 (KJV): "And the word of the LORD came unto me, saying ..."

Zechariah 7:1 (KJV): "And it came to pass in the fourth year of king Darius, that the word of the LORD came unto Zechariah in the fourth day of the ninth month, even in Chisleu."

Zechariah 7:4 (KJV): "Then came the word of the LORD of hosts unto me, saying ..."

Zechariah 7:8 (KJV): "And the word of the LORD came unto Zechariah, saying ..."

Zechariah 8:1 (KJV): "Again the word of the LORD of hosts came *to* me, saying ..."

Zechariah 8:18 (KJV): "And the word of the LORD of hosts came unto me, saying ..."

Angel of the LORD

Genesis 16:7 (KJV): "And the angel of the LORD found her by a fountain of water in the wilderness, by the fountain in the way to Shur."

Genesis 16:9–11 (KJV): "And the angel of the LORD said unto her, Return to thy mistress, and submit thyself under her hands. And the angel of the LORD said unto her, I will multiply thy seed exceedingly, that it shall not be numbered for multitude. And the angel of the LORD said unto her, Behold, thou *art* with child, and shalt bear a son, and shalt call his name Ishmael; because the LORD hath heard thy affliction.

Genesis 22:11 (KJV): "And the angel of the LORD called unto him out of heaven, and said, Abraham, Abraham: and he said, Here am I."

Genesis 22:15 (KJV): "And the angel of the LORD called unto Abraham out of heaven the second time."

Exodus 3:2 (KJV): "And the angel of the LORD appeared unto him in a flame of fire out of the midst of a bush: and he looked, and, behold, the bush burned with fire, and the bush was not consumed."

Numbers 22:22–27 (KJV): "And God's anger was kindled because he went: and the angel of the LORD stood in the way for an adversary against him. Now he was riding upon his ass, and his two servants were with him. And the ass saw the angel of the LORD standing in the way, and his sword drawn in his hand: and the ass turned aside out of the way, and went into the field: and Balaam smote the ass, to turn her into the way. But the angel of the LORD stood in a path of the vineyards, a wall being on this side, and a wall on that side. And when the ass saw the angel of the LORD, she thrust herself unto the wall, and crushed Balaam's foot against the wall: and he smote her again. And the angel of the LORD went further, and stood in a narrow place, where was no way to turn either to the right hand or to the left. And when the ass saw the angel of the LORD, she fell down under Balaam: and Balaam's anger was kindled, and he smote the ass with a staff."

Numbers 22:31–35 (KJV): "Then the LORD opened the eyes of Balaam, and he saw the angel of the LORD standing in the way, and his sword drawn in his hand: and he bowed down his head, and fell flat on his face. And the angel of the LORD said unto him, Wherefore hast thou smitten thine ass these three times? behold, I went out to withstand thee, because thy way is perverse before me: And Balaam said unto the angel of the LORD, I have sinned; for I knew not that thou stoodest in the way against me: now therefore, if it displease thee, I will get me back again. And the angel of the LORD said unto Balaam, Go with the men: but only the word that I shall speak unto thee, that thou shalt speak. So Balaam went with the princes of Balak."

Judges 2:1 (KJV): "And an angel of the LORD came up from Gilgal to Bochim, and said, I made you to go up out of Egypt, and have brought you unto the land which I sware unto your fathers; and I said, I will never break my covenant with you."

Judges 2:4 (KJV): "And it came to pass, when the angel of the LORD spake these words unto all the children of Israel, that the people lifted up their voice, and wept."

Judges 5:23 (KJV): "Curse ye Meroz, said the angel of the LORD, curse ye bitterly the inhabitants thereof; because they came not to the help of the LORD, to the help of the LORD against the mighty."

Judges 6:11–12 (KJV): "And there came an angel of the LORD, and sat under an oak which was in Ophrah, that pertained unto Joash the Abiezrite: and his son Gideon threshed wheat by the winepress, to hide it from the Midianites. And the angel of the LORD appeared unto him, and said unto him, The LORD is with thee, thou mighty man of valour."

Judges 6:21-22 (KJV): "Then the angel of the LORD put forth the end of the staff that was in his hand, and touched the flesh and the unleavened cakes; and there rose up fire out of the rock, and consumed the flesh and the unleavened cakes. Then the angel of the LORD departed out of his sight. And when Gideon perceived that he was an angel of the LORD, Gideon said, Alas, O Lord GOD! for because I have seen an angel of the LORD face to face."

Judges 13:3 (KJV): "And the angel of the LORD appeared unto the woman, and said unto her, Behold now, thou *art* barren, and bearest not: but thou shalt conceive, and bear a son."

Judges 13:13–21 (KJV): "And the angel of the LORD said unto Manoah, Of all that I said unto the woman let her beware. And Manoah said unto the angel of the LORD, I pray thee, let us detain thee, until we shall have made ready a kid for thee. And the angel of the LORD said unto Manoah, Though thou detain me, I will not eat of thy bread: and if thou wilt offer a burnt offering, thou must offer it unto the LORD. For Manoah knew not that he was an angel of the LORD. And Manoah said unto the angel of the LORD, What is thy name, that when thy sayings come to pass we may do thee honour? And the angel of the LORD said unto him, Why askest thou thus after my name, seeing it is secret? For it came to pass, when the flame went up toward heaven from off the altar, that the angel of the LORD ascended in the flame of the altar. And Manoah and his wife looked on it, and fell on their faces to the ground. But the angel of the LORD did no more appear to Manoah and to his wife. Then Manoah knew that he was an angel of the LORD."

2 Samuel 24:16 (KJV): "And when the angel stretched out his hand upon Jerusalem to destroy it, the LORD repented him of the evil, and said to the angel that destroyed the people, It is enough: stay now thine hand. And the angel of the LORD was by the threshingplace of Araunah the Jebusite."

1 Kings 19:7 (KJV): "And the angel of the LORD came again the second time, and touched him, and said, Arise *and* eat; because the journey *is* too great for thee."

2 Kings 1:3 (KJV): "But the angel of the LORD said to Elijah the Tishbite, Arise, go up to meet the messengers of the king of Samaria, and say unto them, Is it not because there is not a God in Israel, that ye go to enquire of Baalzebub the god of Ekron?"

2 Kings 1:15 (KJV): "And the angel of the LORD said unto Elijah, Go down with him: be not afraid of him. And he arose, and went down with him unto the king."

2 Kings 19:35 (KJV): "And it came to pass that night, that the angel of the LORD went out, and smote in the camp of the Assyrians an hundred fourscore and five thousand: and when they arose early in the morning, behold, they were all dead corpses."

1 Chronicles 21:12 (KJV): "Either three years' famine; or three months to be destroyed before thy foes, while that the sword of thine enemies overtaketh thee; or else three days the sword of the LORD, even the pestilence, in the land, and the angel of the LORD destroying throughout all the coasts of Israel. Now therefore advise thyself what word I shall bring again to him that sent me."

1 Chronicles 21:15-16 (KJV): "And God sent an angel unto Jerusalem to destroy it: and as he was destroying, the LORD beheld, and he repented him of the evil, and said to the angel that destroyed, It is enough, stay now thine hand. And the angel of the LORD stood by the threshingfloor of Ornan the Jebusite. And David lifted up his eyes, and saw the angel of the LORD stand between the earth and the heaven, having a drawn sword in his hand stretched out over Jerusalem. Then David and the elders *of Israel, who were* clothed in sackcloth, fell upon their faces."

1 Chronicles 21:18 (KJV): "Then the angel of the LORD commanded Gad to say to David, that David should go up, and set up an altar unto the LORD in the threshingfloor of Ornan the Jebusite."

1 Chronicles 21:30 (KJV): "But David could not go before it to enquire of God: for he was afraid because of the sword of the angel of the LORD."

Psalm 34:7 (KJV): "The angel of the LORD encampeth round about them that fear him, and delivereth them."

Psalm 35:5–6 (KJV): "Let them be as chaff before the wind: and let the angel of the LORD chase them. Let their way be dark and slippery: and let the angel of the LORD persecute them."

Isaiah 37:36 (KJV): "Then the angel of the LORD went forth, and smote in the camp of the Assyrians a hundred and fourscore and five thousand: and when they arose early in the morning, behold, they were all dead corpses.

Zechariah 1:11–12 (KJV): "And they answered the angel of the LORD that stood among the myrtle trees, and said, We have walked to and fro through the earth, and, behold, all the earth sitteth still, and is at rest. Then the angel of the LORD answered and said, O LORD of hosts, how long wilt thou not have mercy on Jerusalem and on the cities of Judah, against which thou hast had indignation these threescore and ten years?"

Zechariah 3:1 (KJV): "And he shewed me Joshua the high priest standing before the angel of the LORD, and Satan standing at his right hand to resist him."

Zechariah 3:5–6 (KJV): "And I said, Let them set a fair mitre upon his head. So they set a fair mitre upon his head, and clothed him with garments. And the angel of the LORD stood by."

Zechariah 3:6 (KJV): "And the angel of the LORD protested unto Joshua, saying ..."

Zechariah 12:8 (KJV): "In that day shall the LORD defend the inhabitants of Jerusalem; and he that is feeble among them at that day shall be as David; and the house of David *shall be* as God, as the angel of the LORD before them."

Angel of God

Genesis 21:17 (KJV): "And God heard the voice of the lad; and the angel of God called to Hagar out of heaven, and said unto her, What aileth thee, Hagar? fear not; for God hath heard the voice of the lad where he is."

Genesis 31:11 (KJV): "And the angel of God spake unto me in a dream, saying, Jacob: And I said, Here am I."

Exodus 14:19 (KJV): "And the angel of God, which went before the camp of Israel, removed and went behind them; and the pillar of the cloud went from before their face, and stood behind them."

Judges 6:20 (KJV): "And the angel of God said unto him, Take the flesh and the unleavened cakes, and lay them upon this rock, and pour out the broth. And he did so."

Judges 13:6 (KJV): "Then the woman came and told her husband, saying, A man of God came unto me, and his countenance *was* like the countenance of an angel of God, very terrible: but I asked him not whence he *was*, neither told he me his name."

Judges 13:9 (KJV): "And God hearkened to the voice of Manoah; and the angel of God came again unto the woman as she sat in the field: but Manoah her husband was not with her."

1 Samuel 29:9 (KJV): "And Achish answered and said to David, I know that thou art good in my sight, as an angel of God: notwithstanding the princes of the Philistines have said, He shall not go up with us to the battle."

2 Samuel 14:17 (KJV): "Then thine handmaid said, The word of my lord the king shall now be comfortable: for as an angel of God, so is my lord the king to discern good and bad: therefore the LORD thy God will be with thee."

2 Samuel 14:20 (KJV): "To fetch about this form of speech hath thy servant Joab done this thing: and my lord is wise, according to the wisdom of an angel of God, to know all things that are in the earth."

2 Samuel 19:27 (KJV): "And he hath slandered thy servant unto my lord the king; but my lord the king is as an angel of God: do therefore what is good in thine eyes."

Appendix 3

The Pelagian Tenets

I quote here from the *Catholic Encyclopedia* the six basic tenets of Pelagius, which Caelestius, a fellow of Pelagius, presented to the Carthage synod of 411.

1. Even if Adam had not sinned, he would have died.
2. Adam's sin harmed only himself, not the human race.
3. Children just born are in the same state as Adam before his fall.
4. The whole human race neither dies through Adam's sin or death, nor rises again through the resurrection of Christ.
5. The Mosaic law is as good a guide to heaven as the gospel.
6. Even before the advent of Christ, there were men who were without sin.

"On account of these doctrines, which clearly contain the quintessence of Pelagianism, Caelestius was summoned to appear before a synod at Carthage (411); but he refused to retract them, alleging that the inheritance of Adam's sin was an open question and hence its denial was no heresy. As a result he was not only excluded from ordination, but his six theses were condemned. He declared his intention of appealing to the pope in Rome, but without executing his design went to Ephesus in Asia Minor, where he was ordained a priest" (*Catholic Encyclopedia*).

I now argue *for* the points listed above and *against* the condemnation of the Roman church.

1. God said, in Genesis 3:22–23, "And the LORD God said, Behold, the man is become as one of us, to know good and evil: and now, lest he put forth his hand, and take *also* of the tree of life, and eat, and live for ever: Therefore the LORD God sent him forth from the garden of Eden, to till the ground from whence he was taken" (emphasis added).

   Can this mean anything other than that man would not live forever unless he had eaten of the Tree of Life? God actually decided later in Genesis 6:3 that "his days shall be 120 years."

   By the way, the life span (not life expectancy) of man is now scientifically established to be 120 years.

2. Because of Adam's sin, sin came to the earth. Adam's sin was neither inherited by his children, nor did it blemish them. Why else would Jesus say, "Unless you become as little children, ye shall not enter into the kingdom of heaven" (Matthew 18:3)? Jesus was speaking of the innocence of a child. We all know that we must be sinless in order to be with God. Jesus gave us the example to follow during the time until He comes again.

   Yes, sin came into the world by Adam. Adam did not bring sin to the earth; Satan did. Adam will have to deal only with his personal sin at his personal judgment. Adam is responsible for only his own sin. I am responsible for my own sin. You are responsible for your own sin.

3. Concerning children being sinless and innocent, as well as subordinate, I refer to the same quote from Jesus, for the same reason.

4. We do not die through Adam's sin. When sin came, death was elevated to a new level, to prominence. Death, because of Adam—not *through* Adam—now accompanies sin and is the only atonement for sin. Men lived long lives (longer than any nowadays) until the time of Moses, and with the exception of Enoch and Elijah, they

all died. (see point 1, above). We do not rise again through the resurrection of Jesus; we rise again because Jesus conquered death. But we are saved by the complete plan of salvation—not only by any part of that plan, and certainly not by any act (crucifixion or resurrection) outside that plan.

5. Paul said the same thing in Romans, chapter 2. Paul's point, however, was that the yoke of Jesus was far easier and the new covenant far better than the old covenant under the yoke of the law. God would not have "stuck with it" for over a millennia if He'd thought it wasn't any good. The law is a guide, as we've shown in this work. Jesus gave us an example of how to live within the law (Matthew 5:17).

6. "The wages of sin is death," said Paul in Romans 6:23. We are told of two men who did not die but were taken by God and did not experience death. Those men were Enoch and Elijah (A=B=C). Concerning Enoch and Elijah, whether or not these two were sinless is a moot point in terms of salvation, in that a sinless human had to be sacrificed—as Jesus was—in concert with God the Father in order to perform the act of the Messiah. Jesus will forever be the only man worthy of sitting in judgment of the world.

Appendix 4

Crucifixion Time Line

Times are obviously approximate. The times of day are shown in our modern twenty-four-hour system in order to get a better feel for when the events took place.

Thursday (6:00–11:30 p.m.)	Last Supper with disciples, Passover meal
Thursday–Friday (11:30 p.m.–1:00 a.m.)	Garden of Gethsemane: Jesus prays in continually deepening sorrow and anguish, waiting for His arrest.
Friday (1:00–1:30 a.m.)	Confrontation in garden of Gethsemane, and Jesus' arrest
Friday (1:30–3:00 a.m.)	Jesus is brought to Annas (former Jewish high priest for sixteen years). Jesus receives initial physical abuse and is then taken to the current Jewish high priest, Caiaphas, and the Sanhedrin court for more random abuse.
Friday (3:00–5:00 a.m.)	Imprisonment at Caiaphas's palace
Friday (5:00–6:00 a.m.)	At the court of all the Jewish elders, including the high priest, scribes, and entire Sanhedrin. They "pass the buck" to the Roman rule to kill Jesus. Jesus receives more abuse.

Friday (6:00–7:00 a.m.)	Jesus' hearing before Roman governor Pilate, who declares, "I find no guilt in this man." Jesus is returned to the Jews and receives more abuse.
Friday (7:00–7:30 a.m.)	Jesus' hearing before Herod Antipas, who had jurisdiction over Galilee. Jesus refused to answer any questions, so Herod simply returned Him to Pilate with a "gorgeous robe" (Luke). Jesus receives more abuse.
Friday (7:30 a.m.–9:00 a.m.)	Pilate tries to free Jesus, but the Jewish leaders will not have it. Pilate has Jesus officially beaten to attempt to satisfy the Jewish leaders. Pilate's soldiers "have their fun" with Jesus. They put on Jesus a crown of thorns and mock and abuse Him further. The Jews demand that Jesus be crucified. Pilate "washes his hands" and issues the order of crucifixion.
Friday (9:00 a.m.–10:00 or 11:00 a.m.?)	Jesus is forced to carry His own cross. Preparation and driving the nails takes place before the actual crucifixion and "raising Jesus on the tree." Mocking continues, Jesus speaks to the thieves, etc.
Friday (12:00–3:00 p.m.)	Darkness occurs as God turns away His face at the "sixth hour." Jesus dies before the "ninth hour," which was when they came to break the legs of the crucified so that the Sabbath would not be defiled.

Here we can also see proof of Acts 2:31, in that Jesus was not physically in the grave long enough for His body to see corruption.

Jesus was taken from the cross on Friday afternoon. The Sabbath began at 6:00 p.m. Jesus was out of the grave and talking to Mary sometime after she got to the grave site on Sunday morning, which would have been after 6:00 a.m.

Jesus was dead for about three hours on Friday afternoon, for twenty-four hours on the Sabbath, and perhaps for an hour or two on Sunday morning. That would be about twenty-eight or twenty-nine hours, tops.

Never are we told that Jesus would remain in the grave for seventy-two hours. We were only told that Jesus would rise on the third day, which He did.

By the way, the soul of Jesus was "not left in hell," which we see in the same verse. Note that the Greek word *hadēs* is interpreted as "the unseen or unknown place for departed souls." The Greeks often interpreted the word to mean simply "the grave." It was the interpreters of the King James Version who told us of hell, Purgatory, and so on.